SONG OF LOVE

SONG OF LOVE

The Letters of Rupert Brooke and Noel Olivier

1909–1915

edited by Pippa Harris

BLOOMSBURY

First published 1991

Letters of Rupert Brooke copyright © by Estate of the late Rupert Brooke 1991
Letters of Noel Olivier copyright © by Estate of the late Noel Olivier 1991
Introduction and Notes copyright © by Pippa Harris 1991

The moral rights of the authors have been asserted.

Bloomsbury Publishing Ltd, 2 Soho Square, London W1V 5DE

A CIP catalogue record for this book is available from the British Library.

ISBN 0 7475 1048 2

10 9 8 7 6 5 4 3 2 1

Typeset by Hewer Text Composition Services, Edinburgh
Printed in by Butler and Tanner Ltd, Frome and London

To the memory of my mother,
Angela

O world of lips, O world of laughter,
Where hope is fleet and thought flies after,
Of lights in the clear night, of cries
That drift along the wave and rise
Thin to the glittering stars above,
You know the hands, the eyes of love!
The strife of limbs, the sightless clinging,
The infinite distance, and the singing
Blown by the wind, a flame of sound,
The gleam, the flowers, and vast around
The horizon, and the heights above –
You know the sigh, the song of love!

Rupert Brooke: 'The Fish', Munich, March 1911

CONTENTS

ILLUSTRATIONS

Preface

As a child, I remember my mother reading aloud a passage about my grandmother, which she had just discovered in the second volume of Virginia Woolf's Diary. Virginia describes meeting Noel for dinner on 17 January 1923, almost eight years after Rupert Brooke's death:

> She looked at me with those strange eyes in which a drop seems to have been spilt – a pale blue drop, with a large deep centre – romantic eyes, that seem to behold still Rupert bathing in the river at Christow: eyes pure & wide, & profound it seems. Or is there nothing behind them? I as good as asked her. Why didn't you marry any of those romantic young men? Why? Why? She didn't know, said she had moods; all Oliviers are mad she said. And Rupert had gone with Cathleen Nesbitt & she had been jealous, & he had spoken against women & gone among the Asquiths & changed. But when she read his love letters – beautiful beautiful love letters – real love letters, she said – she cries & cries.[1]

Then my mother showed me these letters, tied up in bundles with ribbon and string, and stored alongside Noel's replies, which had been returned to her by Mrs Brooke, after Rupert's death. She told me how Noel had never discussed her relationship with Rupert, and had steadfastly refused to allow anyone access to the letters. It was a part of her life which she wished to keep private, until those affected by it were no longer alive.

Reading the letters much later, I gradually came to understand her feelings. Noel would never have wanted the letters censored, and yet they contain much that would have caused unnecessary pain to people she cared about, notably Ka Cox and James Strachey.

---

1 *The Diary of Virginia Woolf*, vol. ii, ed. Anne Olivier Bell (London: Hogarth Press, 1978), pp. 229–30.

For letters are potentially dangerous and misleading things. It should be stressed that, as Noel Annan puts it, they 'do not necessarily reflect the inner man: that there is no one single inner man, but lots of characters often in conflict with each other and presenting different faces to different people'.[1]

This remark is particularly applicable to Rupert, who once admitted: 'I attempt to be "all things to all men"', acknowledging that this made him 'slightly insincere to myself'.[2] These letters provide biographical insight into Rupert's life, but cannot give a complete picture, even of his love life.[3]

What *Song of Love* does is to chronicle one relationship, with all its many vacillations and complications. When I began working on it, I expected that Rupert's passion and wit would outshine anything Noel wrote, and that I would be forever making excuses for her. However, though his words are indeed dazzling, they serve rather as a foil to demonstrate the simple beauty and candour of her writing.

P.H.
London, June 1991

---

1 Written to Leonard Woolf, 6 October 1967; see *Letters of Leonard Woolf*, ed. Frederic Spotts (London: Weidenfeld & Nicolson, 1990), p. 560.
2 *LRB*, p. 73.
3 For more detail of Rupert Brooke's life, see Christopher Hassall's monumental biography. Some of the rest of his correspondence is also available in Geoffrey Keynes's *The Letters of Rupert Brooke*.

Acknowledgments

My first thanks are due to my father, Tony, and my sister, Tamsin, without whose help and support this book could not have been published. Also to Noel, whose habit of keeping undated letters in their envelopes, and of correcting mistakes in any book on the period she possessed, proved continually helpful.

I am indebted to the Trustees of the Rupert Brooke Estate, Professor Jon Stallworthy and Andrew Motion, for their co-operation and for their permission to use previously unpublished material (including the poem 'Princess Angeline'). In particular I would like to thank Jon for his good-humoured support and guidance.

Richard Garnett has been a source of encouragement throughout, and I am particularly grateful to him for reading through the text and making many useful corrections and comments. I would also like to thank the Estate of David Garnett for permission to quote from the letter on p.282.

My publishers, Bloomsbury, have from the beginning shown tireless enthusiasm and dedication, and I would like to thank everyone there, especially Liz Calder and Kate Hubbard, who have been a constant source of inspiration. Also thanks to my agent, Hilary Rubinstein, at A.P. Watt, for all his patience and kindness.

The following individuals have offered me assistance, hospitality or encouragement at various stages in bringing this book to publication: Virginia Allen; Anne Olivier Bell; Caroline Burkitt; Jon Cake; Tom Hall; Laurence Harwood; Tom Hemsley; Ian Kelly; Dr Michael Majerus; Alison Mansbridge; Caroline Mayr-Harting; Dr John Mullen; Virginia and William Nicholson; Emily O'Connor; Jenny Palmer; Keith and Tazza Ramsay; Dr Benedict Richards; Timothy Rogers; Dr George Rylands; Peter Ward.

I have benefited from the resources and staff of the following institutions: Bedales School (David Sykes); Bloomsbury Workshop (Tony Bradshaw and Rosemary Evison); the British Library; Cambridge University Library; King's College, Cambridge, Modern Archive (Jackie

Cox); the London Library; the National Liberal Club (Jo Somerville); the Tate Gallery Archive; Trinity College, Cambridge, Library (Mrs Hughes).

To the three people, Nicole, Eddie and Nick, who, often unknowingly, contributed so much to this book, I wish to send my love and thanks for all they have done.

The author and publishers would like to thank the following for supplying photographs: Rupert Brooke Estate (1–3, 15–18, 24); Noel Olivier Estate (4–14, 19, 22–3, 25–33); Raverat Family Estate (20); Peter Ward (21).

Note on the Text

The complete correspondence between Rupert Brooke and Noel Olivier comprises 170 letters and postcards: 105 from Rupert and 65 from Noel. From these I have chosen 134, of which most appear in their entirety. Any portions of the text omitted are indicated by ellipses in square brackets. My selection of material has been governed by considerations of space, interest and the desire to avoid repetitions. I have also included all the poems sent by Rupert to Noel and some others which can fairly be assumed to be about her.

I have regularized addresses, dates, salutations and parentheses and standardized the length of Rupert's frequent dashes and his spacing between sentences. To avoid possible misunderstandings, I have completed in full their abbreviations of names and places. Such editorial emendations are indicated by square brackets. However, I have left unaltered inaccuracies of spelling and punctuation, as they are an integral part, especially of Noel's writing.

A biographical appendix at the end of the book gives information on the main figures in the text. In the footnotes I have endeavoured to identify minor characters and explain obscure allusions without too much interruption of the text. Since any correspondence is necessarily a record of absence, I have included short editorial narratives, in italics, in order to elucidate the periods they spent together, and to explain relevant events not covered by the letters.

Also, in the footnotes, the following works have been abbreviated:

The Golden Echo by David Garnett (London: Chatto & Windus, 1953)　　　　　　　　　　　　　　　　　*GE*

The Letters of Rupert Brooke, ed. Geoffrey Keynes (London: Faber & Faber, 1968)　　　　　　　　　　　*LRB*

The Poetical Works of Rupert Brooke, ed. Geoffrey Keynes

(London: Faber & Faber, 1970) [All poems by Rupert
Brooke are from this collection unless otherwise
stated.]   *PRB*

Rupert Brooke: A Biography by Christopher Hassall
(London: Faber & Faber, 1964)   *CH*

Sydney Olivier: Letters and Selected Writings ed. Margaret
Olivier (London: George Allen & Unwin, 1948)   *Olivier*

The Modern Archive at King's College, Cambridge, houses much of
Rupert's writing, and when this has been my source, it has been
abbreviated to *KCA*.

I am grateful for the use of material from all the above sources.

Introduction

Rupert Chawner Brooke was born on 3 August 1887, the second of three sons. His father, William Parker Brooke, had graduated from King's College, Cambridge, with a First in Classics, before going on to become a teacher at Fettes, near Edinburgh. While there he met and fell in love with the pretty young sister of one of his colleagues, and on 18 December 1879 they were married.

Beneath her charming exterior, Rupert's mother was a strong-willed, puritanical character, who had no qualms about voicing her disapproval of any of Rupert's friends whom she considered undesirable. When her husband was made housemaster of School Field at Rugby School, she had no difficulty in extending her matriarchal rule to encompass a further fifty males.

Rupert and his two brothers, Dick and Alfred, all attended the nearby prep school of Hillbrow, and it was here that in 1898 Rupert began one of his most important friendships, with a boy in his form named James Strachey. Strachey had an elder cousin at the school, Duncan Grant, but as he was three years above he rarely wasted time socializing with them. Strachey recalls how he and Rupert had the same rather feminine haircut inflicted upon them by their mothers. There was no parting, just a fringe cut straight across the forehead. One day, following a games lesson, they were pounced on by a furious master, who bellowed: 'Back to the changing-room, both of you, and part your hair properly! You look like a couple of *girls!*'[1]

Rupert was not particularly happy at Hillbrow and certainly had no regrets when, in 1901, he started as a new boy in his father's House at Rugby. He was a competent scholar and good all-rounder, playing cricket and football for the school, captaining his House and co-editing a new literary supplement to the school magazine, called *The Phoenix*. His interest

---

1 Quoted in *CH*, p. 30.

in poetry was already apparent, and was enthusiastically fostered by a young man named St John Welles Lucas-Lucas, the son of neighbours in Rugby. Lucas was a French scholar, who later edited *The Oxford Book of French Verse*, though at the time that Rupert met him he was a barrister at the Middle Temple. He introduced Rupert to the work of the 'decadent' poets of the 1890s, as well as to Baudelaire and Oscar Wilde. Two other important figures came into Rupert's life while at School Field, Geoffrey Keynes and Hugh Russell-Smith. In December 1905 the three boys sat the scholarship exams for Cambridge and were all awarded places for the following year.

Rupert won a Classics scholarship to King's, his father's old college, where his uncle, the Rev. Alan England Brooke, was now Dean. Early on in his Cambridge career he met another Brooke, though he was no relative, who was in his third year at Emmanuel. This was Justin Brooke, an Old Bedalian, who quickly infected Rupert with his enthusiasm for drama. In that Michaelmas term Justin was rehearsing the part of the Pythian Prophetess, for a production of Aeschylus' *Eumenides*, and through his influence, Rupert was given the Herald's part. The role was not a taxing one, as he explained to his mother: 'I stand in the middle of the stage and pretend to blow a trumpet, while somebody in the wings makes a sudden noise.'[1] However, his good looks made a strong impression on stage. Years later, one member of the audience, Eddie Marsh, could still envisage 'His radiant, youthful figure in gold and vivid red and blue, like a Page in the Ricardi Chapel'.[2] At this time, Justin was sharing lodgings with another Old Bedalian, a Frenchman named Jacques Raverat. He too provides a record of his initial impressions of Rupert's looks:

> He was undoubtedly extremely beautiful, but with a childish beauty of undefined fluid lineaments . . . His forehead was very high and clear, his chin and lips admirably drawn; the eyes were small, grey-blue and already veiled, mysterious and secret, and with a jerk of his head he constantly tossed back his overlong hair as it fell over his face. It was the colour of tarnished gold and it was parted in the centre.[3]

By the end of his first term, Rupert was already causing a slight stir at Cambridge, and any feelings of alienation he may have felt were beginning to dissipate. Before returning to King's in January 1907, he had a new role,

---

1 *LRB*, p. 66.
2 *Rupert Brooke: A Memoir* by Edward Marsh (London: Sidgwick & Jackson, 1918), p. 20.
3 Quoted in *CH*, p. 110.

as his parents' comforter when, quite suddenly after a short illness, his brother Dick died.

It was not not long before Rupert and Justin embarked on their next dramatic collaboration. This was a production of Dr Faustus by the then neglected Elizabethan dramatist Christopher Marlowe. When Justin failed to interest the University Amateur Dramatic Club in the project, he saw nothing for it but to found a new society. Having gained support from senior members of the University, notably two Classics tutors, Francis Cornford and Jane Harrison, roles were quickly allotted. The cast included Justin as Faustus, Rupert as Mephistopheles, Geoffrey Keynes as the Evil Angel and Hugh Russell-Smith as Gluttony. The production opened at the ADC on 11 November 1907, and was deemed a success, though there were no critics present. This encouraged the participants sufficiently to constitute formally their society the following New Year. Thus the Cambridge University Marlowe Dramatic Society began with Rupert as President, Geoffrey as Secretary, Justin as Producer, and Francis Cornford as Treasurer.

During his first year Rupert was also being considered for membership of another society, The Apostles. Founded in 1820 as the Cambridge Conversazione Society, this secret group of undergraduates soon became known as The Apostles, probably because there had been twelve founder members. James Strachey's elder brother, Lytton, had been elected in 1902 and by 1903 had been joined by two men, Leonard Woolf and John Maynard Keynes, who would, like him, become labelled as members of the Bloomsbury Group. By the time Rupert arrived in Cambridge, his early friendship with James had turned, on James's side, into deep devotion, and he had no qualms about pressing for Rupert's election to The Apostles, once he had himself been elected, in February 1906. The influence of Lytton Strachey and Maynard Keynes had added a noticeably homosexual aura to the society's spirit of brotherly comradeship, so there would have been no stigma attached to James's interest in Rupert. In March 1907 James describes his feelings in a letter to Duncan Grant: 'I have spoken to Rupert again. Nowadays three sentences in the street seem incredibly heavenlike.'[1] Rupert never returned James's love, although he had been attracted to other boys at school. Still he did not hesitate in 1908, when offered a chance to become a member of the University's self-appointed élite. He enjoyed the secrecy of the Brotherhood and became a loyal member, never missing their term-time discussions on Saturday evenings.

However, an even more important aspect of his undergraduate days

---

1 *Bloomsbury/Freud*, ed. Perry Meisel and Walter Kendrick (London: Chatto & Windus, 1986), p. 18.

was his growing commitment to the Fabian Society. His ideas on socialism
had been strongly influenced by William Morris, and thus he hesitated
when a fellow King's freshman, Hugh Dalton, urged him to join the
Fabians. He felt their emphasis on economics was alien to his political
ideas, but agreed to become an associate member while he considered the
matter further. Dalton then introduced him to a third-year undergraduate
from Trinity, Ben Keeling, who was then the leading light in the Cambridge
Young Fabians. He was a charismatic young man, filled with revolutionary
zeal, who had already succeeded in persuading many waverers to commit
themselves to the cause. Through the Cambridge Fabians, Rupert also
made friends with two women, who were to have a profound effect on the
next years of his life. For, although The Apostles and the Marlowe Society
were still all-male preserves, the Cambridge Fabians provided an arena
where male and female undergraduates could work together as equals.
These two women were Ka Cox, who became the society's treasurer in
1907, and Margery Olivier, who was in her first year at Newnham.

Both girls joined a skiing trip Rupert went on that Christmas to
Andermatt, in the Alps, and accompanying Margery was one of her three
younger sisters, Brynhild. Rupert was immediately intoxicated by Bryn's
beauty and unaffected charm, as indeed many would be throughout her
life. A slightly exasperated Margery later wrote: 'It's such a responsibility
taking Bryn about. People always fall in love with her.'[1] Luckily Rupert had
the good sense to recognize his feelings were simply infatuation. Describing
Bryn in a letter written on Boxing Day 1907, he says: 'There is One! . . . oh
there is One . . . aged twenty, very beautiful & nice & everything . . . My
pen is dragging at its bit to run away with me about her. I adore her, for a
week.'[2]

Noel Olivier's family circumstances can be seen as a mirror image of
Rupert's. Born on 25 December 1892, the youngest of four daughters, it

1 Quoted by Rupert, in a letter to Dudley Ward (Sunday ? August 1909, KCA).
2 LRB, p. 118.

was her attractive, articulate father, Sydney Olivier, who dominated family life. For Mrs Brooke's strict puritanism, we find Sydney's liberal atheism. Born in 1859, the son of Arnold Olivier, an Anglican of stern dedication, Sydney had been rapidly disillusioned about the benefits of a religious upbringing. His inability to agree with his parents' beliefs had placed a strain on their relationship and he felt that 'I should have been better under equally moral but secular parents'.[1]

After leaving Oxford, he decided against a possible career as a barrister because he 'disliked what appeared to me the practice of professional insincerity involved in pleading cases and taking money for defending the right or justifying the wrong'.[2] Instead he chose to enter the Colonial Office, where he worked as a resident clerk alongside Sidney Webb. Although from totally different backgrounds, the two men shared many political ideals, and in May 1885 both joined the Fabian Society, which had been founded two years earlier by Edward Pease.

The Fabians advocated socialism as a potential way towards the abolition of poverty, the evils of which were all too apparent around them. Their definition of socialism appears in one of their early tracts:

Socialism means securing equal rights and opportunities for all. The Socialists are trying to have the land and machinery 'socialised', or made the property of the whole people, in order to do away with idle owners, and keep the whole product for those whose labour produces it.[3]

However, they did not advocate immediate revolution, but rather sought to effect social reform through an evolutionary process. This they aimed to set in motion by the circulation of their writing and by holding public debates.

Another of Sydney's Fabian colleagues was George Bernard Shaw, who had attended his first meeting in May 1884, and he provides this vivid account of Noel's father:

Olivier was an extraordinarily attractive figure, and in my experience unique . . . he was distinguished enough to be unclassable. He was handsome and strongly sexed, looking like a Spanish grandee in any sort of clothes, however unconventional . . .

---

1 Olivier family papers, in the possession of Dr Benedict Richards.
2 *Olivier*, p. 30.
3 'What is Socialism', Fabian Tracts, no. 3.

I have enjoyed (or suffered) much more celebrity, or as they
call it now, publicity, than this old Fabian colleague of mine,
though as a man of action I was not qualified to tie his
shoestrings.[1]

Noel's mother, Margaret, provided a sense of loving security to her
childhood. Physically she was tiny, with delicate, fine features and beautiful
blue eyes. Her family was devoted to her and her grandchildren speak of
her gentle kindness, remembering her quietly appearing with warm milk
and biscuits at bedtime.

A year before Noel's birth, Sydney returned from a spell as Colonial
Secretary in British Honduras and finished the conversion into a family
house of two cottages he had bought. This was The Champions at
Limpsfield Chart, in Surrey. In the years that followed, friends and other
Fabians, like the Peases, also gravitated to this area and the Olivier girls
grew up surrounded by the children of their parents' friends. One of Noel's
first playmates was the son of Edward and Constance Garnett, who, though
his name was David, was always referred to as Bunny by Noel and other
friends. He and Noel shared a love of wild creatures and had a fascination
for their anatomy which the Oliviers found slightly unwholesome: 'We
collected skeletons; we stuffed birds; we skinned rabbits and moles and
tanned their skins.'[2] In order to escape her parents' scrutiny, Noel would
often meet Bunny in the dead of night to go exploring. Each of them would
keep a piece of string tied around their big toe, with its end hanging from
the bedroom window, and whoever woke first would hurry to the other's
house and wake their friend with a gentle tug. In his autobiography, Bunny
describes the area as he remembers it:

> Limpsfield Chart in those days was a scattered hamlet with
> cottages clustering behind a big wooden windmill on the edge
> of a strip of common. There was a smithy opposite a large pond,
> now dried up, and there was no church. The common was
> bounded on the south by fields falling steeply away and giving a
> splendid view which extended from Crowborough Beacon in
> the east to Hindhead in the west . . . Half a mile from the Chart
> hamlet the common was bordered by the High Chart – open
> woodlands . . . of beech and pine with undergrowth amongst
> which the whortleberries and bracken grew thickly.[3]

---

1 *Olivier*, p. 30.
2 *GE*, p. 101.
3 *GE*, pp. 16–17.

Robust, healthy children, the Olivier girls would spend much of their time fearlessly roaming these woodlands, or scrutinizing the countryside from a suitable vantage point, high amongst the branches. This freedom, coupled with a certain sense of pride inherited from their father, combined to produce four self-confident, independent girls, whose clannish arrogance often led rather too swiftly to contempt of others. Like Sydney, they could be unbelievably insensitive at times, often hurting the feelings of others over issues which they considered trivial. Of course, though similar, the girls were not identical, as Bunny explains:

> I put Noel first and apart, because for me, and many others, she became far more important than any of her family . . . She was quiet and the least conspicuous of the four sisters. Margery, the eldest, was tall, brown-eyed and brown-haired, handsome with the impulsive warmth and sudden chilliness of her father . . . Brynhild was the outstanding beauty of the four and grew into the most beautiful young woman I have ever known. She was rather fairer than Margery; with the most lovely bone structure, a perfect complexion with red cheeks, and starry eyes that flashed and sparkled as no other woman's have ever done.
>
> Daphne was darker, more dreamy, and, in her childhood, wrapped in the skin of some beast, or crowned with flowers, was exactly as I have always imagined several of Shakespeare's heroines.[1]

In December 1900, Margaret took her four daughters out to Jamaica for the first time, where Sydney had been working as Colonial Secretary for almost a year. While there, the girls each had a pony, and in later years they became skilled polo players. Their great delight would be to troop down to the docks in immaculate dresses and challenge newly arrived naval officers to a match, which, needless to say, they would then win.

Returning to England in 1904, Sydney once again devoted much of his time to the Fabian Society. One new member was H.G. Wells, whose book *A Modern Utopia* greatly impressed Sydney, and by 1906 the two men were working together to amend the Society's Basis, the document setting out the Fabians' aims and beliefs. When new members joined, such as Rupert in 1908, they signed this Basis, which called for the abolition of private property, rent and interest and for the equality of the sexes.

At the beginning of 1907, a great earthquake and fire destroyed most of Kingston, and the Governor of Jamaica, Sir Alexander Swettenham,

---

1 *GE*, pp. 30–31.

resigned, daunted no doubt by the huge task of rebuilding before him. Sydney Olivier was rapidly appointed, and thus later that year Noel found herself once more travelling with her mother across the Atlantic. Her parents became concerned that another long spell abroad would not be good for her education and began to look round for an English boarding school. Up until then her schooling had been a somewhat random affair. While in Limpsfield there had been a succession of tutors, including Carl Heath, a pacifist friend of the Garnetts, and a physics lecturer from University College, London, Dr Charles Burton. The girls had also spent nine months out in Lausanne, learning to speak French.

The school her parents decided on was a predictably unconventional one, Bedales. Here Noel's love of nature was a distinct advantage, since the headmaster, John Haden Badley, believed that the more time spent out of doors the better. Pupils were encouraged to explore the surrounding countryside, and their morning's study would habitually be coupled with an afternoon outside working manually. Badley also fostered a spirit of sexual equality at the school – the ones who really needed sewing and cooking classes were the boys, and they were the ones who got them! The school had a very good reputation abroad, which was what had encouraged Jacques Raverat's father to send him there. It was also responsible for the arrival of a young Hungarian aristocrat, Ferenc Békássy, who became one of Noel's closest friends.

Rupert Brooke and Noel Olivier first met on 10 May 1908, when he was twenty and she was fifteen. The Cambridge Fabians had invited the recently knighted Governor of Jamaica, Sir Sydney Olivier, to speak to them on socialism. Before his lecture they organized a supper party in his honour, in Ben Keeling's Trinity rooms. Lady Olivier, just back from Jamaica, brought Noel and Daphne to Cambridge to hear their father speak and to visit Margery, now studying at Newnham. The last dinner guest to arrive was H.G. Wells, who had to be placed in a window-seat with his plate on his knee. Rupert sat next to Margery and opposite Noel, who watched silently as he cracked nuts and chattered to her elder sister. Though they did not speak, there was a mutual attraction and Noel records being set at ease by his friendly grin. After Sydney had addressed the meeting, they moved on for coffee to Francis Cornford's rooms, where Noel drew unwanted attention to herself by dropping her small green coffee cup.

In the months that followed, Noel and Rupert gradually became better acquainted. The Marlowe Society had decided to follow up its production of *Dr Faustus* by performing *Comus* to celebrate the tercentenary of Milton's birth, which would fall in July 1908. The Master of Milton's old college, Christ's, remembered that one of their Fellows, Sir Francis Darwin, had an artistic daughter who might be able to help with set design. She was called Frances, and was at that point studying painting as a pupil of William Rothenstein. Upon meeting Rupert and Justin, she readily agreed to assist and suggested they ask her cousin Gwen to help with the costumes. Gwen was another granddaughter of Charles Darwin and lived nearby at Newnham Grange.

Once term was over, the cast and production team set to work in earnest. Rupert was stage manager and also learning one of the leading roles, the Attendant Spirit. Since it was to be performed out of term-time, female undergraduates were surreptitiously included, amongst them Ka Cox and Margery Olivier, who were to dance in the Pavane. Noel's contribution was to help backstage, assisting William Rothenstein's brother, Albert, who was painting the scenery. She and Margery had persuaded one of their Limpsfield neighbours, Sybil Pye, to get involved, and she was put to work sewing Rupert's 'short spangled sky-blue tunic'.[1]

The first performance of *Comus* took place on 10 July at the New Theatre, Cambridge, and attracted a distinguished literary audience. The Poet Laureate, Alfred Austin, attended, as did Thomas Hardy and Robert Bridges, though the latter made his exit during the second half. As with *Dr Faustus*, the actors' names did not appear on the programme and there was a polite note which read: 'It is earnestly requested that there be no applause until the Curtain falls.' The production was generally well received and the Attendant Spirit was singled out for praise by the *Athenaeum*, as 'the best of the performers and a better reciter of blank verse than we have heard anywhere'. Lytton Strachey wrote an article about the production, which appeared in the *Spectator* on 18 July, praising wholeheartedly the intentions of those involved: 'How infinitely rarely does one hear, in any theatre, the beauty of blank verse! From that point of view, the performance at Cambridge was indeed memorable . . . The existence of such a body of able and enthusiastic lovers of poetry and drama must be welcomed as at least an augury of a better state of things.'

---

1 *CH*, p. 165.

Mrs Brooke, who had loyally arrived to support her son, was also concerned for him, when she saw how exhausted he was. The production had tired him out and she persuaded him that they should return swiftly to Rugby. However, before leaving, she accepted an invitation to join a party of Rupert's new friends, including Noel, for a picnic up-river.

After this introduction, Rupert tentatively suggested to his mother that perhaps one or two of the Oliviers might come to stay that summer, and an invitation was duly sent, for Margery and one of her sisters. Rupert was in a difficult position, since his whole objective had been to secure Noel's presence, and yet he feared that if he admitted his preference to Margery she might be offended. So he had to keep quiet and wait for Margery's decision. Meanwhile Mrs Brooke had been having second thoughts about the plan, which Rupert described to his friend from St John's, Dudley Ward:

> There is a Young Person at present in Rugby (I've not seen her) who hails from Jamaica – is, indeed, a friend of the Oliviers – is going soon to stay at Limpsfield. Mother met her; said 'Oh yes we're going to have two of the Oliviers to stay with us, do you know them?' 'My, yes!' the Person shrilled, 'the Oliviers! they'd do *anything*, those girls!' Mother (whose '*anything*' is at once vastly ominous and most limited) is, and will be for months, ill with foreboding. She pictures, I think, Margery climbing the roof at night, or throwing bread about at table, or kissing the rural milkman.[1]

However, dates became a problem, as Margery and Noel had to accompany their mother to Keswick, and eventually the scheme was abandoned, much to Mrs Brooke's relief.

It was not until Christmas that Rupert managed to secure another meeting with Noel. He had discovered that she would be accompanying Margery on a skiing holiday at Klosters in the Engadine. Having secured an invitation, he set about convincing his mother that, unless he had a proper rest, his work and health would suffer, as they had done in the summer. Writing at the end of November, he says:

> the only way (I find) I have a real holiday from *my* work, is on a walking-tour, or in Switzerland; times and places where it is impossible to think or read for more than five minutes . . . I think, just a week's mental rest strengthens a mind for some time.[2]

---

1 *LRB*, p. 135.
2 *LRB*, p. 148.

The ploy was successful, and by 18 December 1908 Rupert, Noel and a group of about twenty others were happily settled at Klosters. While there they wrote a short drama, entitled *From the Jaws of the Octopus*, which they performed on Boxing Day. Most of the text was written by Rupert, the singer Clive Carey, and Helen Verrall, the daughter of the eminent Classicist A.W. Verrall. Rupert also succeeded in casting himself as the hero, though Noel's marked lack of acting ability prevented her from playing his heroine. In later life she would pass over this weakness by saying her young cousin Laurence had taken more than his share of the family's acting talent.

The holiday served to confirm Rupert's admiration of Noel. His New Year letter to James Strachey contained the following bulletin: 'Switzerland fair (I morose) Noel Olivier superb.'[1] He determined that, despite possible opposition from Margery and Mrs Brooke, he would see much more of Noel in the coming year.

Since arriving at Cambridge, Rupert's work, particularly Classics, had been a disappointment to his tutors and it was now suggested that he should give the subject up and concentrate on English. Also, it was felt that if he moved out of college into lodgings his work might improve as distractions lessened. Both suggestions were readily accepted by Rupert and he finished the spring term in an ebullient mood.

This frame of mind was further enhanced when he managed to find out from Margery where Noel would be at Easter. The two sisters planned to take a cottage somewhere in the New Forest, together with Margery's Newnham friend, Eva Spielman, with enough room for others to visit at intervals. Rupert decided that he should be one such visitor and selected Dudley Ward as his accomplice in the endeavour:

> Well! if they're in the New Forest, good, I'll go . . . But I leave it to you to learn of their arrangements, discover all, and break to them that we shall be passing their door. I do so because (a) I've been writing to Margery about once a week since January, and she'll be about sick of me, (b) I daren't do it, (c) I have no time: and you have plenty. So you must settle. But oh! be tactful, be gentle, be gently tactful! Perhaps they will hate us? Horrible thought! Do not intrude! apologize! apologize!

Rupert was entranced by the idea of disappearing completely for four days, and he was also aware his mother would never condone such a visit, so his plans were to be kept a secret from friends and family alike: 'I have told [Hugh Russell-Smith] I am going to "seek Romance"! He believes I am

---

1 Quoted in *The Neo-Pagans* by Paul Delany (London: Hamish Hamilton, 1988), p. 54.

going to wander through Surrey disguised in an Italian *sombrero*, with a guitar, singing old English ballads for pence! Ho! ho! But remember, a profound secret. It adds *so* much to the pleasure of it all.'[1]

The visit to the New Forest was not his only plan for Easter. He was also to visit James Strachey, who was staying at Manaton in Devon, and to go with him to a gathering of The Apostles in Cornwall, which would include the philosopher G.E. Moore and the journalist Desmond MacCarthy. As well as this, his father's sister, Fanny Brooke, had invited him to stay, and his parents had made it clear they expected him to spend some time with them at the lodgings they had taken in Sidmouth.

It was by no means certain that he would be able to carry out his carefully laid scheme.

---

1 *LRB*, pp. 160–61.

LETTERS: MARCH 1909
TO JANUARY 1915

Time		*Place*
The black part between	Conditions:	School Field
Thursday and Friday. About	Spring –	Rugby (poor)
the middle		(But soon to be Devonshire)

(But I shan't post it till tomorrow)

[26 March 1909]

My dear Noel,

Lay down your Swinburne and attend.

Why do I write? For many reasons. First, because I am clean and brave, and miles around the wonder grows how well I do behave. (Do you know Prof. Housman's poems?[1] – No; I supposed not). And as for why I am clean, – why, that is because I have just had a very long and very hot bath (which I can't get at Cambridge, so it's the first time for months ———) and my fingers are pink & my hair has turned the dull-green colour, water always turns it, &, being dried at length, stands up a foot into the air all round, like a head drawn by dear Mr Blake. And my bravery, – *that* comes from the same cause, & because I've shaken off the family & am alone (which always produces courage), and because the weather is admirable, and because I have been reading Mr Meredith's poems.

And therefore I write to you. – And therefore, in spite of your cheery and express advice (v.l. injunction) against it, – I write to you.

(This is not a picture of a pear: but a blot.)

---

1 Oh, when I was in love with you,
   Then I was clean and brave,
And miles around the wonder grew
   How well did I behave.
      ('A Shropshire Lad', XVIII)

Oh, but there are many other reasons. One is not a reason at all; but only an attendant circumstance. And that is that all my plans have gone astray; & so the plot I made with Margery, that you were all going to walk from Studland through Devon, & have tea with me in my hut on Dartmoor on the way together with my private plot whereby I was going to stay with my Mad Aunt [Fanny] in Bournemouth (ugh!) to work, in April, & have tea with all *you* in your cottage in the New Forest, – all these plots, I say, were broken & burst for me by the unwellness of my mother & the resulting necessity that I am to be with her the second part of April, from the 13th, in Torquay (pah!). All this may seem mad to you if (as is possible) you are unsure of your plans for your holidays; which I have discussed & decided (with Margery).

(There is no time now, to explain about the Mad Aunt, – a most interesting tale. Another day —— ?)

Anyhow, finding, suddenly, that I was not going to meet you in April, as I had imagined possible, (the possiblity, now, is almost invisible) I had to write what otherwise I should have said.

Which brings me to the third reason; that there were things I wanted to write about.

The other eighteen reasons I will not enumerate. I am growing tired of this way of writing. So no.3 is the rest of the letter, & more.

Well, then –

(You had better come with Margery when she returns to Cambridge on the 22nd April: for you don't surely go to school again then. And, if not, I wonder if you'll be in London on the twenty-third)

(With all the solemnity of youth, and the authority of Dudley Ward, I advise you to lend your immature but pompous weight in favour of your all leaving Studland on the 7th when your lease expires, & Blanco[2] appears. – Why should I prattle? You have once seen Blanco; & that suffices. I prattle only, really, to appease poor Dudley. He had a superstition that you were in command.).

in

(I am going to be extremely healthy, & laborious {on} a place called Dartmoor; with one man & the Minority Report on the Poor Law[3] & Euripides (a dirty fellow).)

---

2 George Rivers Blanco White (1883–1966), QC. Later this year 'Blanco' married his close friend Amber Reeves, a Fabian colleague of Rupert. He did so knowing that she was pregnant by H.G. Wells, with whom she had had an affair – an affair which Wells then fictionalized in his novel *Ann Veronica* (1909).
3 This document, published in February 1909, was the work of Beatrice Webb and a small group of her colleagues from the Royal Commission examining the Poor Law. They had disagreed with the findings of the majority, and were advocating a complete replacement of the existing system by a network of social services.

I am "frightfully" & powerfully wondering if you'd like a book called *The Secret River* by R. Macaulay:[4] & one called *Jumbo* by Algernon Blackwood: & (especially in the first part) Tono Bungay[5] & –

– But I must sink to the Permanent: – Henley?[6] poor Mr Yeats? Old Belloc?[7] Shakespeare? all (in fact) of the moderns, whose names you have never heard before I uttered them –

But this is what I am really writing about. Strewing them on the floor with the wildest laughter I adjudged your photographs (in proof). And, later, Margery promised to give me one of them.

By the Laws of the Land where I live, I must inform you, – even *ask* you – before I take one such. "For" (they say) "if you had one, hanging madly between the Demeter of Cnidos, & the *Penseur*[8] & she knew not, &, even, entered & saw it so, suddenly, & went mad & died".

It is a mere formality; for I despise & detest the Laws, most of which I made; & you are too young to be asked or consulted about anything; it is purely a matter between Margery & myself; & anyhow I have an adamantine will & iron resolve, & should merely take it – Still, just in the way of politeness you know, I should prefer that you should squeak your frail assent. Because I want the photograph, please. (In any case I should have written for it; & why should a merely irresponsible act of the flighty Margery alter the events of the Universe?)

So – my task is accomplished, my labour done. Though my wages are not yet taken; & there is no lark.[9] But I go to sleep.

Heavens! I don't feel sure of your address. And I don't in the least know how to spell it. What if it should be a French word Bî-dêles, or

---

4 Rose Macaulay (1881–1958), novelist, essayist and travel writer. Her uncle was Senior Tutor at King's and her father Rupert's English tutor. She had met Rupert at a tea party in his rooms in October 1907.

5 This recently published novel by H.G. Wells (1866–1946) was awarded to Noel as a school prize the following term.

6 William Ernest Henley (1849–1903), poet, journalist and editor.

7 Hilaire Belloc (1870–1953), historian, poet, Liberal MP and essayist. Rupert greatly admired Belloc's writing and had met him following a history lecture he gave at Pembroke on 31 May 1907.

8 The first statue mentioned is by Praxiteles and is generally recognized to be of Aphrodite, not Demeter. Pliny in his *Naturalis Historia* asserts: 'The finest statue . . . in the whole world is the Aphrodite, for the sight of which many have sailed to Cnidos.' The second statue is by Auguste Rodin (1840–1917).

9 So be my passing!
My task accomplished and the long day done,
My wages taken, and in my heart
Some late lark singing,
Let me be gathered to the quiet west,
The sundown splendid and serene,
Death.
              (W.E. Henley, 'Echoes', 1888)

something. If this letter goes astray & falls into the hands of the Post-
Master General –
    (A) I shall be baffled
    (B) Mr Buxton[10] will be puzzled.
    (C) The Universe will cease.
    (D) You will be saved a good deal of boredom & irritation.

Yours
Rupert

Bedales.
Petersfield
Hants (for short)

3.4.09

Dear Rupert

    I meant to write to you on a postcard, or perhaps on two, as you
approve of them; but unfortunately I had none, nor could I obtain any –
in the time I had at my disposal – for money or love.

    You were right in considering it almost unecessary to ask my
permission. As far as I'm concerned you may have as many
photographs – of me (or others) – as you like, as long as – this
condition must be stuck to – you dont expect me in any way to facilitate
the obtaining of them either by money or trouble.

    Thank you for kind advice about literature. I found Henly here, a
nice man, but he seems dreadfully influenced by tides and winds.
Perhaps you *thought* I hadn't heard of Shakespeare, but I have, I learnt
some of his – poetry, at least part out of one of his plays, this term, so I
know a lot about him. We get quite a good education here, you see.

    I dont know in the least where I am going in the holidays, which
begin on the 6th for me. I *may* come to Cambridge, I *may* be in London
on the 23rd; but I don't know. Why is poor Blanco to be avoided?

    I think I told you I couldnt spell, once. Now you have a practical
illustaration.

from.   Noel

---

10 Sydney Charles, Earl Buxton (1853–1934), statesman. Post-Master General 1905–10.

The cottage the Oliviers finally decided on was at Bank in the New Forest. It belonged to a retired couple, Mr and Mrs Primmer, and had been recommended to them by Ben Keeling. Rupert and Dudley arrived on 10 April and stayed for four days. Rupert's elation is evident in this letter to Jacques, describing his holiday:

> And so I walked and laughed . . . and, in the end of the days, came to a Woman who was more glorious than the Sun and stronger than the sea, and kinder than the earth, who is a flower made out of fire, a star that laughs all day, whose brain is clean and clear like a man's and her heart is full of courage and kindness; and whom I love.[1]

<table>
<tr><td></td><td>after Monday at
Coombe Field
Godalming</td><td>Kings College
Cambridge</td></tr>
<tr><td>Friday May 28 [1909]</td><td></td><td></td></tr>
</table>

At eleven o'clock this morning, I finished the last paper of my Classical Tripos. There were 108 other candidates in the room, but they all stayed the full time, till noon. They write longer, better papers than mine. (They all wear spectacles.) I wrote my translation of the last Latin word (the last Latin word I shall ever translate in my life. Glory!), which happened to be "Good-bye!" The fitness delighted me, and I screamed with laughter, suddenly; & the hundred & eight turned round & blinked. I nodded at a hairless don who was in command, & ran cheerily out of the room, tearing the examination paper to bits as I went. I sang loudly all the way to my rooms, & annoyed all the

---

1 *LRB*, p. 164.

policemen & danced a little; & when I got here I burned the paper, and I keep the ashes in an Urn. I shall never read Latin or Greek again.

All this is quite unconnected (superficially quite; but really . . . – ah! ha!) with the purpose & subject of this letter. I shall state it calmly, and you must be attentive. On next Monday I am going to stay with my Uncle (a prophet called Cotterill[1]) at Godalming; until Friday. I am going to read Shakespeare there, & rejoice. My uncle is writing a book on Brotherhood, Universal Love, Humanity etc. – like the old man in 'Fraternity'[2] . . . To return; I am going on one of those days, probably Thursday, to see Jacques (do you know Jacques? His other name is Raverat, & he is like this and he is an Old Bedalian. But let us proceed), who lives at Froxfield, near Petersfield. He will take me to see Bedales; & talk, maybe, with Badley[3] (or however your man calls himself), who is an old school-fellow of mine, & we have mutual friends, & long to meet each other. Shall I see you there, playing ball, or singing your multiplication table, wearing an Eton collar (or the female substitute.)?

Regard the situation from every side. Shall I just . . . see you about? Or shall I definitely *see* you? (I wonder if that is very clear.) It occasionally seems to me rather impossible, quite impossible. Schools are so mad. And my malign appearance, & influence! . . . Don't you see? I, of course, merely don't know. I don't know the rules of these extra-ordinary games. You perhaps do; and you're happy at making decisions.

Then, you see, you may object to this thunderbolt. I, when *I* was a school-boy, *loathed* the outside world appearing. They looked a fool, & I felt one. So might you object, rightly. Say so. Why should I do more than observe you in a distant crowd? Why, rather, come to Bedales at all? I can talk to Jacques an afternoon, two miles away.

Or, – still another thing, – though I am coming to see Jacques, a school, & Badley; and infinitely incidentally to nod at you, – mightn't *They* (still) object? . . . – O, but you see the whole question; why do I twitter on? I want to see you; and, as things are at present, I shall come

1 Clement C. Cotterill (1860–1932), Mrs Brooke's brother and an advanced socialist. Rupert was influenced by his writings, such as *Human Justice for Those at the Bottom. An Appeal to Those at the Top* (London: 1907).
2 *Fraternity*, a novel by John Galsworthy (1867–1933), published in 1909. Rupert is referring to Mr Stone, the father of the book's central character, Cecilia, who is busy writing his 'Book of Universal Brotherhood'.
3 J.H. Badley (1865–1967), the progressive founder and headmaster of Bedales.
4 Old Bedalian.

over to Bedales, under the high protection of an O.B.,[4] wander about, talk with Badley, and, ultimately, find out if I am allowed to talk with you. You can, and may, evade, or stop me. (Surely we have got beyond the last insult of politeness?) See what you would have. You understand all things in the world (you will even make sense of this letter) and you are a thousand years old, and we know each other perfectly; you must decide.

Oh, and if you talk to me like a schoolgirl, – as you did to the large fool who judged something or other by an international standard – I shall beat you over the head with a stick. Oh, I hope I'll see you. I suppose you couldn't come a walk? You'd like old Jacques, I think; if you thought *very* clearly when you met him.

In Cambridge there is fine weather & picnics as of old. There are dog roses, no water, cows, – oh! everything. But I do not talk about suicide nowadays: I merely splash with a paddle and grin.

And my mother's coming up & going to take out a party of people whose manners are *irreproachable*. And I bathe every morning at 7. And *have* you seen the Banke photographs – the ones you mostly sulked for? And I've forgotten to make you my literary speech. Damn!

Rupert

Bedales,
Petersfield,
Hants.

Tuesday. June 1st. [1909]

There is a period of 2 hours on Thursday – between 4 and 6 P.M. – when I ought to play tennis; but as my duty to tennis is not so great as my subjection to your mighty will – adamantine, I think you called it once – ; If you want to *see* me as well as see me *about*, you might do it then.

I too always have the fear of you – the outsider – looking a fool and my feeling one; but as the last depends on the first, and the first depends on you, I am willing to risk owning to your aquaintance, if you like.

If you come on Wednesday, tomorrow, either you will only see me in the distance, or else I shall have to make a fuss with various othorities and renounce cricket. And you are'nt worth that. I *wont* go for a walk with that wiggly man with the strange & illegeble christian name. My mind refuses to think clearly to order, I'm affraid.

If you come, when will you come, and how long will you stay? It might be convenient to know, & whether I'm to play tennis on Thursday or not.

I wish you could transfer your mind, the part that has the latin in it and which you now no longer need, to me. It seems rather a waste of it to lett it slowly decay in you when I should have so many uses for it.

You have finnished with the University havent you? Did you make that decision which you said, at xmas, would have to be made about this time, or is it still coming, or did it come a long time ago and you quite settled down & used to it?

from Noel.

She wishes you were'nt coming; but she dare'nt say so out right, for fear of offending your pride.

[Coombe Field, Godalming]
Wednesday [2 June 1909]

God (a thing you don't believe in) burn (a sensation you've never had) you (*you!*), Madam (a title given in honour, reverence and admiration to the middle-aged) (now used in the most scathing sarcasm)!
(The whole forming a Vehement Oath.)

You're a devil. *Beginning* by assigning a time, *going on* to water it down, down . . . and *ending* by a post-script in the third person, but referring, as far as the meagre wit Classics have left me can discover, to you, and changing the whole thing, & leaving me cr-r-rushed.

The fact that, old as I am, I vividly remember the feelings & agony of my youth, when the Outsider came, makes me more soft-hearted than ever. Otherwise, I might think it would do you so much good to get over these infantile feelings, that I should appear in my wildest, horriblest garb, & make you a public derision.

Oh, the bouncing elasticity & hard heart of Youth!

Really, it is splendid of you to write an even plainish letter in this ignoble age. You might have been even plainer & spared my poor wits even more. "Offending my pride" you say. I haven't any pride, of *that* sort . . . O, well, perhaps I have. But infinitely less than you think. and it ought to be stamped upon, kicked, maltreated. So you are really very kind to me. Thank you. Lastly, I'm not going to have it shelved, – the responsibility, I mean, – put upon my "adamantine will". (I've got such a will, Ho! yes! but I shan't use it.) If we meet, you & I, we meet, and there you are! We both meet, we both wish to, & we're both responsible. Otherwise, ...

If I knew quite certainly why "she wishes I wasn't coming", – from the outsider feeling only, or what – oh! I'd understand *all* possible feelings – I'd be happier. However, as well as I can, I decide:

I shall go to Froxfield, Petersfield, (address) on Thursday, talk to Jacques, meet Badley (perhaps, see Bedales, you by chance in the distance, or not) – & go to London at 6 that evening. You can scarcely object to *that?* (If you do, I won't even do that.). Play your tennis. Think no more. Be calm & careless.

There! There's Nobility for you!

And if, if, there's anything more to be said, a letter here by tomorrow's first post, or to Froxfield, Petersfield (which I reach at noon) would find me. So if I even shan't see Bedales, you know where & how to stop me. Damn the rain!

R

The Orchard, Grantchester
near Cambridge

[Postmark 25 July 1909]

My dear Noel

He, the Outsider having impudently, offensively and unpardon-
ably *come*, – disguised, however, as a gentleman, and unridiculous, in a
stiff straw hat and very uncomfortable fashionable clothes (it was his
poor best) – and having seen that rather admirable place for hours, and
for seconds, a glimpsed whiteness in the shadowed profundity of a
boot-hole – you – stumped off, quite unreasonably snorting, head-in-
air, to the gloomy station. He wanted to go to the right, and was furious
with the surprised Jacques for insisting on an entirely improbable road
to the left. Turning a still gentlemanly but sloping back upon the vile
spot, I (for I can't keep up the third person; it's too mad) exactly then
relinquished, with a C-Curse, the last vestige of the hope that had
persisted even till then; and then, quite surprisingly, we were justified in
taking that silly road, and met you, illogically coming into Bedales from
the horizon. It was just like one of those terrible plays, in which nothing
happens for *hours* and then, just as the curtain is beginning to creak
down, they all die hurriedly. Then, of course, I was seized by the horror,
my recurrent disease, which makes me talk very quickly about nothing
in a high voice for a long time. I'm sorry. I *can* be nice you know at
times – at least, not exactly *nice*, but much more *intelligent*. I was just ill.
Also I'm sorry I had to be dragging Jacques with me. (Did you
recognize him from my drawing?) So of course, I didn't say about a
thousand things I meant to; and I've quite forgotten everything – every
fact, such as I wanted to know, – that you said. I can't make out, e.g.
whether you're going to stay on at the school or not, and if not, what – .
I didn't see you very long. I hope I didn't waste your time in leading you
to search for us. There are several things I *think* I didn't tell you; and I
can't *remember* having written since.
      For an instance, you must have heard, having been home, that
Margery and somebody are coming to a Vicarage in Somerset in August,
at my Mother's request; and the appendages of this plan, such as my
Mother's rather plaintive remark . . . "we needn't have that youngest
one? she's quite a school-girl, isn't she? – " I imagined you laughing.
You may imagine me speech-making to the cat, to the cows, or – in the

absence of those more intelligent auditors – to Dudley Ward. It would have been very delightful if you'd been invited to come to Somerset, and come: at the dullest moments an exquisite High Comedy. Yet there are compensations in the situation. Before this it was so lopsided, so unfair, the hideosity: merely, I was the Evil Influence, you the Misguidable Young. We have retaliated. You are a Devil, the Leader Astray, the Unmannerly. I the lamb protected from you (a much saner view). My family think (I feel) that your horrible influence may end in my interrupting the conversation of my Elders, eating potatoes with my fingers, or being otherwise – what can I say? – School Childish – Yah!

Oh, well, anyhow, I shan't see you there – this year – (unless you're going to pass through that part of Somerset anytime in August? I wish you were) (Where are you going to be at Christmas?) – and I am writing to apologise for my poor Mother. So that part of this letter's over.

As a kind of *entr'acte* I shall tell you where I am, and what I do. You needn't read it. But I like writing jokes about it. I am in The Country in Arcadia; a rustic. It is a village two miles from Cambridge, up the river. You know the place; it is near all picnicing grounds. And here I work at Shakespeare and see few people. Shakespeare's rather nice. Antony and Cleopatra is a very good play. In the intervals I wander about bare foot and almost naked, surveying Nature with a calm eye. I do not pretend to understand Nature, but I get on very well with her, in a neighbourly way. I go on with my books, and she goes on with her hens and storms and things, and we're both very tolerant. Occasionally we have tea together. I don't know the names of things (like the tramp in Mr Masefield's poem[1]), but I get on very well by addressing all flowers "Hello, Buttercup!" and all animals "Puss! Puss!" I live on honey, eggs and milk, prepared for me by an old lady like an apple (especially in face) and sit all day in a rose garden to work. Of a morning Dudley Ward and a shifting crowd come out from Cambridge and bathe with me, have breakfast (out in the garden, as all meals) and depart. Dudley and I have spent the summer in learning to DIVE. I can *generally* do it now: he rarely. He goes in fantastically; quite flat, one leg pathetically waving, his pince-nez generally on. But O, at 10pm (unless it's too horribly cold), alone, very alone and (though I boast of it next day) greatly frightened, I steal out, down an empty road, across emptier

---

1 Dunno the names o' things, nor what they are,
  Can't say's I ever will.
  Dunno about God – he's jest the noddin' star
  Atop the windy hill.
          ('Vagabond')

fields, through a wood packed with beings and again into the ominous open, and bathe by night. Have you ever done it.? Oh but you have, no doubt. I, never before. I am in deadly terror of the darkness in the wood. I steal through it very silently. Once I frightened two cows there, and they me. Two dim whitenesses surged up the haunted pathway and horribly charged on me . . . And once, returning bare foot through the wood, I trod on a large worm, whose dying form clung to the sole of my foot for many minutes. O Noel, have you ever trodden on a worm with your bare left foot, on a moonless night, in a Dreadful Wood, alone? But when one, beginning to bathe, throws off one's two garments, – then all is surprisingly well. You no longer feel disliked, an outsider. (It's always a question of clothes, you see). You become, part of it all; and bathe. The only terror left is of plunging head foremost into blackness; a moderate terror. I have always had a lurking suspicion that the river *may* have run dry, after all, and that there is, as there seems, no water in it. (I once knew a man who never dared to dive, because he always feared there *might* be a corpse floating just below the surface into which he'd go headlong). For the rest I live an Arcadian existence. There are, indeed, no sheep to pipe to. But I sing a little to the hens.

The second important thing is that you must read E.M. Forster's story in the English Review for July.[2] It is *very* good. Perhaps you never even read his last novel "A Room with a View". (He is a young man).

The second pleasant irrelevancy is that Augustus John (the greatest painter) (of whom I have told you) with two wives and seven children (all male, all between 3 and 7 years) with their two caravans and a gypsy tent, are encamped by the river, a few hundred yards from here. I go and see them sometimes, and they come here to meals. He is in Cambridge to paint Jane Harrison's portrait.[3] The chief wife is a very beautiful woman.[4] And the children are lovely brown wild bare people dressed, if at all, in lovely yellow, red or brown tattered garments of John's own choosing. Yesterday Donald Robertson,[5] Dudley Ward, and I took them all up the river in punts, gave them tea and played with them. They talked to us of an imaginary world of theirs, where the river was milk, the mud honey,

---

2 The story printed by E.M. Forster (1879–1970) was 'Other Kingdom'.
3 Jane Ellen Harrison (1850–1928), eminent Newnham Classicist and member of the 1906 Greek Play Committee, which staged the *Eumenides* in which Rupert played the Herald. Her portrait has been referred to by David Piper as being the only painting ever of a female don.
4 Rupert refers to Dorelia McNeill (1881–1969). The two wives rumour, caused by the presence of Dorelia's younger sister Edie, was further confused and exacerbated when Ottoline Morrell (1873–1938) joined their camp for a day.
5 Donald Robertson (1885–1961), a Cambridge contemporary, who was made a Fellow of Trinity in 1909 and later Regius Professor of Greek at Cambridge.

the reeds and trees green sugar, the earth cake, the leaves of the trees (that was odd) ladies' hats, and the sky Robin's blue pinafore. Robin was the smallest. The sun was a spot of honey on Robin's blue pinafore: which, indeed, duly appeared . . . "What would happen", said the imaginative Dudley, early in the afternoon, "if you were all in a tree, and at the bottom a big bear sat and waited, so that you couldn't come down?" "The bear" they told him calmly would die after a little." It was unanswerable: the end of Dudley's romance. This Sunday morning I was invaded by Gwen Darwin, Helen Verrall,[6] Gilbert Murray and his daughter,[7] who made me take them to visit John. The Professor of Greek was rather nervous at visiting the gypsy Artist: but they all were happy. It was an odd scene. To live with five wild children in a caravan would really be a very good life. I shall take to it one day.

The third and greatest purpose of my writing this letter has, by this morning's post, vanished, or at least got fuzzy. I *was* going to be taken by Justin [Brooke] to your play on Bank Holiday: and I timorously wanted to find out if you were going to be there at the time. But oh! everything is unsettled, the play's on Saturday, and I doubt if I go to it. If I do will you be at Bedale's on Saturday? if not, where are you going to be, where that week-end, and where on Bankkollidy? For I'm going through London about that time, and going to be wandering on foot westward. So tell me if you're going to be at Bedale's for that play.

Life is splendid: but I wish I could write poetry. I write very beautiful stories. One I am accomplishing is about a young man who, for various reasons, felt his bookish life vain: and wanted to get in touch with Nature. He began by learning to climb trees, but in clambering up an easy fir tree, fell off a low branch six feet above the ground and broke his neck. A short, simple story.

I have been Living since I saw you last. I went to a Masked Ball in London, and a reception of Eminent Scientists of the World in the Fitzwilliam, here. Tra! la!

Rupert

---

6 Helen Verrall (1887–1964), daughter of the Trinity Classicist A.W. Verrall. Helen had taken part in the trip to Klosters, Christmas 1908.
7 G. Gilbert Murray (1866–1957), who had become Regius Professor of Greek at Oxford in 1908. Both he and his daughter, Rosalind, remained close to Rupert throughout his life. Augustus John (1878–1953) in his autobiography writes: 'Murray used to visit our camp with Rupert Brooke. Both were charming, good-natured and playful with the children. Rupert Brooke had a blond, robust style of good looks, of which he was naturally not unconscious: a delightful fellow I thought, but perhaps none the better for a too roseate environment.' *Autobiography*, Augustus John (London: Jonathan Cape, 1975), p. 75.

Bedales

28th. July. [1909]

I am not staying "on" till Tuesday, I might have done; but now, for several reasons, I am going back to Limpsfield on Friday afternoon. I shalnt get as far as London but get out at Clapham junction. Also your Mother is quite right, and I'm glad she dislikes me; not that I, or any other school girl, eat potatoes – especially when hot – with my hands; but there are many other, much more important ways in which I am frightfully objectionable, and *quite* a school-girl. No laughing matter at all – very sad.

I know this is a beastly and absurd letter; but few people, and certainly not I, would be capable of answering that – what was it? – *letter* you sent.

I dont quite see how it is you can enjoy breakfast – and all meals – but especially breakfast in a rose garden this sort of weather, I should think the butter would be too hard frozen and the coffee – I *beg* your pardon, or course you dont drink such poisonous stimulants, but milk – the milk too diluted with dirty rain water – dirty with Cambridge soots – to be enjoyable. But no doubt you have a tremendous capacity for enjoyment, only I wish you wouldnt talk about Nature in that foolish and innocent tone of voice – you call it making jokes, and I suppose you think it's nice; but I dont like it a bit – I've told you why lots of times. As for the way you and Dudley – babies both – suddenly in your old age rediscover the charming imaginations of children of 5 and listen to and remember their obvious discriptions of imaginary worlds, when you yourselves have only just left that stage, *that* is a joke – perhaps you meant it as such, but not likely.

I'm sorry – I'm in a very bad rage – because I've been doing easy exams badly – a thing you never did, so you cant sympathise. Dont try.

from
Noel.

Rupert was undeterred by this rather brusque reply from Noel. A few chance remarks of Margery's and some subtle investigation by Dudley had already allowed him to discover her plans for the following weeks. Bunny Garnett had organized a camp, beginning in the last week of July, at Penshurst on the river Eden. He had invited, amongst others, his Limpsfield neighbour Harold Hobson and a Cambridge rowing blue, Godwin Baynes. Bryn and Daphne arrived early on and were to be joined by Noel once term was over. One evening, just as everyone was going to bed, Rupert and Dudley appeared. Forgetting their tiredness, the friends decided to go for a celebratory swim and made their way through the darkness, guided only by a bicycle lamp. Bunny describes his memories of the scene when they returned to the camp:

Soon we were sitting round the blazing fire, Noel's eyes shining welcome for the new arrivals and the soft river water trickling from her hair down her bare shoulders . . . The moon rose full . . . we crawled back into our sleeping bags and slept, but Rupert, I believe, lay awake composing poetry.[1]

Rupert's parents had hired a vicarage in Clevedon, Somerset, for August, but although Margery and Bryn came, there was no sign of Noel. While there Rupert spoke to Margery about his feelings for Noel and asked for permission to take her to London to see King Lear. Margery then wrote to him saying that Lady Olivier had refused his request and adding some fears of her own about the situation:

Are you sure this is final (I'm sorry to be so practical) . . . If it were not and you went on now so that she came to love you, have you thought how it would be with her? (I think I would find a way to kill you). Yet if it is final you can wait and it will be the same with you when she is 18 or 19. What is clear is that you must not bring this into her life now . . . I see I think that when a woman falls in love she does so much more completely and finally, she gets quite lost & absorbed in that one thing and cannot think of other things and her development almost ceases.[2]

However, Margery did relent towards the end of the letter and extended an invitation for Rupert to visit them at Limpsfield, before Noel

---

1 *GE*, p. 170.
2 Olivier papers, Margery Olivier's Estate.

returned to school. Rupert saw no alternative but to accept the compromise, and spent two days at The Champions in September.

Having settled in his lodgings in Grantchester, Rupert was rapidly converted to his new life out of town and began writing a lecture on the subject entitled 'From Without'. It was based on a conversation he had had with Noel, on their picnic trip after Comus, and he intended to deliver it to a discussion society which he and Hugh Dalton had founded in their first year, called The Carbonari.

POST OFFICE TELEGRAPHS

CAMBRIDGE
NO.12.09

Office of Origin and Service Instructions

Steep   Handed } 2.00 P.M.   Received } 2.40 P.M.
               in at   here at

TO {   Brooke Kings College Cambridge

Ich habe genossen das irdische Gluck ich habe gelebt und geliebet by Schiller.[1] Noel

---

1 'I have tasted the fulness of earthly bliss
   I have lived and I have loved.'

These lines are sung by Thekla in *Die Piccolomini* (Act III, scene 7), the second part of Schiller's *Wallenstein*. They also appear, with a further two stanzas, in his *Gedichte*, as 'Des Mädchens Klage' – a poem which Schubert later set to music three times, in 1811, 1815 and 1816.

[Bedales]

Saturday. [13 November 1909]

I trust the lecture was a brilliant success, and that you didn't say: – "and then we feel as the poet, when he cried – 'ich habe genossen'" etc . . . because it wasn't Schiller who said it, but 'ein Madchen" in a song sung by the heroine in Valenstein; which is all very important. This by the way is an apology, and you are quite out of date about hockey and cricket – the latter is a summer game – lacross is what is played this season.[1]

N

The Orchard,

my home = Grantchester,

Cambridge.

Date: The Festival of Bishop Machutus [15 November]
[Postmark 20 November 1909]

My dear Noel,

        This is not a letter. I once wrote you . . . "a letter!" you scornfully replied, meaning that so long and untidy an effort was less or more. Very well. This is a pamphlet. First thanks for the telegram. I am sorry you had to telegraph. Communications, anyhow seemed difficult from your place. The postcard written on Saturday reached King's on Tuesday. The Post Office were very good. They transcribed and transmitted the German correctly. I have sometime telegraphed in Greek, and they have made a dreadful hash of it. The paper was (yes, thank-you!) most successful. It told them about Art and Life, and ended with your quotation. They were a good deal impressed by my knowing German. Rather airily, I said to Dudley yesterday, "Ah, yes in the profound words of the heroine of Wallenstein "Ich habe —— " etc" He said "You have made it up. No German could have written it. He would

---

1 Lacrosse was introduced at Bedales for the first time in the autumn of 1909. Noel played all three games for the school and that summer had achieved a commendable batting average of eleven.

have put genossen after Gluck." is it true? Are you deceiving me? I
baffled Dudley (an easy task) by saying that he was thinking of German
prose: poetry was different. But of course I didn't know. Unconsciously,
your telegram made a stir at Kings. I sat out in Grantchester writing my
paper till 7.30. Then I went to Cambridge. The meeting was at 8.15. I
had left a blank for the quotation. As I entered King's the beery,
suspicious eye of the Porter met me. "Ave you seen your brother" he
said. "No, why?" "E's 'ad a telegram" said the porter in a very deep
groan. I instantly thought my parents must be dead or dying. "What's it
about" I asked nervously. The porter has always suspected me, as a
socialist, of having dealing with Continental Anarchists. "It's in some
foreign lingo, from someone called Noyle", he said. "Good God" I said
and fled to my brother. He was very pale and produced the telegram. I
told him it was from the manager of the Hamburg State Lottery, to say I
had won a prize. It appeared that the telegram had arrived about three,
and was taken, of course, to my uncle the Dean of King's. He is a short
black tired frightened old man, who spends his life discovering errors
in Aramaic texts of the Book of Deuteronomy. He spent the afternoon in
nervous prostration at the shock of getting so passionate a declaration
of Paganism from an entire stranger. "not Goethe" bothered him too, I
gather. I shall not be so petty as to send you 9d. You would only spend
it on sweets and lacrosse-sticks. One day I shall repay you by giving
you an expensive tea, or 3/4 of my first shilling book of poems, or
some such equivalent. Meanwhile my thanks.

Oh! I wrote an inartistic but pleasant poem for The Cambridge
Review at their earnest request: ____ or rather I wrote it last April and
yielded it to them now.[1] The printer and publisher was so mad with
delight that he sent me two copies. I decided to send one to the first
person I write to. *Ecco!* It is your misfortune, not your fault. But you are
indeed a young person who reads poetry. And I always (still) believe
my lowly verse to show promise.

Dear! Dear! It is very difficult, I find, to write a letter ____ a
pamphlet, rather. Instead of getting on to the matter I am trying to write
about, I have an irresistible desire to babble on of a many irrelevant
and, to say truth, rather dull things. It is so easy to write on, whatever
comes into the head. I would like to tell you how some of us bathe in
the afternoon out here, and how fine and sharp and cold and golden it
all is, in setting sun and the wood. I would like to tell you ____ no, I

---

1 The poem, which appeared in the *Cambridge Review* on 11 November, was the sonnet 'Oh! Death
will find me, long before I tire', which Rupert had written while visiting Noel in the New Forest. See
page 24.

would like to write for it's the expressing, not the communicating, ____
about *Pinkie and the Fairies*[2] at the Theatre two nights ago, and about the
man I met in the road, and about my vacillations about going to
Switzerland, and about a book I have been reading, and about a song
called *The Sea View* (I sing it a good deal), and ____ peace! peace!
"Down, little bounder, down!" as Mr Gosse[3] said to his heart. I will
plainly say the things I cannot withhold; and then to my task.

(1) Dudley has got a fellowship at John's £200 a year for 6 years.

(2) Have you read a *Room with a View* yet?

(3) No: well, then, if you want to know what boys feel like and are
like, read *The First Round* by St. John Lucas, when you next get in reach
of the Garnett's Circulating Library. Skip the romance, that's not
particularly true. The rest is.

(4) Have you read Meredith's Last Poems? They're mostly bad.
But there's one very nice thing. It shows his splendour. To grow old like
that! To compensate, and to show up mine, I send it, also cut out of the
Review.[4] Oh, you've probably seen it. But it's good. Better than the sort
of formal farewells of Browning and Tennyson – "I hope to see, My
Pilot face to face" etc. –

I think that's all.

Well, do you remember as I drove away from *The Champions* in a
strangely stuffy cab, weeping a little out of the left-hand window, I
indistinctly cried through the cheering of the multitudes, "I shall write a
letter about it – "? But I expect you never heard. Anyhow, you foresaw it,
when we discussed – or rather when you asked questions among the
flowerpots, and I could not reply, because my mouth was full of biscuit,
and my tongue burnt by the hot milk (which I dislike). By now, perhaps
you have answered your own questions, or discovered new difficulties, or
worked out the Scheme[5] further than I. But in case, – and, anyhow to clear
my mind, and to provoke discussion and illumination from yours (Oh! be
quiet, not *necessarily* on paper!) ____ I do write. You said to Eva,[6] she tells
me, "Did Rupert tell you in his solemn way, or Margery in her flippant

2. This children's play by W. Graham Robertson (1866–1948), with music by Frederic Norton, was
performed at the New Theatre in Cambridge from 15 to 17 November.
3 Sir Edmund Gosse (1849–1928), poet and literary critic, who had been among the distinguished
guests at the Marlowe Society's performance of *Comus* on 10 July 1908, in which Rupert had played the
Attendant Spirit. Rupert met Gosse later that year at a tea party given by A.C. Benson in Magdalene.
4 The Meredith poem published was 'Youth in Age', as part of a review written by Rupert.
5 'The Scheme' to escape the boredom of middle age had first been thought of in early September. Its
originators, who included Margery and Bryn, settled on breakfast time, 1 May 1933, at Basle Station, as
their projected meeting place. (Cf. *LRB*, pp. 192–5)
6 Eva Marian Spielman (1886–1949), a friend of Margery's from Newnham; she had gained a First in
Economics in 1908, and later became a respected educationalist.

way?". The second had happened; but she got a dose of the first after she'd seen you. She was splendidly sensible; in more ways the most sensible in practical arrangements, of all the people with whom I have discussed it. Bryn is very good in that way: and Dudley. Margery is so shy. I believe you to be also a solemn and pedantic person. Then suffer solemnity.

"For ever" was first proposed. Then I (I think), myself desirous of 'for ever' suggested the option of X years. People agreed: but they seem to be hazy about it. Dudley seemed to have forgotten it. He rather frightened Eva by refusing to admit any option. The whole scheme and every detail of it needs to be thought out by us all. Everybody starts level and has an equal right to think of and change details: the babbling neophyte like you as well as the elderly originators, we. The only possession that makes one person more capable of suggestion than another is sense. So your assistance is valuable. My idea is that the Scheme includes, or rather *is*, one or two indispensable things, and the other details must be arranged for utility. Integrally, its a device for getting out of Middle Age by secretly vanishing and starting afresh. Now, all sensible people to themselves have desired to do this, I expect. But they've never arranged it. The thing is to get some impetus powerful enough to jerk the man of 45 out of his world into a new one. The nicest person of 45 can't start out again, because there is no reason why he should start the New Life today and not tomorrow: Monday and not Wednesday, or Friday . . . Therefore a prearranged and much thought of date and place is essential. Secrecy, as a general rule, is also necessary; and the general feeling of starting afresh. That is the kernel of the thing. The question of a time-limit, or none, has certain aspects.
[. . .]
The points in favour of people returning at the end of X years if they wanted to are these. It would get certain people in. To break secretly and clean away, even for 3 or 5 or 10 years, would succeed, even if the people then went back; they would have recovered youth. They would be living at fifty, and splendid, not dead. And the third point is that they *wouldn't* return; some of them. A person, fearful beforehand, might say "I shall only come for X years". but at the end of that period he (or she!) would find it impossible to go back, to leave the world and enter old age, again. The points against a time-limit I'd not realised, till you spoke of them. I see now the danger of it degenerating into a tourist fortnight on the Continent. But I think this, and the kindred danger of people not being serious about it, can be averted by putting the time limit *high* enough; and perhaps by limiting the proportion of those who won't mean to come for ever. But all these

things require consideration: and may have to be altered as time goes on.

Don't you think that once having got away long enough from the greyness into some mad corner or into the whole mad world, one *couldn't* return? The appeal of it now, – of evading smug middle age and tasting the intense best of life, and finding the glory of Earth – wouldn't that be doubly strong when one was nearer the danger, and *in* the splendour?

Anyhow, the one device of going suddenly off that May day must be kept – how, how long, and whither are details that work themselves out. To dish the religious and the melancholy by enjoying things, and finding our heaven on Earth! –

> "Whither soundeth vain as whence
> as word for such wayfarers"![7]

I vacillate dreadfully as to whether to go to Switzerland. I want to go. And I want not to go. I wish you were going. I shall see you in January, I gather.

Rupert.

---

7 This is possibly a parody in the style of Housman's *Fragment of a Greek Tragedy*, which begins:

O suitably-attired-in-leather-boots
Head of a traveller, wherefore seeking whom
Whence by what way how purposed art thou come
To this well-nightingaled vicinity?

SONNET

O! Death will find me, long before I tire
  Of watching you; and swing me suddenly
Into the shade and loneliness and mire
  Of the last land! There, waiting patiently,

One day, I think, I'll feel a cool wind blowing,
  See a slow light across the Stygian tide,
And hear the Dead about me stir, unknowing,
  And tremble. And *I* shall know that you have died,

And watch you, a broad-browed and smiling dream,
  Pass, light as ever, through the lightless host,
Quietly ponder, start, and sway, and gleam –
  Most individual and bewildering ghost! –

And turn, and toss your brown delightful head
Amusedly, among the ancient Dead.

Switzerland
[Hotel Schweizerhof
Lenzerheide]

Friday [24 December 1909]

Dear Noel

    In brown paper is a book: and I send it with this. I tried to put
this letter in the book: but then the woman at the Post Office said I
should have to pay 4fr.50. I got the book in London so it was perhaps
rather silly to bring it out here for the purpose of sending to you. If you

have another copy of this book, send this one back. I don't suppose you have. I hope Henley is not one of the passionate poets who pervert and destroy your young mind. Yet he's rather good.

This is said to be a pleasant place. It is hot. We sit about all day and bathe in the skating rink before breakfast.

On the other side is a drawing of the scenery which saves description.

I send a book you know because tomorrow is your and Jesus' birthday.

Rupert

[On reverse with drawing]

The black things are trees or people. There are more trees than at Klosters: fewer people –

[The Champions,
Limpsfield,
Surrey.]

Sunday 16th Jan [1910]

Dear Rupert

I believe that I met you in London the other day; but I had been to a theatre & my memory, owing to headache, was in an even worse condition than usual. So you see, I write to thank you for the Henley book which I am very glad you sent me, I wanted to have it badly and of course I had'nt got another copy, I never can afford to risk more than 1/- on a book, Meredith's poems, which I proudly posess in red calf limp, were an exception; and now I can never buy anything again, I shall be in debt – if it interests you – for many many years, because the 14 sheep which my brave & wonderful dog killed the other night were worth £22.[1] and my Father is in no way responsible for the disaster, either of the sheep-killing or of my having ever bought a dog. Therefore I rely on the charity of others for my amusements and luckily lots of people are charitable au fond especially one's parents and family and a few nice unrelated people such as you.

My three sisters, who sit in a row at irregular intervals across the fire, send you each their love; Margery and Daphne read, Margery aloud to Bryn who does embroidery, these occupations are typical, so my mentioning them may be useful to you, in fact its deeper than it might at first sound; I am not typical, it always distresses me to write, I cant do it and the knowledge is painfully brought home to me whenever I try. I had better apologise to you for this, I am very sorry about it, & for you.

You dont climb at Easter, so goodbye for some time.[2]

                                                               from Noel.

P.S. In case you didn't realise, the expression to be found about the middle of letter: "au fond" is French.

                                                               School Field
                                                               Rugby

Sunday the twentieth of March 1910

My dear Noel,

I do you the honour of writing on the only non-black-edged piece of paper in the house; I have found it with much trouble.[1] A letter came

---

1 It had been agreed that Noel should have a dog to accompany her on her frequent country rambles. Sydney had acquired a Great Dane from a pedigree breeder in Jamaica and he was named Loge. Later he wrote of the dog: 'His strength was immense: his muscles felt all hard and springy under his warm, shifty, satiny skin. His forelegs and paws were very long and heavy. These, when he fought, were his attacking weapons, to club and punch and buffet down his assailant till he got him pinned beneath him.' (*Olivier*, p. 196)
2 Noel was hoping to go climbing near Bethesda in North Wales.

---

1 Rupert's father, William Parker Brooke, had died on 24 January, aged fifty-nine, and Rupert had been asked to stay at Rugby for the term, as deputy housemaster.

from you once. It found me in bed and high-fevered. Like Antony,   "I did eat strange flesh upon the Alps,
          That some men died to look on."[2] And that caused me to be extraordinarily unwell. I was extraordinarily unwell when I careered with Bryn & you in a bus. The deceptive, hectic flush of the invalid was on my face: but my tongue, throat, & stomach were bleeding and raw. Your letter made me worse by describing the exploits of your non vegetarian dog.[3] I hope he is dead. But – and this is the point – it spoke of Wales. It said I wasn't going – which is true. I am going to Cornwall or Rotterdam. It is not yet decided which. It said you were. *Jacques* said you were going on the 6th or thereabouts. So it struck me you might be passing through Birmingham then. Will you be? Which day? When? For if I go to Cornwall, I shall pass through Birmingham about that day. And in any case, I shall have to interview the exquisite Mr Mountford (my dentist) who dwells near the Burne-Jones drawings . . . So write on a piece of paper & tell me, sometime before then, if & when.

When you see the pale men who teach you sliding wearily & alone round Bedales, pity them. They too are human, & alive (in a way). I tell you this, because I know. I am, so to speak, them. I am in charge, this term, of a houseful of youths, varying from four to seven feet in height. I like it, because I like them. They are a good age – fourteen to nineteen. (It is between nineteen and twenty-four that people are insufferable.) They look rather fresh and jolly too. But oh! the mask like faces that come before me. I am a "master", & therefore a moral machine. They will not believe I exist. Also, I am shy. Occasionally I determine to make a great attempt to pierce to their living souls by some flaming, natural, heartfelt remark. So I summon one. And when he trots into the study, a sullen meekness, I can only say, in a mechanical voice, "Jones *mi*, I hear your Latin Grammar was not sufficiently prepared. Please do me fifty lines." And really, you know, they're quite real, individual persons, rather bloody, of course, with accretions of the public school atmosphere, but human, and therefore conceivably nice. It's really that I'm in a false position; and when I *try* to stretch out a jolly hand to any of them, the shades of a

---

2 Caesar: On the Alps,
          It is reported thou didst eat strange flesh,
          Which some did die to look on.
               (*Antony and Cleopatra*, Act I, scene 4)
3 In a letter to Dudley Ward, Rupert bemoans how his devotion has subjected him to the 'ignominious' fate of spending 'the night in dreaming interminable dreams of Noel's dog'. (18 January 1910, *KCA*)

thousand schoolmasters rise between us, & form a black wall of fog: & we miss each other in the dark. Some of the elder ones are intellectually intelligent, if prim; & they are shocked & fascinated by the things I say about various deep, clear ulcers in their souls. I was not allowed to prepare the candidates for Confirmation. But I take prayers every night. I wish you could hear it, just once. All the prayers about Jesus ——— Some of the elder lads were in the school when I was. And, in those incredibly different days, I was tremendously athletic & played cricket & football with great skill and honour. So they retain the shreds of a worship. But the younger generation despise me as a round shouldered reader of books. As they fear my tongue of vitriol, all is well.

I feel like Ovid at Tomi[4] – but of course you don't know what that means. I am incredibly out of the world – but for a letter or two & a visit from Jacques – and rather weary. I seem to have been here about two thousand years. Last year is infinitely far & dim. Did it ever exist? Is there (for example) a country called Switzerland? Do (I pick at random) you exist?

We leave this house for ever in a fortnight. I wish you had seen it, ere strangers dwelt in the land. It is unpleasant, turning out. One empties cupboard after cupboard, sorts and destroys . . . Many things have been unpleasant. You were right once, in what you said to me (let not your head be turned by this unnatural reversal of the order of things). It was on the verge of the field at Klosters where I didn't jump.

The Prayer-Bell!

I hope you'll like climbing the mountains. I have chosen Holland because I'm told it is impossible to fall off any part of it. Do not fall off Wales. Are you still evil? I regard you with deep mistrust.

Rupert

---

4 Tomi was the town on the shores of the Black Sea to which Augustus banished Ovid in AD 8, and where the poet remained in unhappy exile until his death.

Bedales.
Wednsday, March 23rd. [1910]

Poor Rupert,

        Desease & steady work have unmanned you quite; but you
are wrong to think that yours is the lot & condition of all teachers in
schools. You have given me an 'enormous opening, throug which, to
expand on the great differences & advantages of Bedales over your kind
of school, for the masters here are quite real & happy & no one wears
masks for their benefit, we all realise their humanness and cheek them
accordingly, which they like: but if you will make use of your "tongue of
vitriol" against them, & give them lines with no explanation, no wonder
shortsighted Rugby boys dislike you. If you tried the right way you
could dispell the "shades of a thousand schoolmasters" in ten minutes
– its quite easy to destroy things. But I musn't answer your letter, I
never do. I will just reassure you. I am in existence, very lively & loud,
and Jaques was about right when he said I should go to Wales on the
6th, though it will probably be the 2nd. I dont think Birmingham is a
very good place for meeting people, especially when the train only
stops for about 5 minutes, does Mr Mountford (your dentist) & do the
drawings by Burne-Jones live in Birmingham?
        I shall be travelling with Mary Newbury[1] (whom you met at tea
once) and Ethel Pye[2] perhaps, who are going to Wales too; You might
come & put your head into the carriage & grin at us; but as you
probably wont want to, the real day does'nt matter, and I dont know
yet.
        I wish you'd tell me of some delightful book to read, I am now
working for the Higher Certificate exam (it comes off in June & I shall
either avoid it at the last moment or completely fail to pass) therefore I
have only very disjointed occasions on which to read & nothing, which
isnt delightful quite obviously, will do. You know about books & a little
about me – anyhow Ive explained for the present case – and you like

---

1 Mary Newbery (1892–1985), a Bedalian friend of Noel's. She was the daughter of Francis H.
Newbery (1853–1946), Emeritus Director of the Glasgow School of Art, who had given Charles
Rennie Mackintosh (1868–1928) the commission to redesign the school in 1897. Mary later married
the landscape painter Alix Riddell Sturrock (1885–1953).
2 Ethel Pye (1882–1960), sculptress and sister of Sybil Pye, with whom Rupert corresponded for
many years. Their family lived at Priest Hill, near the Oliviers in Limpsfield.

very much to show off your knowledge, so this is a chance for you – I shall be a very appreciative audience. What happens to you after you have left Rugby for ever? Will you have to go & build a house for your Mother to live in & then write nonsense to support yourself & her? Or will she be independant & let you go back & play & be distinguished in Cambridge? Anyhow, I hope you will get better somehow.

Yrs Ever.

Noel. O.

School Field,

Rugby.

Saturday March 26 [1910]

I descend to normal note-paper, and my official handwriting. I knew you were questionable as an end and infamous as a means in all other ways, but I held a faint hope you might be practically efficient. No; you date a letter Wednesday (though not spelt so) and post it on Friday; and within a week of a difficult and important journey across most of England and into a neighbouring state, you are infinitely dim about even the day you travel on. You do not say that you will make me more certain even when your dimness fades to light. But, if you like, tell me more definitely the hour & day, & I will combine Mr Mountford, it may be, with a little literary advice!

Why do you not think Birmingham a good place for meeting people? It is a most important place. Besides Mr Mountford and the Rossetti & Burnes-Jones & the best Shakespeare library in the world, it contains a race apart, a peculiar people. They look, & are, like no other people in the land. It is impossible to understand England without having stood on that great bridge that runs over the Birmingham Station, and watched the passers. It is almost necessary for you all to get out of your train and view the place – & the people. Otherwise you will not understand Life: as I do.

I may all the more desire to put my head into the carriage, & grin, if Ethel Pye's there too. For she tweets ecstatically about the

Birmingham collection of drawings by the podgy Rossetti. She might even leap from the train and see them.

I will not argue about the relative advantages of Bedales & the English Public School, now. Partly because there are yet one or two points to make clear about our system; partly because you are probably in the right. But it's not so easy to destroy a tradition as you think. Perhaps you have never met a Tradition? *Vires acquirit eundo.*[1]

I can't think of any delightful books you would understand. Possibly Shakespeare or Milton or E.M. Forster (if you've not yet succeeded), or Mr Arnold Bennett's "An Old Wives' Tale". All the best books are in Chinese; & so we can't read them. Perhaps Belloc might do you good.

We don't "leave *Rugby* for ever". We only retire to a wee house in a grey part of it. And my mother is "independent" enough for me to be able to return & be indistinguishable at Cambridge. I don't know what you mean by "playing". And it is very unlikely I shall ever get better. Our financial "independence" by the way, is of the kind known as 'genteel poverty': that is to say, we just fail to live with any comfort on what would support ten "working men" & their families in luxury.

If you read a book in Wales, do not read any book Bill Hubback[2] recommends you, without asking Jacques; & do not read any book Jacques recommends you, at all.

Rupert

Bedales,
Petersfield,
Hants.

Sunday. 27th. [March 1910]

Well, if you will be pigheadedandobstinate – (though you need'nt be furious about it) Mr Badley has just told me that I shall leave here on Tuesday the 5th, so we shall pass Birmingham that day, the afternoon

---

1 It gathers force as it progresses. This is Virgil's description of Rumour in *Aeneid*, iv: 175.
2 Francis William Hubback, who graduated from Trinity in 1907 with a First in History. He was one of the originators of 'The Scheme' (see note 5, p. 21). He married Eva Spielman in 1911, and they had two children before he was killed in France in 1917.

probably – but as I said, there wont be time to get out although Birmingham people are wonderful, and even Ethel is not brave or mad enough to "leap". I too should like very much to see pictures by Burne-Jones & Rossetti.

I saw some in the Tate Gallery the other day, I went there alone & stayed a long time, wandering about with a catalogue; but Shakespeare I cant indulge in off hand. Cant you come to Wales on your way to Holland, or would it be out of your way? I mean in the same train as we do; by the way, you are still more unpractical (whatever it means) for you do not even know *where* you are going yet; you could easily fall off Cornwall.

You were right to suggest Belloc, but I had thought of him, I read The Path to Rome out of doors aloud (not alone) every day, because it is very warm & the book is more successful read so; I believe one can also write – such things as letters & books – better right out in the sun, & can talk better on a walk than in a room, though the actual walking is not necessary – does it also help with speaking publicaly, are the greatest speeches open-air speeches? perhaps though it doesnt apply to great & serious people – only to dawdlers – me etc. You ought to come down here in the Summer once, it is better then than in Spring or Winter, and there are downs; perhaps you have been already? if not, get Jacques to invite you, or Lupton.[1]

I shouldnt take anyone's advice about books now, neither Jaques' nor Bill's: even yours is useless, & I shaln't read in Wales.

Bryn can tell you about trains if you want to know. I am half asleep & unable to be sincere or funny. If you ever write again, dont be scathing, such letters are a dissapointment after the excitement of seeing them in the letter-rack, and not many letters come for me.

Noel.

I have to sit at Mr Badley's table for dinner & tea for the rest of the term, I find him hard to talk to, & the prospect of each meal worries one for hours beforehand, where you awkward when you saw him? He, always give such brief answers and looks so absorbed in his own thoughts and sausages. What shall I say at dinner to day?

---

1 Geoffrey Lupton (1882–1949), an O.B. who had designed and built the school's New Hall. In later life, having gone to farm in South Africa, he was gored to death by a bull.

School Field,
Rugby.
(for four days more)

The Second of April [1910]

My dear Noel,

– Not *scathing*, surely! – I never realised, anyhow! Airy, airy, and perhaps a touch middle-aged: but not more . . . Airy . . . airy . . . airy . . .

Mr Mountfort has returned from his Easter holidays. I think he has had a good time. He *is* going to torment me at 4 on Tuesday. So perhaps I shall see you. Do you know, I still have just an odd fancy for you to let me know the train. It was kind of you to refer me to the rest of the party. I have had delightfully explicit communications in great numbers from them: and I know the time & route of *their* train with startling accuracy. It was the day before yesterday & they besought me to come & look over the bridge as they passed. But as the bridge was twenty-five miles away, & they swept under it at a time when I had to be persuading fifty little boys to take their puddings, the meeting – if so you may call it – did not come off. It may be that you mean that your train is at the same hour as theirs – reaching Birmingham from Paddington at 1.45 & departing soon after. If this be so, you need not answer; if not, I pray you write just even half a card – unless you go, again, on quite another day. I gather that Ethel & Bryn won't be with you, but only the woman with the Florentine hair: – Oh! perhaps others. I am sorry you can't get the train restarted or anything. Wales is, I find, just out of the way for Holland. I am getting so ill that I may only go to Dorset or die here.

Yes, I shall get Jacques to take me 'there' once more (Petersfield, I mean) and in the summer. Or Dudley & I will come in our carriage. Here, we are being 'moved', and it is hateful. All the ugly jolly old chairs & tables one has got up or down from, are reft suddenly from their accustomed places & bound on their backs on carts & carried, pitiful, their legs waving unrespectably in the air, through the public streets.

I hope you thought of something to say to Badley that lunch. I nearly telegraphed suggestions: you moved such sorrow in me.

Rupert

Don't let anybody fall off Wales.

Bedales

Sunday [3rd April 1910]

If we catch the right train we get to Birmingham at 12.10 P.M., if we miss it we shall go by another which gets to Birmingham at 1.45. PM.[1] I hope your dentist wont hurt you very much.

Noel. O

The Orchard
Grantchester

The second of May 1910

Did you? – did you not? – or was it somebody else? – tell me that "Bunny" Garnett was in Letchworth? I think you did. Can you tell me his address? For I want to persuade him to come over here during the next two months, sometime – . And I suppose you're the only source I can get the information from. If you're too lazy "it would be very kind of you" if you would just tell me even, his Limpsfield, his home, address, I don't even know that.

Yesterday it was the first of May and a great many people – Katherine Cox, & Geoffrey Keynes, and that type of person – decided to have breakfast with me. Is the logic of that at all clear? The thing is that they insist on "dabbling in the dew" & being "in the country" on the first of May. I had to get up at half-past seven to give them breakfast: though I had worked until 2. It rained in the morning; yet they all turned up, thousands of them – men and women, devastatingly and indomitably cheery. The world is hard, & I was very bitter. When rain

---

1 Rupert's plans came to nothing, as he related to Dudley: 'I leapt out of the 12.11 directly it touched B'ham: and saw the extraordinarily inexpressive behind of the 12.10 sliding westward out of the station. Nobody seemed to know if she had been in it – or, really, to care. I felt if she had, she'd have had her head out of the window. So I waited cheerily for the 1.45. I searched every carriage in that train. She was not there.' (*LRB*, p. 232)

ceased we put on goloshes & gathered cowslips in the fields. We celebrate the festival with a wealth of detailed and ancient pagan ritual; many dances & songs. We found a mandrake – which is like a Root, but very strange, like this.

2ft

We planted It in Earth & put flowers in It's hair & worshipped it. It was Vegetation God. You will learn about these when you study Comparative Primitive Mythology. Occasionally it fell down & screamed. Once Geoffrey Keynes found a baby slug in a cowslip and put it into It. We composed & intoned a rhymed curse about

> Geoffrey who behaved so Odd;
> Geoffrey who put Slugs in God.

I do not perceive that you are much excited. I only write thus because it is raining very hard; & I ought to go into Cambridge to lunch; and I don't want to; and I feel like a Mackintosh; and

In many ways I am a damnable fool. Sitting talking to myself here in the evenings I discover it. My jokes are so much of the same kind. Laboriously I utter some elaborate jest to myself. I sit & hear it without a smile. It is *too* dull . . .

I forget if I told you about me & Mister Nevinson and Helen of Troy. Isn't Mister Nevinson a friend of yours?[1]

Can you, when you know, let me know what you all *are* going to do in August & September, and when? And shall I really flash through

---

1 Henry Woodd Nevinson (1856–1941), journalist and writer. In April Nevinson had briefly stood in as Editor of the *Nation* and while there had read eight poems which Rupert submitted. While admiring them, he felt certain phrases in 'Menelaus and Helen' were unpalatable and needed changing, for example the concluding description of Helen:

> Oft she weeps, gummy-eyed and impotent;
> Her dry shanks twitch at Paris's mumbled name.
>   (*PRB*, p. 126)

Rupert went in person to the paper's offices to argue out these points. He wrote to his mother describing the visit as a success (c.f. *LRB*, p. 235), although the *Nation* published only 'Goddess in the Wood'. Noel had met Nevinson several times, when he visited her parents at The Champions.

Petersfield on my coach in July? I was glad I did, after all, see you for half a day in April.

Rupert

You must not, I tell you, let your head be turned & your pride inflamed by the thought that *you* find it hard to write a letter, and people of light fingers – like me – find it so easy. If you *knew* how difficult it is! . . . The fog, the fog, the folly & evasion & cowardice . . . The fog . . . the fog . . . the f

The Champions
Limpsfield

Thursday [5 May 1910]

Dear Rupert

Thank you for wanting to know where Bunny lives, and writing about May day, it didn't rain here and Bryn & I & Harold[1] went to look for a camping ground on Ashdown forest, we didnt find one, but it doesnt matter, as we shalnt have time to camp – at least, not yet; nor this year. I dont know what we're going to do or when we have to go to Jamaica, they write from time to time, & suggest a different plan in each letter, we shall probably be let go to Switzerland, which will take up August, & September's to cold to camp; Bunny says he wont be able to come; but ask him about it when you see him; I hope you'l succeed in getting him, you'll find him pleasant, I should think, but dont make him angery about anything, he is very dangerous when enraged & more than once has nearly Killed people who have agravated him.[2] His adress at Letchworth is The Cloisters; but I believe he is down in London now, doing an exam, in which case he will be living at

---

1 Harold Hobson (1891–1973), Bunny's closest friend from Limpsfield, who was then studying engineering at King's College, London.
2 Though Noel writes in jest, Bunny did indeed suffer from terrible rages. For example, in his seventies, he crossed a road without looking properly and was knocked down by a car. By the time the concerned motorist had approached to check he was all right, the furious Bunny was on his feet and laid the man out with a swift punch!

19 Grove Place
Christ Church Road
Hampstead.   his home here is
The Cearne
Kent Hatch
Crockham Hill
Nr Edenbridge
Kent.

I havent heard about you & Mister Nevinson and Helen of Troy, I should like to; but I suppose that is not to be looked for from you, since you have discovered that you too are affraid of writing letters – why, I cant think, the evasion & cowardice succeed very well, which is all thats necessary – O, I suppose thats wrong "Not very good" as you would mutter, but never having been able to evade well, I havent reached a standard whence I can despise the power, I may manage to jump some day; but at present all power seems good.

That too is probably poor, so goodbye
(dont let Bryn shake hands with you in Cambridge)

from. Noel.

24 Bilton Road
Rugby
Sunday July 3rd [1910]

Dear Noel,

I meant to write to you so long ago, and oh! so often! But the life I've been leading, at Grantchester! From time to time great parties of the screaming young descend on me there. And in the intervals and through it all I have been 'working' with no success, and enormous concentration at an infinitely unimportant and uninteresting subject. Every night after the world has gone to sleep I have sat down at a green lonely table and vowed "Now I shall write my surprising letter to her!". And always I felt "I am just too tired for the vital witticisms and exquisite rhymes to drop off my pen. I shall go to bed: and write tomorrow." And, anyhow, nothing in the letter was to be surprising but just the consummate skill that so delicately clothes these "evasions" and indirections you so like and admire, with garments that triumphantly hint the limbs beneath. Have you ever seen a musical comedy?

To it, again, then!

"I am writing to say that" I am coming to Petersfield. Is it permissible? The matter is this. Dudley (a German) and I are going to start from Winchester in a cart about July 16th.[1] We can take Petersfield on the way. Which day, and how long, are undecided, even on other grounds. Jacques will be in Minorca and without him I should be too horribly frightened to come near Bedales. But I thought of trying to get Thomas[2] or Lupton to let Dudley & me slumber in their grounds that night, & give us a meal. If that is impossible, I suppose we shall just pass through the place and hang about for an hour or two, if it's decent or desirable. But I want to see Thomas!

What of you? shall we appear? (you suggested to me that Petersfield was perfect in July . . .) Is it possible you can see us, if, as we shan't, we don't come into the grounds? I understand that there are complications. But here the Jacques difficulty, of not knowing parents, doesn't come in. You may say that I am extremely intimate with the woman who produced you, & have on several occasions been seen to nod to Sir Sydney Olivier. But if you've time, and the will, what can be done? Can you come out an enormous walk? Or can you only come up the hill to tea? or, if those men (Lupton & Thomas) aren't there, is all vain? It is most important that you should write to me, here and now, about this. You may decide or suggest anything; for I am free as the wind, and Dudley an absolute monsoon. And, indeed, if you can bear to wait another three weeks, or if you are occupied with your ultimate examinations or with playing hockey again, warn us and we won't even appear. Three weeks, I say, for I am, oh, yes!, going to your camp at Buckler's Hard. Our cart will land us there. I am – to dip into epistolary language again – "looking forward" to it. I am preparing a quite new accomplishment for it, even. By God, life will be good, in August! I shall make a special endeavour not to die during July.

---

1 Rupert and Dudley Ward had organized a twelve-day tour of the south-west, to campaign for Poor Law reform. Their plan was to address open-air meetings in towns and villages they passed through, and, failing that, 'display the poster, look wise, and scatter pamphlets'. (LRB, p. 243)

2 Edward Thomas (1878–1917), poet and essayist. Already a near neighbour of Geoffrey Lupton's, Thomas was soon to move to Wick Green, a house built by the architect on his own land overlooking the Downs.

So, if anything is possible and all is well, I shall see you in ten days; and *then* I will explain to you the strange Tale of Me & Mr. Nevinson and Helen of Troy (to say nothing of the minor figures in it, legs & Mr. Steevens of Dublin & the Office Boy & Menelaus.). For it would take too long now. And anyhow I expect you've heard it by this. It's all over England.

Strange vaporous ghosts of strange Tales of you have trickled through Grantchester: I look at you with dark and dreadful eyes. Your fantastic life seems to spring up at moments even through the school-girl manner. If I see you, I shall insist on talking to you about your Work: & you will answer in the conversational note you use to Tall Men. (All the same, I do, occasionally, Rise Above conventions. I did *not* shake hands with Bryn at Cambridge. She came towards me with a winning smile and an outstretched hand. I backed against the wall, my hands behind me lest I should be forced; and kicked her ankles till she went away.)

I secured Bunny. I felt I should be good for him, and I knew he was very nice. I contradicted him in such a subtle way that he didn't get (you have a genius for inventing words – I thank you for it) "angery". Or didn't show it. He and I went on to the Broads and joined that uncomprehending tall man,[3] & a lot of others, on a wherry. It was a fat odd life. Bryn was there: Godwin & his woman,[4] and others. Of an evening we sat in rows on the deck & read Swinburne aloud, under a great moon. Wisps of smoking mist curled up out of the river, grew half-real like the people one meets at tea, and fled away in a silent endless procession down the river like the ghosts of a million imponderable businessmen scurrying to keep eternal, non-existent, appointments. Among them stealthy boats from other ships crept up through the half light to hear what was happening, and caught my harsh voice rolling immensely out

"Though the heathen outface and outlive us –
and our lives and our longings are twain
Ah, forgive us our virtues, forgive us,
Our Lady of Pain!"[5]

---

3 This was Dr Rogers, an old family friend of the Oliviers who acted as chaperon on this occasion. As Bunny recalls: 'He was a very large man and extremely gullible . . . but our holiday was not marred by any practical jokes at his expense.' (*GE*, pp. 220–21)
4 Godwin Baynes (1882–1943). Having read medicine at Cambridge, Baynes was now a house physician at St Bartholomew's Hospital. He had camped at Penshurst and been invited to join 'The Scheme'. His 'woman' was Rosalind Thornycroft, a cousin of the Oliviers, whom he married in 1913.
5 Swinburne: 'Dolores', *Poetical Works* (John D. Williams, New York, 1884), p. 70.

and then they scandalizedly slipped off again, with glowing faces, & the discreet regular splash of middle-class oars.

Did you know you were coming up to Cambridge about August 10th for a week? Bryn is going to take part in a play there. It will be splendid. I want to get you a ruined home at Grantchester. I hear, by the way, that you're not coming to the camp for some days, because you're celebrating your abandonment of Bedales. Do turn up as soon as you can. I want to tell you about the Universe, and other things. It will be so useful for a she-doctor to know.

Which also reminds me that you, they say, will after all stop in England next year. Good! Though I could excuse you the spring: when I think of Germany. I must stop: and eat. Answer this, and I will retort with arrangements, & a few more of the things I wanted to say. Even Rugby is gay. This henceforth I write poems all day: superb ones.

ecstatically
Rupert

Bedales,
Petersfield,
Hants.

9th of July [1910]

Dear Rupert

I am longing to hear about Mr Nevinson & curious to hear about the Universe, and if satisfaction on these two points involves being talked to about my work by you, I am willing to risk unpleasantness & listen. So it would be nice for you to come somewhere near here, & perhaps on Sunday 17th, I might be allowed to go for a walk. I shall be begining that happy fortnight in which my exam takes place & perhaps they will think I might catch cold or develope brain fever if I saw you, but what they will think I cannot be sure of till the very Saturday before, when they either will, or will not sign my leave.

Therefore I cannot be sure about seeing you, but as Petersfield – its surroundings – *are* pleasant and as there is Thomas whom you want to see, and also Lumpit, who provides such good teas, both of them living on a hill nearby, your efforts in reaching this district will not have been wasted, even if I have to spend the day in bed. Perhaps you had better find out from the two above mentioned people, whether they will be there.

--- -- -- -- -- -- -- -- -- -- -- -- -- --

Conclusion Come with your German friend by all means & camp in the cart on Lumpit's garden; I will try & intimate to you there, if I can come, & arrange where, when & how.

Is this enough of plans? I hope it will serve as a stoker at least, & that your retort will be enormous.

Yours Ever
Noel.

Are you also living for "pleasure alone"? I have been reprimanded for so doing.

I think Bilton Rd must be horrid.

24 Bilton Road
Rugby

Monday [11 July 1910]

Mr dear Noel,

I'm just a little more precise than I was a week ago. Lupton, in fact, *will* be there. And the German & I are going to stay with him. On the other hand, it will be extremely difficult, not to say impossible, for us to stay for Sunday, the day you are, you think, so free on. It would disorganize the exciting present and blast the gay future, of the Poor Law Organization of the Southern Counties. You don't want to do *that*!

. . . Well, "as things are" we shall leave London on Thursday, & reach
Petersfield 3.32 or 4.45 or some such ridiculous time. And will leave it
again, no doubt, on Saturday morning. Well; what's to be done? We
shan't, you notice, be in our Caravan! We shall be just two gentlemen
with luggage & dressed in oh! the most delightful London clothes. Can
you, if you *can*, come a walk or excursion on the Thursday or Friday, at
any hour and also to a meal? or to one – developing – into – another?
or to which? I think, you know, you'd better make out, on the
information I've given you, what can, may, and shall be done, and tell
Lupton, or send a note to me up there. I'll be here at any rate till mid-
day on Wednesday: so if you want us to appear by or at any particular
hour on Thursday, write straight back & say so. Oh, I hope you're
allowed to have tea & so forth not only on Sundays! It will be ridiculous
to come to that place & not see you. Herr Dudley will never recover. I
will not give you brain-fever. Take an anti-toxin (Matthew Arnold's
prose works). I will talk about quite unintellectual things (like Mr
Nevinson, & the Universe). I will even help your impending exams by
explaining to you, in a low voice, the Method by which one may Defeat
any Examiner: also the Inductive Process. Of course, there's the danger
that I may be suspected of being part of your life of "pleasure alone", so
that your leave willn't be granted. God forbid!

Ah, yes! I've taxed with living for "pleasure alone". The charge is
less frequent than it used to be, though, with me. It is entirely true.
Whether to congratulate you or turn my head, I hardly know. Perhaps
I'm a little uncertain what it means. Have you, like Mr Swinburne,
changed "in a trice

> The Lilies & Languors of Virtue
> For the Raptures and Roses of Vice."?[1]

I love to picture you wantoning among roses and chocolates. But
do you know what is said about living for pleasure in that fountain of
wisdom "The Importance of being Earnest."?[2] There was Lady
Bracknell's friend who did after her husband had died, & her hair
had "turned quite golden from grief." (marginal note – has yours?) –
the symptom of such life being her fondness for muffins. Then, even
worse, there was Jacks poor brother who died in Paris & was "quite

---

1 From 'Dolores', stanza IX.
2 The play by Oscar Wilde (1854–1900), which had first been performed in London on 14 February
1895.

unmarried". "People who live for pleasure alone usually are, I believe," says Miss Prism. And Miss Prism was a governess.

But the post draws nigh. I will see you in four days! I haven't even time to read what I've write. It's probably all wrong.

yours (if anybody's)
continually desperately

Rupert

Together with her friend, Mary Newbery, Noel managed to get permission to visit Edward Thomas for tea, and so saw Rupert before he disappeared on his caravan tour. She sat her Higher Certificate Exams, passing her Biology, German and Essay papers, but failing English, Maths and Latin.

After the tour was finished, Rupert and Dudley went on to join a group of their friends who were camping at Buckler's Hard, Beaulieu. Noel was there, as were Ka Cox, Godwin Baynes, Ethel, Sybil and David Pye, Jacques Raverat and the newly engaged couple, Eva Spielman and Bill Hubback. Later, in his Memoir, Jacques records the impression Noel made on him:

> She had an admirable head, set on her handsome round neck, brown hair, flat complexion, the face very regular and unexpressive, even a bit hard. But it was lit up as if by the beam of a lighthouse when she turned her large grey eyes to you. One could hardly bear their gaze without feeling a kind of instant dizziness, like an electric shock. They seemed full of all the innocence in the world, and of all the experience also; they seemed to promise infinite happiness and wonderful love for whoever could win her.[1]

One evening Rupert and Noel walked off alone, to collect wood for the fire. Rupert took the chance to declare his love for her and was overjoyed when she admitted that she loved him too. They decided to become engaged, but, knowing the resistance such an announcement would meet with, to keep their pledge secret. It is interesting to note that this change in their relationship came at a time when the whole nation was in a state of turmoil: the government was at loggerheads with the House of Lords; the Women's Suffrage movement was growing more clamorous; King Edward VII was succeeded by George V and the art world had been rocked by Roger Fry's first Post-Impressionist exhibition. In her Memoir of Roger Fry Vanessa Bell notes: 'That autumn of 1910 is to me a time when everything seemed springing to new life – a time when all was a sizzle of excitement, new relationships, new ideas, different and intense emotions seemed crowding into one's life.'[2]

The Marlowe Society had been asked to repeat their production of Dr Faustus on 17 August, for the benefit of fifty visiting German students. Francis Cornford, who was now married to Frances Darwin, was chosen to play Faustus, with Rupert as Chorus. As it was not an official University

---

1 *Memoir III*, p. 22. Quoted in *The Neo-Pagans* by Paul Delany, p. 89.
2 Quoted in *A Very Close Conspiracy* by Jane Dunn (London: Jonathan Cape, 1990), p. 147.

production, Bryn was to play Helen of Troy, and Noel was permitted to understudy one of the seven deadly sins, Envy! The Olivier and Pye sisters stayed in the house next to the Orchard, which was called the Old Vicarage.

As Noel left Cambridge, once the production was over, both she and Rupert knew that it could be some time before they met again. Both had been invited to stay with Jacques in France, but Noel felt Rupert's presence might make her feel awkward and suggested he decline the offer.

> Rooftree
> Walberswick
> Nr Southwold
> Suffolk

Tuesday September 6th [1910]

O Rupert,

I'm very affraid to write, but you said I might, even that I had better; so I trust that this wont be received with too much irritation by you, who sit among the permanent joys & satisfaction of books & work. I only want to say that Prunoys[1] is settled for Bryn & me & we shall go proabably on Monday the 12th, also that I still feel that you'd better not come & have discovered reasons too; those referring to me are rather complex, but now I hear of your serenity it is obvious also that for your sake it should not be broken.

I dont know how long ago it was that we left Cambridge but I seem only to have read five books at the most, all of them little short ones too; so I suppose the intellect is not being developed sufficiently.

---

1 Jacques Raverat's home in France, the Château de Vienne, Prunoy. Noel, Bryn, Gwen, Ka and the Cornfords had accepted the invitation, which Rupert later reluctantly declined.

There is a strange new atmosphere here, Walberswick has been famous for many years as a resort for landscape & other painters; they come down in quantities every summer & stay in lodgings & villas (?Ls?) till September. The Newberies, who are the parents of the woman with the Florentine hair & with whom I am, are also of that kind & know them all. So I get taken round to teas & tennis and into lovely drawing rooms after supper to see exquisite furniture & hear music, also I am introduced into picture shows & elegant studios, coming out saturated with bewildering ideas & sensations about minor artists & their work. How I shall go back to Bedales as a sane & vulgar child after all this & France on top of it I cant tell, it may be a failure.

The other thing, what happened at Camp & at Cambridge, will not affect my manner so much. I shall not pine & I do not; if I think of it it just makes me gloat & dance & other people dont notice it, except Bryn, who was always a sympathetic person.

I have a permanent notion that I shall see you in about a week, the time never gets less, but the idea keeps me quiet. Perhaps you will write & shatter it some day.

Yours ever
Noel.

24 Bilton Road
Rugby

September 6th 1910

It is an *amazing* length of time. Only my firm intellectual grasp of thir ·s, and my grim faith in my own memory, convince me that it *wasn't* all an illusion. I refuse to believe it was. But remember how suspicious of my memory I got after twenty-four hours, and reflect on the probable effect of nearly twenty-four days. Yet I refuse to disbelieve that something did, somewhere, happen . . . In that faith I write.

Isn't it queer that this is the first letter I have ever written to you? Who wrote all the others, and to whom, I can't exactly say. They are very old, now. Today is the sixth of September. It's funny to think that one day one'll be able to look at that "September 6th 1910" and think of it as just as funny dead a date as October 1st 1904, or January 8th 1879, and the rest of them, seem to us now.

– Oh, I don't *at all* want to go on telling you just what blithering thoughts trail through my mind every second. In any case it would take too long. And I refuse to write a long letter (like those prenatal ones). As you refuse to reply at any length, it makes it very unfair. And anyhow I want to use the time in writing a poem on Dining Room Tea, not waste it writing unlucrative letters to you.

But I'm irresistibly compelled to write to you, just to tell you – God knows what! One or two details of fact anyhow. One is, that it's possible – there are even chances – that I shall go abroad, with my mother, *before* Christmas, say December 15th, leave her & go on to Munich & return, – God knows when, April or later. Also I shall be here, probably, till September 28th, then Cambridge or London. So, if all that's so, don't you see that we'll not meet for more than half a year? Isn't that carrying the discipline rather *too* far? (– But what's to be done?) I may decay beyond recognition by next April: there are seeds of it in me already. I warn you, I am feeble. Of course, there's Prunoy: which is possible, though difficult, – on all other grounds I mean. *You* never said anything very definite, in conclusion. And I cannot make up my mind. But even that would leave September 21st (the date, roughly, when I'd have to return) to April nth. In these last three weeks I have been extremely hilarious & triumphant, and quite calm. I think far less often of you than I used to, & far less feverishly. (Whether to praise or blame myself, I don't know. Sometimes I feel rather ashamed of it. Though, as I rather set out to do this, feeling it somehow the thing worthiest of us & the situation I *could* do, I don't see why I shouldn't be pleased at my success.) But there are moments (this is one) when I get rather despondent. You see, I am feeble & mean & empty and a fool & a devil & rather a beast. And I feel that with proper treatment something might be made of me. Only, the proper treatment, I suspect, includes more of – you. And without that I, as I say, decay and decompose, – and occasionally dislike myself.

At that point, I went & had tea. And now, do you know, I feel quite cheerful again. That's the worst of writing letters. They only give the writer as he is during a certain hour; not the writer as he is during a month or a year: nor, possibly, just – the writer. I might easily write during a time when I didn't care twopence whether you lived or died or what you did, & convey a false impression that I'd fallen quite out of love with you, and so (conceivably) relieve, or irritate you –

unnecessarily. Or, what'd be even, perhaps, tiresomer, I might write during one of the horrible periods when I realise that unless I'm thinking of you every minute, and unless I'm Tristan-drunk all the time, I'm not being fine enough for you, not treating you worthily. (There's a flaw in that, isn't there? I hope so. Do assure me it's all right that I – we – should enjoy ourselves under the circumstances, quite heartily.)

But, just now, – and pretty often – I'm immensely cheery. I go bounding through life. "Do not" I say to the parlourmaid "look at me as if I was a Common Person. I am not. I am Unique; Marked out above all men. I will explain." And I dance to her the reason. Yesterday I stopped before the fat policeman at the corner. "You look as if you thought you were Important;" I told him, "Know then that I barely realise your existence. I soar above you. – Ah, but you've never met Noel, eh, Old Thing?" And later "Great, green, wood! Pah!" I said, snapping my fingers at the greengrocer in High Street. – Oh, I don't know where I've got to. Do you loathe this oafish & imbecile pirouetting? Shall I plunge into some strong simple stark sticky sugary sentimentality?

No!

[. . .]

I've a million things to discuss tell, & ask. That's partly why I must see you, sometime. I've never had time to mention you half the things I wanted to spend hours in explaining. If ever we do meet again, we might make a rule that we are to spend at least two hours in rational conversation every time we're together. It'd be good for our characters anyhow!

I went to the Fabian Summer School[1] a week for conscience' sake. I rather loved it all. There was, I discovered, a Bedalian there, with her brother, whom I know, – one Sargant-Florence.[2] She's just left & going to take to fresco painting. Is she good? She knew everyone connected with Bedales, I did, even Jacques. And had very good judgements on them all. I thought her rather fine, for four reasons (1) she had a large, sensible head (2) she always sat or stood absolutely still. (3) She displayed a right judgement about you (at that point I dragged her off &

---

1 The Fabian Society had begun organizing annual Summer Schools in 1907 and Rupert had first attended in 1908. In 1910 it had fallen to Beatrice and Sidney Webb to direct the six weeks of 'teaching, learning and discussion', with 'some off days, and off hours, for recreation and social intercourse', which took place at Llanbedr in North Wales. *Our Partnership* by Beatrice Webb (New York: Longmans Green, 1948), p. 457.

2 Alix Sargant-Florence (1892–1973) went to the Summer School with her brother Philip, who was just about to go up to Cambridge. Alix too studied at Cambridge, although she first spent a year at the Slade School of Art. It was while she was with the Fabians this summer that she met her future husband, James Strachey.

talked to her for an hour – oh! about Art) (4) She understood what one said and answered exactly sufficiently, always to the point, & always with an appearance of thought. I may have been misled by an insignificant Bedales' manner (which I approve) and a reflected glory that occasionally glistened about her. But tell me she is sensible. It is an important thing to be.

It fills one with the oddest feelings to imagine that you (unless your executors) will be opening & touching this with these exact hands, & the envelope will be lying in your lap, on those precise and very clothes. And you'll be reading it quietly with an unmoving face, & there'll be perhaps a person or two near you, waiting for you to talk with them, or breaking in on you & laughing something external to you, that'll make you laugh in reply. Damn them! – No! that's wrong. But I'm very mean & unpleasant.

Yes, dammit, I *am* glad you're existing away from me among & for other people; just that you're exisitng, quite glad, quite fairly glad.

I do want to see you. But don't reckon that. I'm very happy.

It's *very* queer, this should be <u>me</u> writing to <u>you</u> –

How do I end up this? I'm afraid. I shall just write my name. –

                                                            Rupert

Oh, I want to go *on* writing, so!

N o - e l !

                                                    The Champions
                                                    Limpsfield
Saturday 10th [September 1910]

Dear Rupert

        I think its almost necessary that I should write, to answer two letters of yours.

All *was* vain, for I went up on Friday & did lots of things in London all day alone. Bryn wouldn't come and in the evening I went to the houses of many relations and tried to get a bed for the night, they were all away & I finally came down here by the last train minus 4d. When I got to this house in a panic at some time past 12 at night I woke up four people with the banging I made, some of them came down & let me in & I discovered that they were the very relations whom I had sought in vain in Hampstead; they had filled the house & I had to creep into the foot of a bed containing a small cousin. So today I am sleepy & I shall not go to London again till on the way to Prunoy.

I am rather glad that it was impossible to carry out those unspeakably horrid plots, the letter full of them came just as I was leaving Walberswick and it made me ill & mad all the way up in the train.[1] If we cant meet without schemes I would rather, by far, not see you for half a year – when you will be "decayed" (I dont know what it means) & I shall have cut off my hair, or put it up. Now, I dont see whats to be done, I go back to Bedales (with luck) on the 23rd & shall probably get back from France the day or hour before I have to pack up a school trunk.

I didnt read the other letter among people who laughed & waited; neither did I wear any clothes, but the envelope became saturated on the edge of the bath, and the water got tepid as I tried to make you out.

The most inteligible & most exciting thing in it was that you met Alix (Sargent Florence). She always struck me as being overpoweringly sensible, and good because so strong. She was the best person at Bedales, but too indifferent to be a success there, she drew "cleverly", but I rather doubted whether she would ever be good, perhaps frescos will develope her better than characatures could. What you saw & understood of her was true, she does not pose nor adapt herself. Unfortunately although she didn't mind me, I shall never probably know her again. Did you like her brother? I sha'nt write another sheet it would be exceeding the limit & therefor unsafe.

"Yours Ever" is as good now, as it ever was & it is a permissabel form of considerable freedom; how about

Love from
Noel.
?

---

1 This letter is missing.

Rugby
But on Tuesday   Grantchester –
Sunday September 25. [1910]

I see you hating to get this. But I *will* defend myself. And you needn't
answer. About "unspeakably horrid plots." (Oh, I loathe myself & I
loathe you, that I upset you that day – made you "ill & mad.") . . . (I
feel more & more flushed & foolish & gobbly & undignified & sinking
into the unfathomable mud of your cool disdain . . . No, damn you, I'm
right. And you're a sentimental schoolgirl. I shall go on.).
      I could, I feel, argue it out on the basis you put it on. I could find you
thinking *yourself* noble and high-minded and honest & open & self
restrained & dignified & in general the ideal of the English public school
clergyman ("playing the game" eh?), and *me* mean and hot-faced &
undignified & sneaky & scheming & flustered & underhand & rotten &
low; and (perhaps) I could leave you realising *yourself* a sentimental,
flighty, priggish, silly, romantic, sloppy, infant, and me an ordinary,
commonsense, sane, business-like, ardent, middle-aged lover. But I
won't. I won't argue on that basis. I bow to my fate. I realise that one of
the disadvantages, for us common place, level-headed, people, of falling
in love with flighty, poetical, fantastic, unaccountable dreamers is that we
have to fall in with their dear old silly poetry-book-cum-pulpit ideals.
"La! la!" we say to ourselves "I wonder where she'll be fluttering off to
next! The dear lady! . . . (Do you remember the admirable region below
the crook of her elbow on her right arm, about an inch each way? . . . and
do you remember how she moves round . . etc. eh) . . . ." and go on
with our knitting. It is part of the penalty we pay. Perhaps it is worth it.
      So I'll always advertise extensively in the Morning Post whenever
I'm going to meet you. And we'll all be healthy. (Of course, though, you
must remember that it's recognized that you take it all much better than I,
and that your calmness must sometimes disregard my fever. O adorable
calm goddess, I often wish I could achieve that stone serenity, –
            "But at my back *I* always hear
            Time's winged chariot hurrying near;
            And yonder all before me lie
            Deserts of vast eternity."[1]
It's queer you don't.)

---

1 From 'To His Coy Mistress' by Andrew Marvell (1621–78).

I shall argue it – "argue's" the wrong word, I shall *refer* to it – this way. I take you by those live shoulders and shake you, saying "you silly old thing, don't – though young, – though wonderful – though strange – though holy and from afar – don't, my dear good Creature, – don't be quite so very passionately solemn!" Be debonair! Be fantastic! I thought passionate solemnity was *my* bit . . . Really, if you can't *see* the amazing *fun* of madly meeting for ten minutes in an absolutely unheard of place in the middle of Essex on a mud plain, I can say no more. Really, did you actually swallow 'Milton' & 'Shakespeare' as being *necessary?* Oh, I *cannot* talk to you with a straight mouth. It was only that that damned post went, or you'd have had an enormous & elaborate code I'd planned with words for every eventuality. I meant to work through all the British Poets & go on with the Cheeses. There was the elaborate seaside part – "Gorgonzola", I recollect, meant "appear on Sunday morning at 8.30 at Clacton, & bring a shrimping-net" . . .

But if you've neither commonsense nor humour, what are you? A Christian, no less.

And now you're in your convent. At least I hope so. I sat on Friday & thought of them all shining welcome & surprised joy to see you. Damn them! and you! I shall write a letter to you (this is an explanatory postcard.) sometime. I'll restrain myself as long as I can. You can write on November 5th and – if I don't see you first – September 29th (Gladstone's birthday). I suppose I shall soon hear from some of those people of You-in-France. Has the experiment of my not going worked? That's what I want to hear from *you* – on November 5th. I end by loathing myself; but you – to you I am as a paralysed protozoon is To God. But I sing all day; and I wait.

"With love" – no – "Love from"
Rupert

The Orchard, [Grantchester]

[Postmark 26 October 1910]

Most holy

Just to get in touch with you, to get the right attitude, I've been up to look at you. You sit on my garish bedroom mantel-piece now (you wrinkled a vast nose of disapproval, you remember, at your continual, traitorous, presence in *this* room). Occasionally I go and stare. You never say anything. You are brown and discreet. Once or twice, though, you've begun to smile . . .

I wish I knew what you most *liked* me to write to you about. (Even how often is very difficult.). Art? Food? Life? Dudley? Cambridge? Mr Dawson?[1] the ten new little pigs? The Fabian Society? You? —— What? For I always feel rather frightened you'll be saying "This stuff again . . . !", and shivering at my sentimentalities. I imagine that you may, in a school, & a crowd, & hockey, have thrown out about yourself an atmosphere of winds and waters and clean rushing things that shrivels up and sweeps away my creeping mists; a wood, still, where my faint literary phrases are forgotten dust. Oh, I know this is all wrong. It's queer, isn't it, how being in love brings out all the worst parts, flunkeyism, jealousy, meanness, distrust – in me. *You*, of course, do it splendidly, wonderfully, in the grand manner. O most dear, and most lovely, and most glorious! – God! if you knew what a beast you make me feel! – But that too's not allowed now, perhaps. But it does show one up, all this business of being in love.

I've been finishing off a poem I began & planned in the spring.[2] It's a bit out of date now. But illuminating. The position is this. – I worshipped. I once ridiculously hoped you'd fall in love with *me*. But that was blasphemy. It would have meant that holy serene far off splendour would be shaken by desire for – of all miserable meannesses – *me*! Shaken & spoilt & defiled. So that it was very good that my impossible intolerable prayer wasn't granted. – I felt that, very acutely, then. Part of it, indeed, I feel now. But I also thought myself fine, and certainly clever, to feel that. Oh, my cleverness! My poor grubby

---

1 Rupert refers to the bull-terrier Pudsey Dawson, who would often accompany him swimming at Byron's Pool and had a penchant for eating frogs.
2 This was the sonnet 'Success'. (*PRB*, p. 104)

cleverness! that couldn't at all foresee you falling in love, and yet doing it in your own perfect & gracious manner. The poor poem is rather knocked on the head – not, as might have been thought, by the impudent presumption of the supposition that you could fall in love with me. *That* miracle has happened, and all the horror seems to have vanished. You carry it off. You can carry any-thing off. You only become finer. Perhaps it is the mark of genuine goddesses that they can even descend. Artemis has come down! And yet I am not consumed by fire. And Artemis is still Artemis.

La! what an inconceivable world! What can I do? Gratitude, and protest, are alike grotesquely too tiny for the situation, infinitely irrelevant. I can only bow my head in silence. And find your hand on it.

People come and see me here occasionally, – Margery, Daphne, Eva, & Ka, once; and Gwen; and Dudley; and Mr Edward Thomas; and so on, – and just occasionally mention you. (Gwen, as a matter of fact, talked a lot about you – you in France – and Bryn; and I scowled to think what I had missed. Gwen's ever so in love with Bryn. Thomas referred to you – quite spontaneously and in passing – as "the least good-looking of the Oliviers", but also with profound respect for your mind and character. It would take pages to disentangle and explain my state of mind for a minute after that. The world's a jolly place.) And when you're mentioned I have the most amazing feelings – like the Holy Ghost's when he hears people talking about God, or a maggot's, which is inside an apple, and hears the people at desert commenting on it's rosy appearance – feelings of secret omniscience and an infinite calm smile. I try to evince a languid and ignorant interest in your doings. I think I succeed very well, – better anyhow than I used to. My soul is shouting within me "The air is full of gold, This tea is irrelevant. I (= the soul) shall go & sit with Noel under those trees." My lips are saying "Ah! yes! I hear she's goin' to Jamaica." . . .

Oh, I was very angry when I heard that you were summoned there. Damn them! As if *you* couldn't decide your own life! (As if, – where the comedy of their just-too-lateness comes in – you *hadn't* decided it!). Bryn, whom I think an extraordinarily noble person, was extremely optimistic that she would persuade them to let you stay after all. But you're to let me know about these things. They affect my plans.

Oh, I know you'll go to Jamaica, and be very ill, and marry a negro, and settle down there, and have piebald chocolate children. And then my life will be ruined for at least nine months.

I rather expect you won't go, though. But if you do, I must see you first. We've so much to say. I ought to see you for a month. Even then,

I'd not finish half. I don't suppose I shall go to Germany before January. I want to talk about Germany. And again about female doctors. And even about my own profession! – Oh, I wish you'd been here lately. I've refused two "careers" in favour of poetry! But I'd like to have thought it out aloud. Isn't it worth while to take the chance of writing good poetry, though the odds are all against it, if there does seem to be a chance? But it's not very lucrative! I was sorely tempted to take the offer of lecturing in English at Newcastle, the other day. It is so comfortable to see ones life stretching solidly out in front, beginning with three hundred pounds a year at least, & climbing up to about a thousand, when I'm thirty and my mother dies. That's wealth! It means we could lead our lovely separate lives, and see each other when we liked, and you could do what you liked and have children & go where you wanted and heal the world! Tell me the amount of good in the Universe is greater if I sit in a house with almost no money, and write poetry for eight years, and never see you except one weekend a year at The Champions. For that's the only consolation, and stronger in theory than in practice.

Oh, my dear, the feeling of you tells me that I'm being my tiresome self again. Did Antony worry about the draughts in the palace at Alexandria, or do archangels in heaven wonder if their ties are straight? But, I tell you proudly, I'm getting to do it more in your style, becoming serene and stupid like a sunset. There are weeks when I watch the hours drift by in gold and each of them is just full of singing about you. Occasionally I'm even led to make a protest: why should you drag me up into the inhuman the intolerable serenity of the gods? But then a swirl of you in a tree, or the wind reminds me of August: and I sit on a golden Universe with you, placid and winged and naked, both. Until I remember that after all I'm only a droopy man wandering about a field after sunset, in Grantchester, and you're only an unthinking young person down in Petersfield, and we aren't meeting at all.

Nonsense, all that, you say. I quite agree. I see even more deeply than you that all my literary words against your vast inarticulateness are the dust blowing against the Sphinx. But what am I to do? I thought of writing a very formal letter thanking you for the privilege of having seen you. My God, the glory of it! For that, which is shared by many, is nearer being expressible. But then all memory of it is swamped by the one thing I have alone. The only way I can begin to express that is by the gigantic conceit I display nowadays. I talk to friends, or dons, or geniuses, with a vast slow smile that spreads round and through them, and beyond, with the immense and immovable irrelevance of eternal things, such as the sea.

I cease. I wonder what you're doing – oh! you're asleep now, probably. You look holy but stupid when you sleep. I saw you asleep at Camp, once or twice.

The worst of it is that *I* don't know, even vaguely, what *you're* doing at each moment. What I mean is, I don't know Bedales as an existence and a background, so that I can't *see* you. But you can, *me*. I roam about Grantchester, and you know Grantchester. On the other hand I have a pull over you, in that you are here. I don't know if you've ever been in this room (I write in bed now between 12 and 1 at night). But the room below is full of you. And in the night over in ⤴ that direction, a clump of trees stands, I know, suddenly up, a sentinel. And ⤡ there are some willows: and elsewhere trees – and all the ways of Grantchester are full of your comings and goings. You have shone here. I am not lonely.

Send me, once, if not on the dates suggested – a post-card. For you're a female of eighteen; and females of eighteen are changeable they say. They *always* change, they say. They wake up and find that their first emotions were just the faintest dreams. Will you be the one exception, here as everywhere else? Oh, but I fear. Perhaps you're not a goddess at all, but only a small square girl; and I'm a blitherer; and you're so far away; and the world's full of vast forces . . . But at least say you've not wholly woken up, yet.

Bosh! Pooh! Damn! I adore you. You are Noel. You are supreme.
>   as a flea to god
>   – no, as equal to equal –
>   most hungry for you, and most happy,
>   very passionately
>   Rupert

George Hotel
Chatteris

9.30 a.m. Wednesday Nov 9 1910

(*Mummia*   When those of old drank mummia
= mummy,   To fire their limbs of lead,
i.e. what   Making dead kings from Africa
Egyptians   Stand pandars to their bed;
are now)

So drunk on death, so medicined
  With spiced and royal dust,
In a short night they reeled to find
  Ten centuries of lust.

So I, from paint, stone, Tale, and rhyme
  Stuffed Love's infinity,
And sucked all lovers of all time
  To rarify ecstasy.

Helen's the hair shuts out from me
  Verona's livid skies;
Gypsy the lips I press; and see
  Two Antony's in your eyes.

The unheard invisible lovely dead
  Lie with us in this place:
And ghostly hands above my head
  Press face to straining face.

———   ———   ———

Woven from their tomb and one with it
  The night wherein we press:
Their thousand pitchy pyres have lit
  Your flaming nakedness – – –[1]

This is a very rough unfinished copy of the sort of thing I shall send you
on a postcard if you don't write to me, – even ten words to say you exist.

1 The completed poem appears as 'Mummia'. (*PRB*, pp. 81–2)

Don't ask how I got here. I leave in five minutes. I live at
Grantchester.

I dreamt (three hours ago) that we were going to a lunch-party
given by my preparatory schoolmaster & his wife (whom I've not seen
for eight years: and you never), and that we spent so long talking in the
garden, you and I, that we only arrived in time for pudding.

Farewell. Imagine, most unapproachable, a little figure stumping
across the illimitable fens, occasionally bowing to the sun because it
reminds him of you.

Yours (what's good in him) your equal-inferior and lover

                                                    Rupert

                                                    Bedales,
                                                  Petersfield,
                                                       Hants.

November 13th [1910]

Dear Rupert

        Your threat is too horrible. But I was waiting for November
the 5th, which seems to have passed, by the way.

I was going to write once just after I got back from Prunoy; but
suddenly that awful thing of yours came, which quite bewildered me.
As a matter of fact I had almost got resigned to your having recovered
from any kind of passion. I had mourned you for 3 days & nights in
France & in England & had started off with fresh & independant plans
of life.

I suppose it had changed me; I cant explain how, if I ever saw you,
you might understand it better than I can. I think you would try &
classify it, (my state of mind) call it the purity of instinct or some such
unsuggestive name. I'm affraid it is a very unresponsive mood, & you
will think this letter hateful; but let me rest – I shall get better – or worse
– soon.

Lots of very exciting things happen here – we play matches, and last week a boy died, it was extraordinary & I cant forget it yet.[1] It affected the whole school & for a little while there was an atmosphere which changed everyone.

Dont write again about me, I am disgusted with myself – as a worm – at present; & anything which doesnt abuse & hate me seems unharmonious. If this is just the effect of being nearly 18, write to me about yourself, who are 23 (-4-5?.) & pull me out of it.

I dont know whether I am going to Jamaica at Xmas or not, they are waiting to see Bryn before they decide.

Jaques also thinks Bryn is trusworthy & splendid. She is someone worth admiring; I dont think I can rely on anyone as I can on her.

from *Noel who is horrid.*

The Orchard
Grantchester
near Cambridge

November 15th 1910

(It was just because the fantastically suggested November the Fifth *had* passed, fruitless, that I sent my imbecilely jocose letter from the wilds. I gave you a two month's silence . . . ! . . .)

Oh, Noel, I don't *understand*, I don't understand *a bit*. At least, I don't think I do. I can only guess – a million things. Oh, letters are hateful: writing is no use. It leaves everything dim. If one can *see* people, and Talk . . . If I could only talk to you, & ask you things. Two sensible people can say anything, – anything in the world – to each other.

Forgive me for writing – for you asked me to "let you rest". It's filthy to bother you: yet it's right. For I don't understand – It may be my fault, or your's, or letter writing's.

I can't remember just what I said in the letter which I sent you

---

1 The *Bedales Chronicle* records the death of L.W. Carter on 6 November 1910, aged thirteen. The cause of death is not given.

after you'd got back from Prunoy. It was inspired by the loathsome self-martyrdom of one who hadn't been to Prunoy: – I'm like that. When I've hurt my toe, I talk of nothing else. But couldn't you wipe *that* away, & forget it. Perhaps you did – And then, I remember, I was partly righteously offended and offensive about *your* – but we can't go nosing back into "But you said I said you said" stuff. Anyhow I can't remember anything there that was "awful" and "bewildered" you. Oh, but I'm sorry, I'm sorry. What *did* I do? I'm grindingly, blankly, sorry . . . But, next, *why* did you think I'd "recovered from any kind of passion" in such a way that you should "mourn" for me three days and nights" and then "start off with fresh and independent (as if you *weren't, anyhow*, utterly & forever independent: oh, Noel!) plans of life"? Why did you think everything had slipped into infinity and mud between the 20th of August and the 20th of September, and never a word said? What did I do? – I understand nothing. Oh, that I have the mind of a journalist and the pen of damned imbecile, and eyes of a mole!

– But that's the *past*. Don't mess yourself with grubbing at it, if you don't want to. It's more the present and the future, I want to know about. – But I forgot. I'm to leave you alone – because you'll "get better, or worse – soon." You're right. And I'm an infinitely vulgar nuisance: though I suppose it's comprehensible that I should want to know if my facing the truth in August has made you unhappy. For you seem to be, in a way, – queer. And it wasn't to.

But you say something's "changed" you. And I ought to know, sometime, to *what*. For it seems to affect everything; my plans, anyhow, – to be practical. What's to happen? *Generally*, first; – do we continue? or have a two year truce, in which I see you as I see Daphne?, or shall I "let you rest" altogether for two years? or till the Judgement Day? And then in *particular*, – Am I to see you before I go to Germany? If so, when? and how? Some of that, of course, can't be decided till you hear from Jamaica. But supposing – and I assure you I think it easily conceivable and right – you don't want things to be disturbed at present, I should go off to Germany straight, & Jamaica wouldn't affect me. But, if you *don't* go to Jamaica, are you going to Land's End with Ka? And (for instance) I want to regulate my foreign trip – and you *might* enter in as a factor in determining time.

My dear, I repeat, sensible people can say *anything*: if it's the truth. You're not a worm. The world has given to you that you may have any emotion – violent lust, eternal hatred, infinite indifference, – to me or to anyone else in the world, for as a long or a short a time, & at any moment, you like. That you have, or don't have, it, is *you*. Things are like that. And it's always possible to say so. And sometimes necessary.

Oh, my platitudes! forgive them. I'd better – hadn't I? – put it on your manners, or your mercy, to submit to this confused and noisome worrying and to tell me what's what. You're a mountain of sense: and I'm an abysm of receptivity. Pity my stupidity. While you're you, the world stands fast.

This is damnably confused. Shall I "sum up", as people do in papers on abstract subjects.

(1.) I'm sorry to be disgusting and a nuisance.

(2) I don't think your letter hateful; but

(3) When you can, and even sooner than you like, I wish you'd write and tell me at least some of these things, –

(a.) What in God's name I did or wrote:

(b.) What the devil you mean:

(c.) What the bloody hell is going to happen –

(4.) Writing is awful: I wish I could *see* your face, and talk, *to you*.

– Oh, I won't "classify" with "unsuggestive" words, damn you! about instincts. I'll be as intelligent as I know how, & as well-meaning. I know you are you. But tell me what that is, more clearly, won't you?

Ever

Rupert

Oh! **Write! Write! Write! Noel!**

Bedales,

Petersfield,

Hants.

November 24th [1910]

I dont know, Rupert; as I said, I cant quite understand it myself, and I believe it is only a passing phase. I didn't mean it to sound so important as to frighten you into suggesting that things – we should stop; yet it does affect me, & I suppose us.

I believe that I must be mistaken about the cause – it cant be just that madness which I had after Prunoy. It was madness, you did nothing, & I am to disgusted to understand what I did. You just wrote an excellent letter, full of ingenious plans which I was afraid to carry out and warned me in it of misterious & terrifying things in you, which you called weakness & liability to decay – I didn't understand; then you sent a poem to Jaques,[1] which I didn't understand & which I agreed with – or rather sympathised with my incomprehension of it. (I cant write properly, because I'm in a hurry & its very important that you shouldnt have to wait any longer). And after that something happened to me & I must have lost all the sense I ever had & I took it that you had gone on to better things.

And I came to think any one liking me very much was not doing the best thing & that marriage (all that business – children) was a poor thing to wait for & look forward to. And my mood consists in hating the idea of it & feeling that you & your life are far more important when separated from it, and mine ought to be etc.

But as for "stopping" – "two years" – "like Daphne"; it wont do. I ought to see you soon. I am not going to Jamaica – (my poor Mother has yeilded reluctantly) at least it depends on my own choice. I havent yet found out what to do at Xmas – M[argery] & D[aphne] *will* go to Switzerland, Jaques has a scheme for Wales – but all is vague.

Will this do? I must stop

Noel.

---

1 Noel refers to the sonnet 'The Life Beyond', which Rupert had sent to Jacques at Prunoy. See p. 63.

THE LIFE BEYOND

He wakes, who never thought to wake again,
  Who held the end was Death. He opens eyes
Slowly, to one long lived oozing plain
  Closed down by the strange eyeless heavens. He
  lies;
  And waits; and once in timeless sick surmise
Through the dead air heaves up an unknown hand,
Like a dry branch. No life is in that land,
  Himself not lives, but is a thing that cries;
An unmeaning point upon the mud; a speck
  Of moveless horror; an Immortal One
Cleansed of the world, sentient and dead; a fly
  Fast-stuck in grey sweat on a corpse's neck.

I thought when love for you died, I should die.
It's dead. Alone, most strangely, I live on.

The Orchard
Grantchester

Tuesday November 29th 1910

I was glad of your letter. You *did* frighten me. And I felt rather a beast. And – but first this: – Jacques & Ka & I arranged to go away somewhere about Christmas time – any time, indeed, between December 16 and January 7. When Jacques heard you were to be in England and unattached in December, he fairly blazed into the suggestion you should come. Ka too, when we saw her, caught fire. I, having had your letter, which declared for seeing me in the holidays, allowed it to go forward you will hear from Ka about it.

The time, as I said, we can arrange, – coinciding with the Swiss visit, perhaps? The place, too, – Jacques is keen on Lulworth, which wouldn't be bad. Or Cornwall, which is hot. We have a passion for the Sea, because Jacques & I are going to bathe on Christmas Day. But it can easily be extinguished – I know, for instance, a place on the edge of Dartmoor . . .

Oh, Noel, you'll be able to come, won't you? Ka will be responsible: – & perhaps Gwen'll be there. But anyhow Ka arranges & satisfies *everybody*. She can talk to Margery, if that good lady fears to abandon you to the wilds. That side of it anyhow, I feel, is all right. It's only a question if it's a good thing. *I* think so. But I'm rather imperceptive and coarse – I mean that when I want a thing I generally think it's a good thing. But what do *you* think? If you think it better, only one of us would go, and we'd meet, sometime, otherhow, before I go to Germany.

So decide. But oh! it will be great, if you do it. We four (or five or six) will be working (you must bring some intelligent books), and walking immense distances, & talking. We will talk of *everything*, & decide everything – I grow priggish; But theres no fear of that with Ka there. Sometimes we'd pack the others off, and talk ourselves. I've yet a million things to tell you, & to hear – whatever terms we're on! I'd try to be more intelligent, and you could try to be – oh nothing different, but *you*. "We are the Masters of our Fate",[1] we could control everything to our wish, settle how & what we wanted, for the occasion, to be, & be it! Command, & I obey.

Oh, Noel, it sends me mad with hope & happiness to think of going great walks over those downs in the rain with you there, or sitting after tea, or talking. Do do it! Just for one great week! to see you every morning, again, and all day, & every evening! We could just live so and be perfectly happy, and never worry about things past, nor about the future. We shall understand a thousand things – letters are so stupid – by a word or a look. Whether the "passing phase" of your "present mood" has passed, or is still there, does it matter? Don't ponder on your dullness of feeling or my "purity instinct" generalisations, don't foresee marriage, don't worry about lives being spoiled by the future. Those things are irrelevant. If you feel any better or happier (I say even

---

1 It matters not how strait the gate,
  How charged with punishments the scroll,
  I am the master of my fate
  I am the captain of my soul.'
(W.E. Henley 'Invictus. In Mem R.T.H.B.', *Echoes* (1888))

'impossible' shuddering horrible things) if I'm there, isn't that enough? If you don't, – there's still my side of the account to consider, in the eternal balance.

I have the pen of a stock-broker, and the mind of a cab-driver. I only want to say how right everything is – or rather with what a bias that way everything begins. Shan't we realise that rightness, if we see one another?

Oh, I'm sorry for my letter of *mysterious* (note the 'y'!) hints, and for that bloody sonnet. I am wholly a fool. (It may interest you to know that the sonnet was thought out, & half written, last April.) Remember for ever, or for as long as you know me, that I'm a fool. I ramble on, in letters or elsewhere, pouring out whatever I think of. You don't understand the psychology of gushers. You sit with amazing things going on behind that amazing mask, and speak deliberate words. I babble on, & change every hour. At breakfast I love you with my soul, and at lunch-time with my body, and at tea-time not at all, and I pour it all out. (But always – can't you *see* it? – you're so immensely in the middle, central, – which means, I suppose, that I actually am unchangingly in love with you all the time). When I write, or wire, or say, to you on Monday that I don't care whether you exist or not, & again on Tuesday, & on Wednesday, & every day for ten days, *then* you may begin to think I perhaps have got a headache.

And, I tell you, I often remember that I am disgusting & filthy & contemptible after all, & wonder when you'll realise it, . . . & *that* breeds in me a dull irritation that poisons a letter.

And so on.

I wrote you foolish letters: and you were even foolisher, and took it that I'd "gone on to better things". (Better things = writing reviews for the Spectator! Doesn't that make even you feel there's something wrong in the scale of values?). Noel! for what you say of your mood – *why* should you have marriage to "wait for & look forward to", in that way? Of *course* you "hate the idea of it". My God, I won't have it. I once talked of your children. You know, you *ought* to have some, sometime; just & merely because you're fine. Who's their father, doesn't matter. But of course I can't understand your feelings. But all that doesn't matter. *Damn* Children! and DAMN Marriage. It's a million times to be damned, as a thing to look forward to. I won't see you degraded & pulled down in such ways. All, in looking at the future in that way, I care for, or anyone else, is that you shall be eternally you; & have your will. I dance with fury at your attitude. I love you: & if, as you once ridiculously suggested, you're fond of me – oh, my dear, you can make, *you* can make, Life what you like.

But that "anyone liking" you "very much" was "not doing the best thing" etc. – oh, there are moments when the inefficiency of letter writing become intolerable. This is one. Sometimes, I have learnt from my preceptors, moral reproving is no good for the infinitely dull school-child, physical castigation is the only thing. If I could only beat you suddenly on the nose, very hard, or pull your hair with painful and unexpected vehemence – Oh, Noel, but I must see you. I weary you with another long slushy letter. I mistrust myself, letterwriting. I know I often fail to convey the effect I desire. And when I succeed, I only make it clear how stupid and dull I am, how entirely I fail to understand your feelings. So I trample clumsily. O forgive me, and see me. I'll not write how I want to see you. For words are mawkish. – Perhaps I am. But I want, want, want. I hear from Margery you may appear next week end. It would be great if you did, (though I should have thought you'd not be allowed.). We could talk about Christmas. I'd be free all the time. If not, I'll hear from you or through Ka. Let's pretend that your madness – it may be so – makes you owe me an apology. And pay it by coming at Christmas. Don't go to Switzerland or anywhere. Come! Come! Come!

I've been canvassing (ugh!). I'm rather tired. I'm going to bed. I've a great hope. Oh, we'll talk & laugh & be content with just being there. Damn your future! That present will be sufficient.

Good night! Noel.
Rupert

National Liberal Club,
Whitehall Place, S.W.

Tuesday morning.
[Postmark 6 December 1910]

I don't know if you've written to me, or to Ka, this last day or two. I left *The Orchard* yesterday. Tomorrow I go to Rugby (24 Bilton Road.).

I had a long talk with Ka last night: and promised to write to you.

Ka was in Cambridge for the week-end. She went on Monday morning to talk to Margery, "to ask leave", – or at least to mention it, &

accept responsibility as a chaperon, & so forth. She found Margery (&
Eva, who was there, – *Eva!*) hopeless. Having got accustomed to Bryn
being in England, I had forgotten all people weren't like her. If only they
were! And all this begins again! Poor Ka! she was very sad & perplexed.
She hadn't understood; and I had to explain, which was rather painful.
Of course I didn't explain far.

Margery *is* a damned fool. I am very angry. I cannot contain my
wrath. I am afraid I shall burst out at her – only luckily I shan't see her
for a long while. She bleats about "getting out of touch with you" &
"wanting to see more of you", & taking you to Switzerland, & you not
being disturbed. I see red, and pant. – It may be that you don't want to
go to Lulworth. But that's not the point; & she doesn't *know* what you
want, – or *think*. The foolishness, and the damned impudence, of her
thinking she can interfere with you – with You. I feel furious. Ka, too,
quite agrees with me.

However, if you didn't go, Ka said, it made it very difficult for *her*.
For no other female could be found. We discussed this & that – &
found ourselves hampered by not knowing, in this or that case, what
you'd prefer: – what we'd prefer we did know, & Jacques we could
guess – anyhow he was attainable. But you were out of reach. So I was
to write.

(A) We've neither of us heard if you even wanted to go as we
originally suggested. *Now* Ka's going anyhow to Lulworth Dec 26 for a
week or ten days. So is her mother in law – a nice person aged 30 – & a
"baby" (aged 7 or 8.)[1] Jacques'll be there: & Gwen probably. (B) If I'm
not there – & therefore you can go without all the thunder of an
outraged family, & the Heavens falling – will you prefer that to going to
Switzerland, or where ever else? (They'll be a less bloody lot.) (C.) If I
go, & it is considered that you may be there, as the widow Cox & child
will be (which 'permission' is very unlikely) do you think it worth
while? (D) In fact what the devil do you want, anyway? *We* don't know.
You may be yearning to go to Switzerland. (E.) (my own subsection) If
I don't see you at Lulworth, when, & where, & how? And how are you?

Poor Margery! she's very sad that she hasn't heard from you, – all
about "getting out of touch." That makes her anxiouser to get you to
Switzerland. And, of course, she fills everything with back ways &
mutterings. "Ka isn't to tell Noel that Margery said it wasn't to be . . ."

---

1 After the death of Ka's mother, her father, Henry Fisher Cox, remarried and had two more daughters.
He then died suddenly in 1905, leaving his widow to bring up their young daughters, as well as act as
occasional chaperone to the elder girls.

& so on. Ka, hating that sort of thing, is going to talk to Noel though. Ka's a good woman, & wise. <u>Damn</u> Margery. I hate her muddled shiftiness. Also I hate myself for bothering & worrying you. Oh Noel it's impossible to write to <u>you</u> out of this place. Jews & smoke around me. I suppose if you once entered this room it'd all fade, to dust. And it's stupid & feverish. But forgive, and answer. Oh, answer, directly, to Rugby, by return. For I must let Ka know immediately. Many people's plans hang on it. We want to know your general attitude & feelings. *I* know that the whole thing's even more complicated than Ka thinks. But tell us.

I <u>am</u> horrible. Shine out over everything.

With love
Rupert

I have had two proofs of a bloody poem (8 months old) sent me. I only want one. Here's the other. Ugh!

Mary Brooke, Rupert's domineering mother.

Rupert, Mrs Brooke and Alfred in fancy dress, 1898.

Alfred and Rupert, Rugby, 1900.

Sydney Olivier, Colonial Secretary to British Honduras, 1890.

The Olivier sisters, Limpsfield, 1896.
Daphne, Bryn, Noel and Margery.

Noel and Daphne, 1898.

Margery, Daphne, Bryn, Noel and Sydney.
Kingston, Jamaica, 1900.

Noel, Bryn and Margery, 1902.

Margery Olivier, 1909.

Bryn Olivier, 1909.

Daphne Olivier, 1909.

Noel Olivier, 1909.

Sydney Olivier, Governor of Jamaica, 1907.

Margaret Olivier, Jamaica, 1910.

Rupert, Evelyn Radford, Margery, Dudley Ward, and Noel, outside
Mrs Primmer's cottage at Bank, April 1909.

Ka Cox, Cambridge, 1910.

SONNET

Breathless, we flung us on the windy hill,
  Laughed in the sun, and kissed the lovely grass.
  You said 'Through glory and ecstasy we pass;
Wind, sun, and earth remain, the birds sing still
When we are old, are old' . . . 'And when we die
  All's over that is our's; and life burns on
Through other lovers, other lips,' said I,
– Heart of my heart, our heaven is now, is won'!

'We are Earth's best, that learnt her lesson here.
  Life is our cry. We have kept the faith'! we said;
  'We shall go down with unreluctant tread
Rose-crowned into the darkness'! . . . Proud we were,
And laughed, that had such brave true things to say.
– And then you suddenly cried, and turned away.

                                  RUPERT BROOKE

Don't go reading anything into it except itself. I've *never* seen you "cry
& turn away"!

                                      Bedales,
                                  Petersfield,
                                  Hants.

Wednesday 7th. [December 1910]

I couldnt *possibly* have written before; but I am glad you reminded me
that everyone is waiting.
    Answers to questions:
    (1) I do want to go to Lulworth, or wherever it is, very much.

(2) If you aren't there, I should still like to go.

(3) If you are, it will be quite & completely worth wile.

(4) ("what the Devil do I want anyway?") I should like to go to Switzerland & see Margery & Daphne – I should certainly be very happy there; but I've got to get certain "work" done in the holidays & ten days out of England means 10 days slack – also its costly. Lulworth I cannot quite imagine, but (here your own private question comes in) if I dont go there, there doesn't seem to be any other chance of seeing you; I suppose you *are* going to Germany.

It goes like this:

$$\text{Lulworth} \equiv \text{Switzerland}$$
$$\text{Lulworth} + \text{Rupert} > \text{Switzerland}$$

If poor old Margery does'nt understand & wont allow, I expect I shall go with her. But I *did* arrange with Jaques to do things in England, *long* ago.

I shall write to M[argery] & D[aphne] – (I believe the latter is more practical) about plans; but I suppose final decisions rest with them. Tell Ka I'm very sorry that I have'nt answered her letter & if plans depend on me (I wish they didnt), I want to come, but Margery knows best.

It is painful to think that now you will always have to explain what you *dont* mean in a poem whenever I read one; I ought to be able to reform by myself after this.

I have'nt any opinion but I liked the old mummy poem better than this "we flung us" one.

Love from Noel.

Praescript. I ate so little last term, that I'm <u>very</u> sick – also, I love habits. Shan't I, then, give you a book? a lovely book? are there any lovely books? Do tell me. Or would it be a scandal? Of course, giving you a book doesn't matter now, from *our* point of view. But it's great fun. It makes me proud of myself for <u>days</u>.

24 Bilton Road
Rugby

Wednesday 14th [December 1910]

Thanks for answering so swiftly.

    I began a letter, a week ago, like this – "YOU ARE A SHEEP." – but I didn't get any further. It was rather foolish, wasn't it? Not untrue, maybe; but out of proportion. I've remembered, since, that you're other than I (other, by now, perhaps, even, than you), and that we had it all out, – the difference – long ago. For I've been stamping and foaming about the absurdities of the situation. I'm a fool and fretful; you're serene. You can't imagine what my mind's lately been like; and I won't describe for you don't like it.

    Still, though serenity's fine, I feel a wish you would flare out a bit. Mightn't it pay if you did? Oughtn't you to? I feel so distant and ignorant about your position and your feelings and what you want, that I just humbly suggest, not lay down. You are eighteen. But even that isn't the important way to look at it. The important thing is that you are you. And you ought to be able to, you <u>must</u> be able to, choose things for yourself. Margery's conduct is idiotic and wicked. It is the oldest, most hopeless, folly for one person to try to interfere with another. It's wicked. And it's useless.

    (It is, of course, actually useless, in this case. Because Margery thinks she may succeed in preventing you being "disturbed" (amazing word) by anyone (in this case, me) till you're 25 or so. But, as we know, she's plaintively shutting the stable-door, after the horse has escaped – somewhere or other, wherever it may be now. But I don't mean that. Interference is <u>always</u> useless. "No man can save the soul of another. He must let that alone for ever."[1])

    There are two points.

    (1) It's a matter of Principle. It is <u>intolerable</u> – you <u>must</u> see this –

---

1 Unidentified.

that you shouldn't be allowed to do what you like. That you'll be pretty happy if you don't – even that you *ought* to do something else – are irrelevant. It may be best for you, or me, or the world, that we shouldn't meet. But *we*, and no one else, must decide and arrange that. There are limits, of course. Society makes some; it forbids you to put a knife into me, for instance. Your family *might* be excused for making others. It might enforce six month's reflection on you, if you wanted to run away with a green grocer. (I think it certainly oughtn't to.). But this is not conceivably a case. Choose not to go anywhere; and there's no more to be said. But you must choose; not Margery, nor any one else. This is certain, and important, infinitely important. And Margery must learn it.

(2.) *Practically*, my Noel, – stand out that you may be allowed to do what you think good. If Margery is allowed undisturbed to have her way of guarding you round from "evil influences" thus, it means that every holidays – every month – it'll happen again. If you don't go to Lulworth, & if you want to, – though you're happy enough in Switzerland, and though you like Margery, you must tell her her position's wicked & intolerable. If you don't think it's worthwhile doing so, have pity, O Splendid, upon my fretfulness; for *I* think its too important to be Scandinavian about. We must meet, if we want to, you & I. Time's short: & we've a deal to say. And By God, I tell you, the World's finer when we do meet, you & I.

On these two grounds, the matter of principle and our (damn it, your & my) particular advantage, I'm trying rather confusedly to urge you to make a protest against idiocy & wickedness. Don't show a Christian spirit. Thunder! Even if you're not used to thundering. You, *you*, can thunder. Is my advice impudent? No. Nothing's impudent, between us, now. And don't think it's all my hysterical selfishness. I'm right to begin with. Superbly right. And if you don't believe me, – everyone agrees, except cowards. Ka agrees, obviously. And she's fine, and wise. And think of Bryn! She's sensible. Margery must be made as sensible. You mustn't humour her.

So make a push for it. And let me know what happens. Noel, I must see you. I love you. If we don't, by any chance, meet at Lulworth, if you're back at Limpsfield by January 4th or so, shall I see you there?

You liked the (unfinished) mummy poem better than this last. You are amazing. Because it probably *is* better. Though the most intelligent judges can't see it. (I'm thinking of one or two who have seen the sonnet). You have besides *everything* else – even taste! Devil! Do hurry up & grow a year or two older, & then we'll be able to give up pretending that you aren't a million times wiser & cleverer than my cultured self in every way.

I'm publishing a frightful book of poems; and I wanted to be able to ask your counsel about some, at Lulworth.[2]

And another thing I'd ask you, if you were there 🗡 , in that chair, the other side of the fire, (God, that you were!) is this. I think Margery's absurd and wicked, & oughtn't I to tell her so? Because it makes my position to her so odd. If one likes a person very much, & knows them very well (longer, "thou whom I long for", than you – & that's 2½ years!), and thinks them wicked, *oughtn't* one to say so?

I'm going to stop, and learn my German lesson. Writing about this, and in a hurry, I seem feverish and horrible. Oh, I'm fretful and grimy and bad. But sometimes, I do assure you, I'm better than that. Though I'm hungering often for you, and though I'm of little faith, and full of jealousies and fears, sometimes I step back a bit and look at the world and me and you; and realise the glory. Noel, most glorious and most dear, do you ever reflect on it all, very quietly, like one reading a book about old past things? Think of it, stand back, slip away, and think of it. That the world should soar about us unconsciously, and we sit here – I writing and you reading, – and all this knowledge and understanding between us. Do you remember those meals at the Old Vicarage when our feet were touching under the table, and above we all talked and laughed and ate, each, apparently, no more to each than to the rest? The whole thing's like that, the whole world. And isn't the secret, the amazing secret, part of the glory? When the secrecy's over, it'll be different, better far, maybe, but different. You & I, across England, now, with memories, and with That between us – and the rest of folk dropped millions of miles away down.

Last week, a few days, I was working so hard at elections,[3] all day & half the night, without moving, on occasional coffee and bread and butter. But that, or working, or writing, or meeting old friends in the streets, – it's all so vague and dreamy, compared with realities. For *you're* reality, and there I live – you coming up the Old Vicarage Garden, or in a field, or in camp, and the light on you, and the way you move, your mouth and hair and face and body, and the feel of your hands. You say things haven't changed much for you – that, I mean, it was the same before as after. But even with you it *must* be

---

2 Rupert's plans for publication were vague at this point. Interest in his work had been loudly voiced by his friends, particularly the Cornfords and Jacques. A colleague from the Cambridge Fabians, J.C. Squire, who was now working in publishing, had been tentatively approached earlier in the year, but nothing concrete had been decided.
3 Rupert had been put in charge of organizing transportation for Labour voters in the general election, no easy task when only twelve cars were available in a constituency containing ninety villages.

different. Look on it, what has happened, and me writing to you, as I could write to no one else in the world, the truth about everything; – think of what Noel, or Rupert, of a year ago, would say, seeing this!

It may be that I'm wrong, or hurting, writing so. For you've been mad; and I a fool; since. And what you are now, and are feeling, perhaps I don't know. For I can't see you; and how can I tell, how can I tell? But it won't be. I'll not have it. If we could meet, once, it would all be right. Do you remember that bold strong clump of trees, off the path to Cantelupe Farm? They stand straight. It mustn't change, or grow strange. Noel, Noel, Noel, I'll not let you go. I'll hold you by the shoulders tight, tight, tight. I can almost feel you. You <u>shall</u> not <u>change</u>. Except to grow more glorious; for you'll burn more amazingly, and I'll do finer things, the finest in the world, for you. But oh! I must see you!

Your lover
Rupert

The Champions.

22nd December. [1910]

Dear poor Rupert.

This is a horrible muddle. I seem to be going to Switzerland. My Father has told me not to & you are angry with Margery because you think its her fault & that she schemed it all. And I, as usual am damnably placid & indifferent, & wanting to do about three incompatible things at the same time.

I believe that now, perhaps, you can understand what I meant at Camp when I complained that I was to compliable & considerate. "Considerate" was the wrong word, so was compliable almost; but I was referring to this beastly indifference in me, this absence of any determination which could help me to do things whatever anyone else wanted. I think I've heard you complain a little in some of your letters; you call it "serenity" & are polite about it as such, but you have muttered ocasionally & almost wished that it wasn't quite so apathetic.

Your quite right to object. I hate it & feel that it will prevent my ever achieving anything, "even of any kind". Do you remember how "it" lost the train for us at Beaulieu Rd? It has done worse than that tho' & probably will do still worse.

I hope you grasp what I mean. this thing (wretched trait of my character) is entirely responsible for the present state of affairs. Margery is as innocent as – oh anything, she wrote & asked me whether I wanted to go to Switzerland, said it would be nice, & on that I decided to come. For goodness sake dont abuse her anymore, she understands about you as well as Ka or Bryn or anyone! She may be a little less efficient, thats all.

Your coming down here when we get back from Switzerland & I shall have to entertain you as they try & work.

I am suddenly summoned to a train. Cabs are bad to write in.

Love from
Noel

Despite Noel's denial that Margery had interfered, Rupert spent Christmas in Rugby brooding over her treachery, and left for Lulworth in a frustrated mood. Ka too was in a depressed state. Having rejected Jacques' avowals of love, she now realized that the match between him and Gwen Darwin, which she had initially encouraged, would leave her very much on her own.

Ka had become Rupert's confidante over his difficulties with Noel, and now each looked to the other for the emotional support that was lacking elsewhere in their lives. One incident in particular served to demonstrate to Rupert that his feelings for Ka were growing stronger. Ka had wanted to buy him a book for Christmas, and Rupert hurt her feelings by seeming to be unconcerned about which book it was. On perceiving his insensitivity, he was consumed with remorse and began to realize just how much he did care for her.

After Lulworth, Rupert saw Noel briefly at Limpsfield, and told her about the incident with Ka, for, even though nothing had really happened, he felt their relationship should be as open as possible. They managed a hurried farewell in London, before she returned to Bedales and he left for Munich.

Pension Bellevue
30 Meresienstrasse
München
Bavaria

January {23 and
     24
    1911

That, oh lovely, is my address; and letters here, it is to be remembered, cost $2\frac{1}{2}$d. (The name of my pension, written badly above, is Bellevue – a French word, meaning "lovely sight" a misleading name.)

How we circle, and fly apart, and together, and apart! And now I'm writing to you from Munich . . . ! . . . Everything's very amazing; and we most of all. I turn Northward and a little West and see a glow on the horizon, over Munich. It is you. I bow towards you.

Note, lady, that the supper was a mistake. Or wasn't it? I, anyhow, thought it wasn't worth it. My nerves weren't up to it, all the while you were dressing in that accursed room, or even when you were at supper, I kept thinking that the minutes were slipping away – not *very* profitably – towards another four-month's-gulf. Being, in time or space, very near the great glories, yet not in them, is so shattering. *Now* there's five hundred miles between us, & I can't see you, and I don't much mind! I can take the wider view, and see all the splendour of you, and the blinding wonder that you love me, – that we love each other. But *then*, five yards away, you were gleaming, as you changed your dress, and the minutes were running out, and I couldn't go to you. I could only bite my nails. In Time, too – tonight *I'm* writing in my bedroom (where I work half the day), and *you're* going to sleep, or asleep, away there in Petersfield, but yesterday it was the same, and will be tomorrow. But ten days ago, the difference between Wednesday night . . . , and Thursday night with you at a dance in London, and me sea-sick in mid-channel – it was too immense and breaking. Oh, there was some excuse. Even you ("Serene"!), at the last moment, thought so. To turn my Noel, from You, even to this glorious amazing tumbling world that I love, is a precipitous leap from Heaven into darkness. Still, I was a baby. I was reduced to pulp. I couldn't say anything to Ka. And I spent the time in the train, alternately sure that you'd been abducted by the taxi-cabman, and certain that I should be drowned. Oh! The degradation of pulp! Are you ever pulp? I daresay not – I suppose not. But it *was* wicked; when

all fears and confusions had been driven away and outshone and
everything was so splendidly right. You must, after these months, be
getting sick of my whinings. Ignore them! But I am getting better. Know
that I glory highly, and am filled with long periods of ecstasy. –
      Yes, I was seasick: for the first time in my life. It was not, I found,
very unpleasant. The prelude is worse, far worse. But the whole thing is
exaggerated. This time, anyhow, it was worthwhile. In the National
Liberal Club between 8 and 9 Jacques, Dudley, & I found in the evening
papers that there was a terrific storm in the channel, that the mails had
been turned back because they couldn't get to Calais, & that there'd
been several wrecks. It finished my collapse. I mentally composed
touching letters to you, to be found in my breast-pocket, when I was
washed up off Normandy. I offered to Jacques & Dudley that I should
write down the secrets of my life & put them in an envelope, to be
entrusted to them. If I got across the Channel they were to burn it: if
not, to open it & settle up the affairs. They jumped at the offer; but I saw
unfaithfulness in their eyes, glinting; & withdrew at the last moment.
They were awfully sick.
      The sky had cleared; by the sea, under $\frac{3}{4}$ of a moon, was amazing. I
hired nautical clothes & sat on deck talking to a sentimental simple
business man. The edge of the ship kept going under and receiving the
upper portion of a wave on board. So our legs got wet. The business
man kept telling me about his ungrateful *employés*, and about marrying
for money. As we left the ship, he wrung my hand and said "I like
talking to people . . . If we had not spoken on this ship, two souls
would, perhaps, have gone to the grave and never touched one
another!" He paused; and added in a gruff voice "It is a small world. It is
a small world. Good-night!" He was quite young. It made me happy all
night. I forgot to say we both, at intervals, noticed the Awe Inspiring
Majesty of the Sea.
      Here I talk very bad German with infinite pain, to old ladies at the
dinner-table. I know very few words. I met a man in a *café* who used to
be at school with me. He was in the same position, learning German
here, last year. To one middle-aged German spinster he tried to say "I
know all the every day words in German." What he *did* say was "I know
all your little vulgarities!" rather roguishly. She went white & left the
room; & he was nearly landed in a duel. I'm always doing that sort of
thing. The company at the pension is astounding. Two English ladies, a
Romanian economist, his brother, Professor of Physics in Bucharest, an
Italian count who is a cavalry-colonel, an Australian sheep-farmer, my
age, a Franco-German dancing-master, and about eight Germans, male

& female. One of the last is a dowager of sixty-five with white hair & a bright yellow face, that reeks of sin. She is the most hideous thing in the world; & fascinates me. The Professor (just alas! gone home to Bucharest) is a nice little dark strange Slavonic creature, with whom I am going to stay. You should have heard me explaining Philosophy on a vocabulary of 10 words & 20 gestures to him & the Australian in a *café*! The Australian has never been outside Australia & is the simplest man in the world. His taste is awful. I like him.

Oh, they're a queer lot at meals. I occasionally wish you were there. My God; the faintest thought of you makes them & the dingy room retire to a dim background. If you *were* there the whole crew would just vanish. Isn't a queer feeling that makes me sometimes want you there, just to share the funniness of something? – But then I have it rather about several friends, too, Jacques & Ka & Dudley & Bryn & people you don't know. Do you have it?

Outside, I wander & stare & dream & am very happy. An hour a day I'm in galleries: & concerts, operas, & theatres every evening. My dim attempt at a musical education proceeds apace. Two hours Wagner on a good orchestra for 3d. But oh, I'm not & never shall be *musikalisch*. You, I expect, rather are. Another gulf!

The Germans – oh, it turns out to be very simple about the Germans. They're Soft. That is all. Very nice, but ... Soft. It comes out in their books, and everywhere. All their views, of everything, just blur a little. Their grasp is of a fat hand. Pictures, books, ideas, faces – it is all the same. It's rather amusing, though, to find out what Soft Ideas *are*. I talk to Germans about scenery & the country. I explain laboriously why towns are often better. They are *always* shocked. Every German I have met has said to me. "*Ich habe gern die Natur*". They all – just vaguely – "love Nature". Nature has a capital N. Thoughts of English Nature lovers creep into my mind. Oh, it is so easy and so troublesome to love Nature – *that* way. The sentimentality and Fudge come out better with Germans, than with some English nature-lovers, more shapely. You hear and see a so fat, so greasy, so complacent and civilized German roll up his eyes and wheeze "*Ich habe gern die Natur*" – and the whole thing flies to pieces before you. You have a picture of that coated belly in the woodlands, waddling helter skelter from Pan, or Diana's hounds – But I talk of things I know not. Oh goddess, all the world lies about "Nature" (a soiled word) except you & me. For you are of Earth, and (if not in words) say so: and I am not, & say I'm not. On the peaks no one but you shall live, you alone. And I, below, shall wait in a town, and meet you every month half way down the mountains, where the woods end.

... And that vision also fades, as less true than the other that puts us alone, above everything & everyone. Noel, we're equal and immortal and alone, and give and take as equals, & freely. I *can't* write. I wish I could tell you what we are. Oh we love & will love finelier than it has ever been done. Go out and take the splendid things of life, and clothe yourself in them, & crown yourself with them and we'll meet with all the world for a gift to each other. Damn you, read the truth that is under all this fustian I'm writing. You are more glorious than God: and I – Because you have taken me & kissed me the good outweighs all the evil there could possibly be and because we have kissed & you have, wonderfully, loved me, (I don't only say with lips "Noel", but with every inch of me thrills & strains to you when I think the word) the world's an ecstasy, and there's no time to learn German or eat or do anything but sing. Read, and forgive, and glory. Noel, stranger, *I*, Rupert, am writing to you, I am afraid at the sound of your name, & of my own. Throw out arms across sea & lands to you. I love you.

Rupert

You may write to me, sometime. Not a long letter, & when you like – but to show you can. You have almost only ever written about arrangements, or about misunderstandings. Write – once – for the letter's sake! Write yourself – *you.*

Bedales,
Petersfield,
Hants.

Feb 10th [1911]

Creature!

Last night I thought. For some years now I have hardly thought at all, about once or twice only; by day I say things on impulse & write on impulse & everything I do is unprepared & unexpected; if anything remarkable happens, I consider it again afterwards, & exclaim at it, if it is very important I go through the circumstances again & again & that keeps me awake, but it is not thought. No wonder then that I never know how things stand in my own mind, & that when they ask: "are you a liberal or conservative?" I stare. And that when you are with me & ask me questions about myself, I can only groan & grin & feel disgusted that I canot answer. Last night was an exception, why it happened to be, I cant think, only two things have happened to me lately, & they could have very little effect on my brain: I gave a lecture to the Scientific Society here, which meant that I had to speak continually & consecutively for an hour for the first time in my life;[1] and I am lame. Does that, (do they) account for the following? . . .

I thought: There is Rupert in Germany, very wise & clever (he is probably learning more German in one month than you have ever learnt with all your years of study); he seems to know about all the most important things, except music, & that he is trying to appreciate (I wonder if he ever will properly, why not? I've learnt to be excited by some pictures just through trying); and he is very beautiful, everyone who sees him loves him; when I first saw him cracking nuts in Ben Keeling's rooms with Margery, I fell in love with him, as I had fallen in love with other people before, only this time it seemed final – as it had, indeed, every time – I got excited when people talked of him & spent every day waiting & expecting to see him & felt wondrous proud when he talked to me or took any notice. When he talked for a long time on the river I got more & more in love & said so to myself when he was there. After Cambridge I placed him so: there are people (family, friends) & there is Rupert; with them I live generally & it is their influence which forms my ways & ideas; when Rupert is there, none of these ways will do, I must work up to his, I must talk about the important things, the only ones which he considers – I am ashamed at many parts of my mind, the way I think, but it is because they are bad & when he's there I realise it. At camp at Penshurst I was driven silly with love & it was perhaps at that time that I felt it most strongly.

Since then I have gradually begun to know him better, & would I think, have looked on him as a friend, a person whom I loved better than anyone else but from whom I neither needed nor expected more than to see him at times & talk to him; I wanted him to prefer me to others but not to everything. There is probably a good deal of sympathy in me. With many people I have known, I have sympathised so well that

---

1 Noel delivered her lecture on 'Blood' on 4 February, dividing her topic into three sections: Historical, Present knowledge and theories, and, finally, Comparison of circulation in different animals.

I could help them in no way by giving fresh suggestions (here, you see, my thought became obscure). And it was like that with Rupert, when he bowed his head & said the truth about what he felt; I understood & was sorry & I loved his head so I kissed it & then he & history made me believe that I was a lover as well as he.

I'm not, Rupert. I'm affectionate, reverent, anything you like but not that. And so I get worried & sorry when you look devoted & I dont mind about Ka or German Duchesses at all, & I never feel jealous; only affraid of your loving me too much.

I hope this sounds true. I think it is interesting, it explains things & relieves me extraordinarily to have discovered it.

I will write again when I've heard from you.

> I shall always love you.
> Noel

God grant I've put the right number of stamps on. Do you admire them?

> Ohmstrasse 3
> Gartenhaus I
> Munchen

March 15 1911

Noel, whom I love!

> I am a worm, a crawling thing
> "Buried and bricked in a forgotten Hell,"[1]

because I have not written to you for months, and because I did not write to you straight after your last letter – of nearly a month ago. For a time there was Carnival, and then the quiet funny red-haired Benians[2]

---

1 Unidentified.
2 E.A. Benians (1880–1952), St John's history scholar, who was visiting Munich on the Travelling Fellowship he had won the previous year. He became Master of St John's in 1933.

(you've met him?) came to stay here a week and demanded to be shown Munchen and then, just as peace settled slowly down, came the strange great news from England, and I've been pondering over letters from Gwen and Jacques and Ka, and thinking the situation out, and writing to them[3] . . . Eh? no! all that's not an excuse. I am your perpetual disgrace. But, see you, most glorious lady and my Noel, it demands a clean hair and heart to write to you – Hippolytus had to bring his Dewy flowers with a morning step in sunshine to Artemis – and nowadays there's so often a tired dusty superficial German urbane dirty Rupert – But that, again, is nonsense.

   Oh, Noel, your letter! – Look here, I write damn good letters. I am a most clever creature, and can sometimes, write better than almost anybody in England. My God, I write well! And some of the letters I write to you – hoo, superb!! . . . My dear, the best I can do, the best attempt I've ever made to express my disgusting self to you, – it's all fudge, sham, self conscious journalism, irritating weakbacked shifty eyed phrase-making – compared with your letter. Oh, I despair! If I (knowing what you are) could write you down one tenth as well as you (not knowing) write yourself down – I'd be the greatest poet England ever produced. Oh I don't mean that you're a *litterateur* (or whatever the feminine may be). God, no! Only, when I opened the letter, out stepped, very present and visible and true and there and oh! glorious, Noel! I didn't read the words. I heard them. I saw the expressions on your face as you spoke. Oh you stood and moved there, so real and living that I got thin and transparent and wavy, a vague little wisp of a ghost of a lifeless fool in Germany; you were real, and the sunlight on you.

   And the things you said! You think rarely, but – so to speak – completely! I'm glad you got it all clear. It's so much better so. And you're happier.

   It seems to fit together. It's all very queer. I'm just a trifle frightened when I look back over it all, with your help. At least – I hold my breath. For instance, you say you were worst at Penshurst. Do you remember that evening there, when you snatched some wooden thing, or some ball or something from me, and vanished with it into the darkness, me after you? You were like an amazing animal. You tried to turn quickly – anyhow you fell, right out in the middle of the field. I could point to every spot. God, how I nearly threw every thought in the world away, and kissed you like a flame. Why didn't I? I suppose I'm

---

3 Jacques and Gwen had announced that they were to be married in July.

too old and wise and cold. I just didn't. I wish I had, rather. Would everything have been very different, by now? I seem to think not. But anyhow we – no, damn your eyes! We, – should have been a year and a half old, instead of half a year.

There's lots of things to say about your letter – not in the way of questions or corrections or additions, I think, -- merely comment. Not, that is to say, important, perhaps; only, perhaps . . . interesting! I'd so much like to talk to you, immediately, and not over 36 hours. But that is not possible, even by telephone. This must suffice!

One thing is that your letter made me extraordinarily happy. Do you know the kind of emotion that makes it necessary to do something – physically – to express it? Do something, I mean, more than shouting, even. When things hurt a great deal, I'm driven to take a strong stick or bar of iron in my hands, and try to break it, and strain till I'm tired out. So your letter at intervals forces me to do something – generally bang with my fists in a gentle and absurdly complacent rhythm on this vast ridiculous yellow stove. Occasionally I wave a handkerchief in a fitful and solitary way. Once I did a demure step down the street, till the suspicious glances of the police frightened me. Why I feel happy is not quite clear. Partly because (after a bit of muddling) it all seems very clear and fine – you've put it so clearly and finely (you really are a very fine lady!). Partly, also, because, as I say, you came so actually yourself in the letter. And your actual presence is a livening thing. Really, of course, I ought to be also a trifle melancholy. I am. Only melancholy isn't the word. How could you describe the feelings of a despicable and desperate worm who amazingly found himself in Heaven, but also discovered that he hadn't been selected Archangel? Even that is totally misleading. It suggests that he wasn't satisfied! God! As if I wasn't utterly utterly utterly satisfied! To use the word is a profane filfthy and unspeakable imbecility. But I dare, now, be even imbecile to you. Only, I mean, let it be completely obvious and understood that I'm not wanting anything more. My state of mind is practically at no moment that of wanting anything more. I don't mean it is the same as yours; it has it always in reserve, so to speak. But I'm not crying for the moon. I haven't time. I have infinite riches given me – oh, that wouldn't stop me wanting more, I know! I could cry for the moon, if I liked. I could cry for anything if I liked. But I don't. You see, Noel, it's rather, I think, this way. It takes two to make a quarrel; and it takes two to make bodily love – which, with your kind permission, I will proceed to refer to as lust. (Understand, most clear eyed of women, two things: one, that lust has not a bad connotation, it can be very fine: two, that it means not the actual act of copulation, but the desires and feelings, the passionate state of mind, connected more or less with the idea of copulation). The situation's thus. To begin with, I am in love and lust and everything else with Noel. I centre round her radiate towards her. 'Lust' not overwhelming, but there, and on a level with the rest. But all this (when you are still unknown and unapproachable) is incomplete; the whole range of emotions is one-sided, hypothetical, not on the highest level of reality. (They're amazing & fine, oh God! they're fine enough!). For example, at that period, Love means at moments, perhaps. "I want to kiss Noel." (You'll understand that this is scientifically & absurdly bald: it'd take too long to put in all the glory and heaven swimming round the words in 1909). But that really implies "I want to Kiss a Noel-who-wants-to-kiss-me" (with a codicil "which is unthinkable") Noel = not Noel-dead or Noel-unwilling or Noel-impassive or Noel-thinking-I'm-some-one-else but (profanity!) Noel-wanting-to-kiss-me. And so on all through. *Nicht wahr?*

Well! Then consider the next stage, when the unimaginable dream of August had changed all. Love meant something different thereafter. The hypothesis was fulfilled. Each emotion that didn't wing away into the void, but met its fellow and complement took on reality, became a million times more glorious. Love then meant "I love Noel who *does* love me", "I kiss" implied "am kissed". (I daren't comment in brackets. I should lose the last semblance of coherence!) Only poor little "I lust" is left in the old condition. All his brothers have gone up to heaven, fulfilled and deified. He stays, a shadow, an hypothesis . . . When the rest were so, he could take his part among them. Now, he is shunted down, eclipsed, negligeable, forgotten. If ever he joins them, the chorus might be fuller . . . So *he* says. But, look you, in Heaven one does not make plans. If he never joins them – there's an excellent mathematical rule, my Noel, that if you take a finite number from an infinite number, you don't make it less. Is that clear? I feel that you understood it all before. But I thought I'd prevent any possible discomforts. It's nicer to have it said, accurately. It's part of our glory, Noel, that we say all things – or can say all things – you and I.

My 'melancholy', though, extends just a trifle further – when, at least, I'm weak, tired i' th' evening. I trace, and plague myself with tracing, a horrible development in you. At Penshurst, you say you felt it most strongly. After that you "began to know me better" and would have regarded me "as a friend" whom you loved most in the world. Only your sympathy tricked you for a bit. But you relapse into that, that you're "affectionate, reverent, anything you like, but not" a lover. "I

appreciate you very sincerely, Mr Brooke. I shall always be a granddaughter to you . . . "! But the melancholy development suggested is,
that you had a youthful adoration – some people have it for actors,
some for bishops, some for long-haired undergraduates, – which, when
you "knew me better" (= "began to see through me") began to pass.
The Ideal – became a not faultless, a pleasant, an admiring, . . . friend!
And with friendship the time will pass, till, one day, the real thing
comes, and Noel, the grown-up, is in love! But not – it doesn't happen
that way – with the friend! Oh, Noel, it's a silly suggestion. But you see
how it fits the facts; and it's plausibility, as I say, pinches me when I
can't sleep. Of course, at bottom I see through it; for you do – you have
said so – love me. And that's the beginning and end. Lo! a laughable
sight! Rupert at one time reproving Noel for worrying about the future,
at another, fumbling and worrying himself! Noel, Noel, we've now,
we've next May. These things we know. The rest . . . . For the rest we
shall see when it comes. We shall manage it better then, for managing
finely now. That future will find so glorious a Rupert and so splendid a
Noel that all it's tricks and meannesses will fail before them. Oh, Noel,
Noel, don't write to me "I shall always love you"! It's dangerous. It's
terrible. You can't know. You mustn't say it. Say only "I love, love, love
you." Say "My love's the greatest thing in the world." Say "I hope I shall
always love you" – if you're mad enough. But not the other thing.
    My Great Noel, write four lines to me and say what you're
thinking and what you're going to do. I'm at this address till April 7th.
Then I think of roaming and of coming back in May. If it were possible,
and if you wanted it, for us to be together in April, I'd come back – oh,
like a bird. Other things being equal, however, I've a dim fancy I'd be
completer if I stopped abroad a month longer. But tell me what you
think about this Noel whom I love.
    I've such a passion to see you again, and talk, having kissed you.
We've denied ourselves so much, there was Prunoy, and now Munich!
We deserve something. And these hurried snatches at bliss – they don't
admit of certain calmer longer glories. I must see you some time for a
long while, day after day. Oh, Noel remember Grantchester! I want to
sit and talk and talk and talk, and see you, in every light and mood and
position.
[. . .]
    I've got such a queer, deep happiness on me, because youre
somewhere in the world, and we're lovers. I wish I could tell you, what
it is. Sometimes – for instance when I was writing my last letter – I love
you so much that I feel frightened at our very names. To think of them,

of us, seems to reveal the strangeness of everything as by a flash of lightening; and I'm frightened. Tonight I'm different, so secure and content. The universe stands so fast and fine, and full of such glories for you and me. I'm going to write to Jacques and Gwen and tell them how great they are. I'm glad they're in love, and going to be married soon. You've heard? Quite sudden. And they're very radiant. And Ka's a little sad, but glad and very fine. And I wrote putting them all right . . . I tell you about it all one day. Tomorrow, if you like. Have you written to them, or to either? Will you? Your letters are more than you think. And Jacques and Gwen are worth writing to. They and Ka worked everything out greatly. Be proud.

Yes, I shall write to them. Tomorrow I shall feel a passion for the French lady (a most violent affair). On Wednesday I shall hear Wagner . . . And before and afterwards and always I come back to you. All else is finer for your sake. We are great, Noel; and we shall be great; and we have made a great thing. Good night! – damn, I wish there were words for you!

My dearest dearest – I love you
Rupert

[24, Bilton Road] Rugby (till Saturday)
a.d. VII. Id Mai.
[8 May 1911]

O iucunda et amoena et cara felixque atque benigna et pulcherrima, in uno corpore atque eodem tempore Ceres tu et Proserpina, ut arbor vel ut collis tacita et serena et dea praestantissima, amo te atque adoro.[1]

Jacques (I'm writing to say) is in Paris and so won't be able to take you up till tomorrow week, when he intends to. I have written to my publisher to say I must see him in London, & bidding him choose a

---

1 O, joyous, pleasing beloved, happy, kindly and exquisitely beautiful, at the same moment and in the same body, you encompass Ceres and Proserpina, you are like an arbour or a silent and tranquil hill, and a most dazzling goddess, I love and adore you.

Wednesday. So beware! The next item is, Gwen's going to invite (probably) you & Virginia Stephen[2] & Bryn for the same week-end to Newnham Grange, & Jacques & an artist or two to The Old Vicarage[3] – a joint house-party. On the 27th. I give you so much warning: that you may decide.

There's a rumour that you & your mamma are coming to Cambridge this week-end. If *so*, let me know <u>promptly</u>: for I must arrange to see you.

And Ka & others want to get up a camp in July, the second half, that you're to be at. All this, to put you in possession of the world, & its doings.

Grantchester was subtly smiling and queer and still and full of you. Do you (you don't) know how Italy's full of wayside images of saints & gods? I'm putting up 19 small shrines to you in various places where you are known to have trodden in Grantchester.

Oh, oh! I hoped to have escaped, but it's worse than ever; all back again and more. I love you in your own degraded bucolic and godlike style, as a lettuce loves a cabbage. I am infinitely happy & serene: and I die (as lettuces die, a slight thing) to be with you. We <u>must</u> be together three weeks this summer, My Nowell.

Very soon I write you a letter full of mirth and pleasant amusement. Now I eat. It was very good of her Ladyship to invite me to Limpsfield.

Yours in the common way of love,
Rupert

---

2 Rupert had first met Virginia when their families both holidayed at St Ives, in April 1893. Rupert and his elder brother Dick would join the Stephens to play cricket, a game at which Virginia distinguished herself, with some ferocious bowling. The planned joint house-party never came to fruition, although during this year Virginia did become acquainted with many of Rupert's circle, notably Ka Cox, whose friendship she came to value enormously.

3 Rupert was to move into the Old Vicarage, the house next to the Orchard, and had invited Jacques to stay with him. His new landlords were called Henry and Florence Neeve.

The Old Vicarage,
Grantchester

Friday [19 May 1911]

It's very wonderful, you know, about your nose – I thought I was going to write you a long letter, full of meat, but somehow it hasn't been done. But this is just to carry on the tradition, you know. Jacques saw you on Wednesday. And got the idea you were all coming up quite soon. Is it so? Oh! Look here, my mother's coming to Cambridge (not Grantchester) from Friday June 2 till Monday June 5, *or* from Saturday June 3 till Tuesday June 6. If it's being discussed and you're in the discussion, use your mighty influence to prevent them coming at that date. It's merely for my convenience (so don't give the reason). *You* ("that youngest Olivier girl – I hear she's left school" . . .) needn't meet my mamma. Only it'll give me more time to see you, if it's another period. Oh, the next house to Glen Veagh is *To Let* for the summer – and I very nearly took it for June in your names.

What'd been the perfectest, would be if you & Bryn alone came up for a while. Bryn could wander off on her giddy rounds and (as she leaves you to do what you like) you could roam out here and talk to me – as long as you could stand it.

However –

Oh, woman, I've got flatter. You must pull me up again, and make me the complete cabbage or meadow or whatever you make people.

I'm sitting in an infinitely dark room – the dining-room, which Mr What's-his-name used to have. Outside I can see rain. La! and it was so fine on Monday and Tuesday. Also I can see a new antique the Neeves have put up, a gigantic white vase, of marble, which now holds one geranium. Grantchester's much the same. Come back to it! Here'll be dog roses soon. Mrs Neeve, Byron's Pool, the Trees and the Village Idiot – all the old landmarks waiting for you.

Aren't married people impudent? Jacques, realising – I suppose – that I was so mixed up in his beastly affairs, thought he'd like (oh! mostly in the friendliest cheeriness!) to know (damn him!) about my states of mind. And said (the other day) with coarse directness and suddenness "Are you & Noel in love?" Remembering you on Reticence I waved my hands in a way that indicated "My dear fellow! The scaly cheeriness of the Engaged Person!" "I *think you* aren't" he went on "and I *know she* isn't!" I made, again, a foreign-looking gesture, which meant "Define

Love, and I *might* answer you!" And darted off on to a side issue. Lor! We are rum, you and I. It's really very remarkable of us, don't you think? To begin with, its the best thing either has done – better than your quietness, or your horse-riding, or your playing inside left at hockey, or your matriculating or even your being born, and better than my cricket or my Scholarship or my poems. And anyhow, it's so very peculiar: so very much our own, the way we've worked it out; those ordinary plunging affairs are so common (one sometimes unforgivably thinks) and usual – Bill & Eva's or Jacques & Gwen – by the side of ours. Ours is quite different from everything and everybody's else. Think of the history and nature of it! That extraordinary Noel! That extraordinary Rupert!

In fact, this is to say that I want to go on with it. By which I mean that I'm tired of not being in London on Wednesdays, and that I make this proposal. Will you be free next Wednesday from ten to two, & from four till 11.55? And we'll go to some theatre. Just let me know, for if so I shall go up to London on Tuesday and see *Nan*.[1] – Oh, I say, is there *any* chance of you being there on a Tuesday or a Friday, for I'd love more than anything else to go to *Nan* with you –

For Wednesday, I'd not mind missing one meal, or meeting (e.g.) David Garnett or Bryn, at one meal. But I want several hours. If not, what about Wednesday week?

Last night I dreamt you were passing through Munich and stopping there 2.30 till 8.30 p.m.: and I was showing you round.

Sometimes I'm seized by a vast desire, not to   kiss you
                                                  or marry you
                                                  or see you
                                                  or write about you
but – to know every smallest detail of the whole of your life, thoughts, mind, appearance, gestures, and everything. Queer!

                                                  Ich liebe dich
                                                  Rupert

P.S. You are a funny devil
P.P.S. But (it's my secret) very wonderful.
P.P.P.S. Write!

---

1 *The Tragedy of Nan* by John Masefield (1878–1967) had been revived at the Little Theatre for a run of eight matinées. It was produced by Harley Granville-Barker (1877–1946), whom Rupert had met at the 1908 Fabian Summer School.

The Champions,
Limpsfield.

Saturday. [20 May 1911]

Rupert

Jacques was very pleasant last Wednesday & I think he is right in the conclusion he came to after talking to me. Poor Rupert! I'm glad I wasn't there, to see you trying to conceal and protect this thing that you will insist on calling our love. If Jacques had asked me that question I shouldn't have had the determination to answer anything but a frank "no!" because I dont believe we are, I know its dull to say so after, I seem to say it every time I write, (when I see you I only talk nonsense) but you dont seem to agree. You seem to *want* us to be in love so much; why do you? I dont want to do what Jacques & Gwen do & I dont want their emotions, I know quite well what they are like, they destroy all one's judgement & turn one into an ape. I refuse to be blinded to anything about you, good or bad, & I should see nothing but good, if I was smitten with this here illness.

So sometimes I hate your seeming to be in love with me, because you dont realise sufficiently how beastly I am, in most ways. Look at this foul letter! You'll hate getting it.

Not next Wednesday. I must go to Lawson Dodd my dentist; & there is a possibility of my not being in London at all. If, by the Wednesday after, you want, in spite of dissolusionment, to see me; why, I shall be there & shall want to see you; perhaps you know of a place in the metropolis, where one can spend an hour or two in peace.

I cant come to Cambridge until my exam is over, about the 15th of June, Bryn will want to go sooner. This I also told Jacques, but his mind is a little mixed.

Did he hate Father? Somehow, I am anxious to hear from you. So answer this.

With Love. fr.
Noel.

The Old Vicarage

Tuesday [23 May 1911]

Oh! <u>Damn you</u> !
If people in love are blinded to the other person's real nature, I too am certainly not in love. For I see plainly that you're a codfish.

– One point of fact, by the way, I must protest against. It wasn't after last Wednesday Jacques made his judgement: it was a week before.

Very well, then; we're not in love. As you say not. – Oh, it's easy enough to prove a negative case as you do:

> Jacques and Gwen are in love:
> therefore people in love are like Gwen and Jacques.
> We are not like Gwen & Jacques:
> therefore we are not in love.

We are not in love. But what we *are* is very queer. Define that next. I guess it's mostly quarreling about words. It's at any rate rather queer that I should want to go to London to see you for an afternoon: and I can't believe that you find me indistinguishable from any other male of twenty-three. Oh, it's agreed long since that, in one sense, we're not "in love". But if we don't love each other in every other sense, then you'll have to find a new and madder word for our relationship. Why does walking from Oxted to The Champions at midnight stand out from the rest of life as a quotation from Shelley stands out in a modern novel – the most noticeable thing being that it's quite, quite different? Noel, do what you will, there are some things you can't help giving me, and part of our relationship you can't deny. Thank God I'm (and it's) partly independent of you, partly free from your clutches "trying to conceal and protect this thing you will insist on calling our love." By God, you are a <u>Bloody</u> woman!

However –

Next Wednesday, 31st, I'll be in London. (a) Can you also come to *Nan* on Tuesday, – be in London Tuesday & Wednesday? (b) or *Nan* any other Tuesday or Friday? (c) On Wednesday when and where? – as much and as long as you can. (d) If nothing else recommends itself, we've always Dudley's empty rooms to go and have tea in. (e) Will you be able to stop for a theatre? – do. (f) I wish it wasn't so far as eight days away. (g) Mind you come *after* the 15th to Cambridge. (h) In

future, to avoid offending you, I shall refer – if at all – to either
unsere}?} Liebe or Noster Amor.
unser } }
Your letter made me rather sullen for a while. But I think you're
too morbid. I want to know if you're fairly satisfied, rather. And swear to
tell me if I worry you.
On Wednesday we'll talk most brightly of the Insurance Bill[1] &
New English Art.[2]

with (you know) love
Rupert

Will Bryn be in London Tuesday or Thursday *if you're not*? I'm jolly
glad about Wednesday,

The Champions,
Limpsfield.
Saturday. 10th [June 1911]

Rupert, mon ami,
Ne te fache pas tant, puisque je t'aime assez!
As far as I can make out the interval you speak of, between
Tuesday & Thursday, must be Wednesday, – ? Well then. I finish my
Latin paper at 1.0. on Wednesday & have no more to do that day. There
may be a matinee (of an Irish play) there may be a concert (& you so
musical!) or there may be a sun & sky, in which case a walk at
Hampton Court (as you suggest), or elsewhere, would do.
Bryn said she saw you, & that you snorted when I was mentioned;
but how weird you are! I believe that you are quite cured & sane as long
as you are'nt writing or talking to me; so ought'nt you to stop doing

---

1 The National Health Insurance Act of 1911, which had been brought in by Lloyd George and John
Burns, caused anger among the Fabians. For, although it was a step forward, introducing health
insurance for the unemployed, it ignored the suggestions of Beatrice Webb's Minority Report and left
the Poor Law unaltered.
2 The New English Art Club had been founded in 1886, in opposition to the traditionalism of the
Royal Academy. However, by 1911, it had also grown to be regarded as too conservative by many
artists.

those things? If you can stand Wednesday, do come, for I fear I can stand anything.

If you walk up that street, (we walked up to meet Bunny), at Sth Kensington at 1.30 or after on Wednesday the chances are that you will meet me.

Till then a Dieu! or write to me
    c/o Mrs Cox[1]
      11 Briardale Gardens
      Platts Lane
      Hampstead.

                                  love from Noel.

                                        Grantchester

Monday [12 June 1911]

Centre of the world,

    We are all sitting in the window of The Old Vicarage, for it's raining. Ethel & Daphne opposite me: Hugh[1] to one side. But they don't know who I'm writing to.

I read your letter during lunch, under the table.

I dreamt last night that we met – I was looking in all directions for you as usual: and as usual you saw me first, & came up behind, & put a hand on my shoulder – And you *were* nice. By God, you <u>were</u> nice! There was such a feeling of security about. However . . .

    I think I can "stand" Wednesday. What we do, we'll settle then. I'll be in that road if I can find it. I don't exactly know which it is. Could you let me know the name? I imagine one walks through an arcade,

---

1 Noel was staying with her grandmother, Margaret Lucy Cox, whilst sitting the entrance exams for University College.

---

1 A[rthur] E[wart] Popham (1889–1970), known as Hugh; a friend from King's, who later became Keeper of Prints and Drawings at the British Museum. He was a cousin of Maitland Radford and had come to the camp at Buckler's Hard, Beaulieu. Hugh had fallen in love with Bryn and made an unsuccessful first proposal to her in October 1910.

from S. Kensington station, and then on? But if I don't know, I shan't go far from the station.

1.30? If you get out at 1, that gives you more than 20 minutes. O let's say 1.25.

I suppose you mayn't sit up *too* late. *But arrange, I pray, to give me all the time you can, including dinner.* We can lounge in Dudley's new rooms.

Also if there's anytime Thursday Friday or Saturday, *keep it clear!*

You'll notice I'm not very much "cured", now. Because I'm writing, you say. Hm . . . ! But *of course* I snorted to Bryn. What would you have me do? Blush? Giggle? Faint?

With love

Rupert

I wish I understood French. "Assez" . . . ?
My address'll be c/o A.Y. Campbell[2]

King's Clere

Northcourt Avenue

Reading

Oh, I'm so keen to be seeing you again. You're very lovely & very kind & very good.

[Grantchester]

Sunday [2nd July 1911]

Oh, it *is* the <u>only</u> place, here. It's such a nice breezy first glorious morning, and I'm having a hurried breakfast, half dressed, in the garden, & writing to you. What cocoa! What a garden! What a you! And oh! damn! I've got to go into Cambridge & fetch out a punt for Dudley

---

2 A.Y. Campbell (1885–1958), the Greek scholar, who had performed opposite Rupert as the Elder Brother in *Comus*. He was made a fellow of St John's in 1910 and in 1922 became Professor of Greek at Liverpool.

& his German women,[1] who are coming for the day. Damn them. Fetching a punt, entertaining them, & taking the punt back – there's a whole day gone. And I wanted to <u>work</u>. I've just been two days in London, seeing the Russians,[2] drinking wine, – oh! oh! As for the Russians – I'll tell you one day – no, I'll take you one day: when they have their best programme.

But now, business. I see my days filling up: and I want to be free, if there's any arrangement for seeing you. I have invited a man to stay with me for the week-end 21–23 July: & I want to know whether to put him off.

So please say, if you know, when or whenabouts any Camp or any river expedition or any other show is.

Answer immediately: and give your address. I am in a hurry: I shall write again. I do want to see you, so.

With all love
Rupert

2 Rawlinson Rd.
Oxford.

Tuesday 4th [July 1911]

Must you put off your man (the one who wants to see you from the 21st to the 23rd) at all? Why shouldn't you come here in the middle of a week?

A veteran uncle will be the final week-end visitor here from 15th – 17th, and after him – no one. Come any time you can after that. Margery will be back from Ireland, so it will be quite sensible (you remember, she asked you to come). And Oxford is lovely, at least the places in it & outside it are. There is nothing quite so well arranged as

---

1 The women were Dudley's future wife, Annemarie von der Planitz, and her sister, the dancer Clothilde von Derp.
2 Diaghilev's (1872–1929) Ballets Russes had opened their celebrated Covent Garden season on 21 June 1911. The company included Nijinsky (1889–1950) and the designer Léon Bakst (1866–1924). Before the year was out, Rupert had been to see them perform fifteen times.

the Backs; but Worcester & the Magdalen are better than almost anything else. You probably know the place though.

Strangely, I have been thinking about you often for days, and not horribly as I did last Autumn; you would be quite pleased, if you knew.

Write a longer letter soon, and say, when you want to come here.

from Noel.

What *fun* Dudley is! "just fancy!"

The more I remember that Hedda Gabler,[1] the more I like it. It was *most gorgeous*.

I'm no musician!

Grantchester.

Tuesday July 12
[Postmark 11 July 1911]

What the devil's it supposed to be – I sang it, whistled it, played it, even, on the few whole notes of my piano. But I couldn't recognise it. It comes after a reference to Hedda Gabler. Is it meant to be a musical rendering of your emotions at that play. Oh, what *is* it?

My plans, after a week hence, are wholly dim. I've to be in London sometime, in Oxford, sometime, in Rugby – sometime. Does it matter, my dimness? Are you settling irrevocable things for the near future? Tell me what they are.

---

1 The Edmund Gosse translation of Ibsen's play had first been performed in 1891. This production opened in May 1911 at the Kingsway Theatre with the part of Hedda played by Lydia Yavorska.

I chiefly want to know how long you're all in that dreadful provincial town, and if anything of a wilder nature I'm likely to be invited to, is shadowed forth. If it came, you see to a choice, between a week middle at Oxford with you, and even only a week-end in the wildness, I'd go for the latter. It's delightful to hear that Margery "who invited me" (did she? does she know?) will be "back from beyond." But I've seen her. The people I really want to see are you & Bryn, whom I've not seen. Oh, when must I say definitely when I can come? At a pinch I'll say between 23–28. (between = within. I don't claim the whole week!) First week in August'ld be even more likely. But <u>do</u> tell me if you're going to sail down a river in a canoe or anything, in August. For I've the smell of last year's Camp in my nose, & it makes me kick. And I hear that any idea of Camp this year has probably fallen through, owing to complications & inertia. Oh, I could have brought – if an expert had been wanted and it had been in the second week in August – poor old Geoffrey Keynes to fill a gap. But even he's *almost* engaged for the Broads.

What's that bouncy woman Bruin[1] doing? I'd hoped she were organizing some party of wild adventurers & that my meek, silent, upturned face'd possibly secure an invitation . . . Anyhow, you're in the (lately so remote and silent) centre of things. "I rely on you" to let me know how the world wears itself out . . .

I'm so frightened, you see, of your family at Oxford. They'll not want, or like, me. If I *did* come I should have to be working (did I tell you?) in the Bodleian – Would that be insufferable, or a relief?

There's London, meanwhile. I'm looking out for a good Ballet show of the Russians. If there is one – next week e.g. – could I get two seats? You rather promised . . . Or would it be *too* crude? I shall perhaps be in London next week . . .

My fish supper. And then the post. Oh! Oh! I shall write again, tomorrow. Shall I? Perhaps tomorrow'll slip by like all these days, bathing and working. I read, read, read, the dramatists. And for hours bathe, & lie out in the sun naked; still reading. Oh, *why* aren't you here? What are you doing all day, in – Oh! God! – "2 Rawlinson Road"? Oh, my Noel! I'm drifting like a paper-boat. I *must* see you!

with love
Rupert

---

1 Virginia Stephen had nicknamed Ka Cox 'Bruin' or 'the Bear', presumably because of her gleaming brown hair and cuddly appearance.

Grantchester

Saturday morning [15 July 1911]

Oh God, the weather's changed!

I can come in the middle of this week coming: i.e. and e.g.
Tuesday next – Friday. Or in the following week. What's to be done?
Am I really expected at all? Can I bear it? Can all you bear it? I must go
somewhere – I am in the last stages of exhaustion. The week I am not
with you I shall be in London. I am working like a steam-roller. Half the
day I read plays; half the day I patch up poems. For a man has suddenly
expressed a morose desire to print my poems immediately – *quam
celerrime.*[1]

Had it all better collapse? Will they, I mean, loathe my
thrustingness? Your father despises me. Your mother detests me. I
can not bear your family. Yet, if I've got to look at the Bodleian, it seems
reasonable to stay at 2 Rawlinson Road . . . Oh, God!

The day is, grey. There have been ten amazing days. Ka comes
from Newnham every day, & we read Bergson, together. I've got very
fond of her. But as she's got a lot of old-fashioned and silly prejudices,
the only thing they'll allow her to do is to marry & have children. As I
don't want to marry, and can't afford to marry & have children, & as
she's very old, she'd better, I discovered, not waste time on me: she
doesn't seem to be able to attend to two people at once. So I'll see no
more of her.

A bloody woman. Oh, a <u>bloody</u> woman! I must go & work.

A card! a card! I don't know what to do.

Rupert

---

1 The interest in Rupert's poems had come from Frank Sidgwick, founder of the publishers Sidgwick &
Jackson, who did indeed publish his first volume of poetry, on 4 December 1911. Frank Sidgwick was
called up in 1917 and killed on 23 September the same year.

2. Rawlinson Rd
Oxford.

July 17th [1911]

Rupert, *darling!*

[. . .]
    Next week Eva will be here too, but there will be a small bed in a cupboard for you at night and the Bodlean library for the day time; so come on Monday, or Tuesday, or Wednesday & stay for as long as you can like it – (4 days, or five).

    The sailing here is more comfortable than it used to be at Beaulieu, even I have never felt sick at all yet, so you might do that too. Yesterday & to day we sailed up a little way & bathed from a haystack by the river; I'm affraid I shall never accomplish a beautiful running dive, I always go flat, but even so its as good as Daphne's. Could you teach us? athletic one!

    No, but it is all lovely – Rawlinson Rd is a dream, we've never lived in so ugly a house, but it charms us, so that we sleep & eat well & smile all day. And I always go quite absurd every evening (which accounts for the begining of the letter) & I shall be dangerously affectionate at times; so please, if you come, be stern with me, because I should hate to find myself drifting into a relationship that I can not maintain with you; last summer was glorious at the time, & now I love it for that; but it was sometimes so dreadful, when I felt remorseful & wished I had'nt gone through it all, that I feel I shall never want to do quite the same again.

    Perhaps that is more disagreeable than I meant it to be: at this moment I regret nothing, but I have a great dread & suspicion of *repititions* (and Oxford keeps on startling me by being so like Cambridge). I know, though, that when you come, you will be cool and, as always, sensible; so that we shall sail through the four (or five) days excellently & very fast.

    I think, that when you say you hate my family, you mean that you like Bryn & Margery & you dont mind Mother & Daphne (Father fits in too, as you will see); but that you find them abominable as they live: together & forming a "home" – nicht wahr?

    Well, you will get a good dose of that, and you may escape finally, loving the exquisite though comfortable isolation of Ka, living with her sister in a flat. I wish you wouldn't call Ka "bloody"; she isn't, & it sounds as though you were angry with her; you have no cause to be. Perhaps you will explain more about your conversations with her? Oh, it would have been so much better, if you had married her ages ago! And you told me, once, that you could be very rich (& support a huge wife & family) if you wanted to.

Perhaps you dont want to tho'

Love from Noel.

[. . .]

The Champions
Limpsfield.

August 8th. [1911]

Dear Rupert.

You may have noticed that I didnt send you a birthday present. Were you angry? I looked wherever I went for something great or fine to get you, but could find nothing good, or cheap enough. So from now on till Xmas, you may daily expect a belated gift from me; after xmas it will be a celebration of mine & Christ's birthday, not yours.

Only one depressing thing has happened since I saw you; apart from that, life here has been very happy. Yesterday I cleaned out the work shop with Father & we lit a bonfire; today I have been doing laundry work. Every night one sister & I sleep out in the chart woods with Bunny & Harold [Hobson] & any one else, who choses to come; it has been very merry, the climax was last night when Daphne & Bunny & I danced "the dance of the beasts", whilst a beautiful greek lady[1] played the acc(h?)ordion (it might be spelt six ways). And it was at this

---

1 This was possibly Antonia Almgren (née Cyriax), a friend of the Garnetts, who was staying at the Cearne, although Noel is wrong in thinking she was Greek. Bunny had a brief affair with her that summer: 'It taught me something about physical love, but the lesson that a liaison is not satisfactory for more than a few weeks, unless one is in love, was not in the least what I had expected, or what I wanted to know at nineteen.' (*GE*, p. 227)

same sleeping out business that the sad thing happened. Hugh Morgan[2] was down for the week end, and as he was settling down into his sleeping-sac, he asked me: "who are coming to the camp, after the O.B. camp." I gave him the list, as we had arranged it (it now includes Bunny for sure) and he said "you seem to have forgotten me." So now he is coming, & quite pleased to stay the whole time. Perhaps it wont be as bad as I immagine – his being there – but at first I thought all was hopelessly muddled. what do you think?

Old Margery went off to Switzerland, with her heart full of forebodings that she wasn't going to enjoy herself, we all had to summon up our powers of imagination to describe the beauties of the land to her and it needed all the eloquence of the family to induce her not to return her ticket at the last hour. Apparently we were'nt so wrong; for she has written one post-card and what it contains sounds happy; she has bought an ice axe, slept in a chalet & is going to walk far & high over the mountains from now on, for a fortnight. Then, if she has money, she will come to camp.

Ho Rupert! you said you would write to me because you had an idea in your head, what is the idea? I should be very pleased to get a letter from you, I have almost forgotten, what you look like at all; I suppose this is natural: but I could realise you daily, quite easily, untill yesterday morning, when I suddenly thought "why, I've quite forgotten about old Rupert and he is to me, as a street in some strange town; that I passed through ten, or more, years ago!"

I sometimes look in the papers to see if your book is recorded in the "Poetry of the day" department; I may have missed it, but up till now I've found no notice of it; perhaps you will send me a telegram when it is published? nicht?

What can I do to keep from becoming dead? I am distressed, because I see that no one is so rotted as me; and that though none of them are good enough for the world, I am worse than any. Besides being sleepy & dull, I am not even heavenly sereen; for, as you saw, I can become vilely ill with sulks & jealousy. I move about this place, where there are excellent people; Sybil, Bryn, Bunny & more, & can not talk to them, nor get anything from them; I had far better be living alone. And that cant be done; there are lots of plans, the most approved & latest is for me & Bryn & M[argery] & Mother to live in a flat in Hampstead & come here at times. Other vaguer plans are: me to go to

---

2 Hugh Morgan, an O.B. who had been a member of the Klosters skiing trip, where both Rupert and Noel developed a lasting dislike of him.

Newnham for a year; . . . us to take a house in Oxford for a year or more; but nothing is settled, & my poor Mother seems worried to death by uncertainty & Daphne equally anxious because of Mother's anxiety. Yet I am happy: I hope you are

With love from Noel.

P.S. when the elder-berries are ripe, I shall make good jelly!

Grantchester

Thursday [10 August 1911]

[. . .]
Oh, woman, woman, what does she know of the serious things of life? You live my girl, in an Unreal Fairyland. In the real world, one doesn't say one moment "I shall publish a book!" And the next moment it's out! There are months of dreariness. You needn't scan the lists till October. And anyhow before its published I shall give you a copy.

(a.)   There's haggling about Terms.
(b.)   There's making up one's mind to sign the Agreement (a bloody business.)
(c.)   There's writing the book.
(d.)   There's waiting while its printed.
(e.)   There's correcting the proofs.
(f.)   There's letting it mellow in the publisher's cellar till he see's a good chance of putting it on the market.

Each of these stages takes some weeks. At present I'm in a. b. and c.
The agreement's wonderful. " . . . as between Rupert Chawner Brooke, of The Old Vicarage, Grantchester, hereinafter to be referred to as The Author, his heirs, executors, and assignees; and . . . "
I've just been reading what of the book's written, again; and my sorrow is changed to joy. For a week I have felt it is so bad I about decided to give everything up. But today I find its GOOD. I tried to think out some hidden way of dedicating it to you. "A La Jesus de nos Jours" oder so etwas. But I can't work it out.

It's very nice of you to have been searching for a present, my funny Noel. But don't worry. Send something slight & typical & inexpensive – a rose-leaf or a sigh. Or even your nice letter may be taken as filling the place!

Oh, you are a dear!

Best of all, attend to my idea. You are going to O.B. camp & then the other; altogether nearly three weeks. You'll get very sick of it. Obviously what you want is a break of two or three days in the middle. Very well then. Our camp begins, say, the 24th. You meet me some forty or fifty miles away on the 22nd: and we'll turn up on foot on the 25th. We might meet up Crediton way, or down towards Ashburton, or down at Bridstow or even Tavistock, and come back across the moor. It would be great (if you didn't walk too fast). Fancy, dashing across Dartmoor alone, in the most superb weather, you & I with lightish rucksacks & three books, & careless hearts, & those amazing Dartmoor sunsets! And Camp to look forward to! It would be the wonderfullest thing ever was. Write and say you can do it. Places & dates we can fix up later – my dates are frightfully tangled. You needn't tell your beastly family now – But say it's possible. Oh, I could write pages of the glory of it. I'm getting exhausted by this beastly work. I must have something like that to revive me: or I shall be horribly snappy at Camp. Never mind about whether you've forgotten what I'm like or I'm only half what I used to be or love's a delusion . . . just come & walk & we'll be as merry as anything & sing (no, you'll sing: I shall speak) & meet extraordinary adventures & perhaps even sleep out & rag passers by . . .

I must go & work. Write me a short reply. I am all kinds of a beast – but that'll save me.

"Rotted" – not you; You're all right. You'll be better when you've been alone a bit. But you're all right. What's that about sulks & jealousy? When? What fun? I didn't notice. Of all your plans, Newnham sounds best. Not because Newnham's any good, but because you'd be fairly separate & individual & alone. If you come to Newnham, though, I shall leave Cambridge. London, if you could be fairly alone, 'd be better for you. And if you're at Newnham, how shall I be able to take you to Tristram & Die Walkure[1] & the Russians, in October? Eh?

Why aren't you in France, and Bryn? Oh, you *ought* to be. It's better than laundry-work at Limpsfield. Why aren't you? It would have been rather superb. Aren't you going? Damn!

---

1 Wagner's *Ring* cycle was to open at Covent Garden on 19 October 1911.

I'm glad David's coming to Camp (David Garnett). But why didn't you tell Hugh it was Justin's camp, & you couldn't allow people without his leave? It wouldn't even have been quite untrue. Have you told Justin? Perhaps he'll be able to manage Hugh: who oughtn't to come the whole time, I imagine.

Happy? *Lord*, yes. It's wonderful here, in the solitude. But you *ought* to be here, or I with you: almost a year ago today . . . It oughtn't to be August, & we apart. But we'll meet!

with love
Rupert

P.S. How did you like Virginia?[2]

O.B. Camp
[Clifford Bridge
Drewsteignton
Devon]

Tuesday. [15 August 1911]

That idea wont do; you must wait until I'm 21. Also, having come late to this camp, I am not likely to get bored for months. You have got the latch key of that hotel near Charing X, which M & I went to on the night of the Russian Ballet;[1] Margery put it in your pocket & you never

---

2 They had met Virginia Stephen by chance at the beginning of June. She had not been particularly impressed by Noel, as she writes to her sister Vanessa: 'Her beauty was marred by protruberant blemishes; as she wasn't beautiful, only a pretty chit, perhaps she wasn't Miss Olivier.' *The Letters of Virginia Woolf*, vol. i, ed. Nigel Nicolson and Joanne Trautmann (London: Hogarth Press, 1975), p. 466.

Virginia was on Rupert's mind at the moment, as he, Jacques and Ka had succeeded in persuading her to come camping, and she had also agreed to visit him in Grantchester before the expedition began.

1 On 31 July they had gone to see *Shéhérazade*. Before the ballet, Rupert had organized for them to have supper at Eustace Miles's vegetarian restaurant, and here Noel met James Strachey for the first time. He had seen her once, the previous summer, at the performance of *Dr Faustus*, and had written prophetically to Lytton: 'She certainly looks intelligent as well as beautiful. I expect you'll hear more of her before you die.' (18 August 1910: British Library)

returned it, with the result that we almost slept on the Embankment.
The woman at the hotel is anxious about it, you must send it to her, if
you know the address (some place in Buckingham Street, Strand) or
bring it here & I can ask Margery. Dont fail.

yours N.O.

Virginia Stephen was not the only one to try camping for the first time this summer. Maynard Keynes appeared, as did the Oliviers' Limpsfield friend, Maitland Radford. James Strachey arrived late one night and was discovered in the morning, shivering under a bush with a blanket round him. This was enough hardship for him and he retired to join his brother Lytton, who had taken lodgings at Manaton, near Becky Falls. Lytton had no intention of risking the elements, and was busy working on his first book, Landmarks in French Literature. *Rupert also spent time working; he was writing a dissertation called 'John Webster and the Elizabethan Drama', for a Fellowship at King's, which needed to be finished before Christmas.*

The days were filled with play readings and walks, and at night there would be singing round the camp fire, led by an O.B. named Paul Montague, who had a passion for Elizabethan music and had brought with him his hand-made cittern. His parents lived nearby at Crediton and invited them over there one afternoon for tea. It was this occasion which encouraged Rupert to complete his poem 'Dining Room Tea'.

DINING-ROOM TEA

When you were there, and you, and you,
Happiness crowned the night; I too,
Laughing and looking, one of all,
I watched the quivering lamplight fall
On plate and flowers and pouring tea
And cup and cloth; and they and we
Flung all the dancing moments by
With jest and glitter. Lip and eye
Flashed on the glory, shone and cried,
Improvident, unmemoried;
And fitfully and like a flame
The light of laughter went and came.

Proud in their careless transience moved
The changing faces that I loved.

Till suddenly, and otherwhence,
I looked upon your innocence.
For lifted clear and still and strange
From the dark woven flow of change
Under a vast and starless sky
I saw the immortal moment lie.
One instant I, an instant, knew
As God knows all. And it and you
I, above Time, oh, blind! could see
In witless immortality.
I saw the marble cup; the tea,
Hung on the air, an amber stream;
I saw the fire's unglittering gleam,
The painted flame, the frozen smoke.
No more the flooding lamplight broke
On flying eyes and lips and hair;
But lay, but slept unbroken there,
On stiller flesh, and body breathless,
And lips and laughter stayed and deathless,
And words on which no silence grew.
Light was more alive than you.
For suddenly, and otherwhence,
I looked on your magnificence.
I saw the stillness and the light,
And you, august, immortal, white,
Holy and strange; and every glint
Posture and jest and thought and tint
Freed from the mask of transiency,
Triumphant in eternity,
Immote, immortal.

                              Dazed at length
Human eyes grew, mortal strength
Wearied; and Time began to creep.
Change closed about me like a sleep.
Light glinted on the eyes I loved.
The cup was filled. The bodies moved.
The drifting petal came to ground.
The laughter chimed its perfect round.

The broken syllable was ended.
And I, so certain and so friended,
How could I cloud, or how distress,
The heaven of your unconsciousness?
Or shake at Time's sufficient spell,
Stammering of lights unutterable?
The eternal holiness of you,
The timeless end, you never knew,
The peace that lay, the light that shone.
You never knew that I had gone
A million miles away, and stayed
A million years. The laughter played
Unbroken round me; and the jest
Flashed on. And we that knew the best
Down wonderful hours grew happier yet.
I sang at heart, and talked, and eat,
And lived from laugh to laugh, I too,
When you were there, and you, and you.

The Champions
Limpsfield

September 20th [1911]

Dear Good Rupert

Margery wants to read "Tom Jones" & as I think that
the book can do her, & in fact anyone, a great amount of good, I've let
her start on the first vol. I know you are generous, can your generosity
stand this? For sure, I know that when Margery has got hold of the book
Daphne will also remember, that she has been wanting to read it all her

life; & then Bryn will start, & the end will probably be, that she will lose the whole galoot. Thats but a risk; but it is certain that, however smoothly matters go, *you* wont have a chance of reading "Tom Jones", or even begining it, for a month to come. If you cant bear this, let me know at once, & I promise you, I'll lay hands on the work at once & post it to you by return. But if you dont mind at all, then could you turn your attention to the sending off of the other vols, which you still have: 3, 4, & 5. I am waiting for them eagerly. It is a good work, in many ways; & I've never felt so "moral" (in Justin's sense of the world) in my life before, as I do now. To me too, the actual writing seems awfully good; is that so really?

And here are some of your letters, found in my poor blotting pad, all that it now contains instead of many fine stamped envelopes & a packet of postcards & lots of writing paper. Oh the casual folk at camp! how, by resembling me, they make me see what a fiend & vagabond I am!

But it *was* fun, & now already I'm fast forgetting all about it, except the smell & the scenery, which things, as you know, can affect me more than all else in this land.

Daphne and I are going to colaborate & write short striking stories for the monthly periodicals; apparently it is quite likely that we shall turn many an honest penny that way! How we shall look down on you, poor serious searching poet, from the heights of our rich literary success! She is going to supply the imaginative literary style & I the common sense & general restraint & tidiness. I feel we shall have great influence & do no end of people a lot of good.

We haven't yet found a flat or house; but as time gets shorter, the family's ideals come down, so we shall probably be satisfied very soon now. They wanted to go to all sorts of awful places; even such holes as Hampstead & Bloomsbury were thought of; but I managed to persuade them by an exhibition of violent feeling, how dreary those parts would be to live in; now the choice lies between the Maurice Greifenhagen's house in St John's Wood[1] (which I am very keen on) & one or two more or less horrid flats in such places as Marble arch, Buckingham place or Baker strt. Where are you going to be, do you know yet?

Dear Rupert, I think after all you are about the most tolerant person there ever was. For, once you have liked a body, you can bear them through thick & thin, & tho' you criticise them at times, your criticism generally leaves them quite as agreable to you, as they ever

---

1 The house which the Oliviers soon chose, 12 Loudoun Road, belonged to Maurice Greiffenhagen (1862–1931), RA, who had been Head of the Life Department at the Glasgow School of Art.

were. Now, things like "The Olivier" can bear with all kinds of folk at first, extracting from them what is good until they are, as it were, boiled dry; whereupon we at last look at them critically, & seeing at one time all the objectionable qualities, which we had at first been blind to, conceive for them a bitter contempt & ennui. Thus it is, that such as us have many delightful acquaintances, it may be; but few good friends. Now *you* – etc. etc.

And its none of it true neither; but it is an idea I just had for the moment, & it may entertain you.

Its very pleasant to be an ordinary person (this is again, "just an idea"); but its tedious, sometimes depressing; you are well out of it. For whether you'r nice or nasty or indifferent, you are so in a slightly extraordinary way.

What you ought really to do, is to bow & thank me. Do you? Or shall I receive by the next post a torrent of denials & encouraging kind words? If the latter, I shall never write you an *idea* again. Oh horror!

Rupert, I cant keep sane. So please excuse the above, & send the other three vols of "Tom Jones" as soon as posible.

You *are* nice

Love from Noel.

Grantchester

1911 October 2nd.

It was *so* exciting when so fat a letter from you arrived a fortnight ago. I trembled, without daring to open it, a long while. What could you be going to say? You'd never been so voluble. It must be a Crisis. Was it the End of Everything? Or a lengthy reasoned proposal to fly together by the Tuesday's mail To Suez? . . . At length I opened it. My surprise was quadrupled. They were all from different people! You, mother, Mr St John Lucas, Frau Ewald,[1] Fraulein Kanoldt[2] and my publisher. What

---

1 Frau Clara Ewald (1859–1931), painter, who had been one of Rupert's first friends in Munich. He had been given an introduction to her by E.J. Dent (1876–1957), the musicologist from King's.
2 The Kanoldt family had also befriended Rupert during his stay in Munich.

could you all be doing together! What sort of a Joint Letter <u>could</u> you be writing – you, my mother, St John, Frau Ewald, Fraulein Kanoldt, & my publisher? The sane world seemed to have fallen away. I reeled in dismay. I had a dim incredible – credible vision of a too wild reading party going on, secretly, in some fantastic corner of Surrey consisting – oh, God! – of my publisher, Fraulein Kanoldt, Frau Ewald, St John Lucas, my mother, and you . . . At last the truth leaked out. But I was shattered all day.

This letter has got too much like that inferior song *Widdicombe Fair*.[3] I sent you Vols 3 & 4 of Tom Jones, rather coldly. I hunted for days for Vol 5. Then a man told me there were only 4 volumes. Is that true? If not, I must get no.5. Tell me. Coldly, because as I'd solemnly and happily *given* you the book, I thought your anxious apologetic asking if Margery might read it was overdone and unnecessary. Silly old thing! I'm glad you like it. I've not read it, so I can't judge. I shall read it. I don't understand, from your description, exactly how it makes you feel.

On Wednesday I go to London for a day. I shall talk to my publisher. He turned rather Green about that sonnet called *Lust* & wanted it left out. I wrote him a LETTER and he, more or less, gave in, crumblingly. Now we're wrangling amicably about the size of the page.[4]

Then I go to Rugby till the 16th. After that I spend Saturday to Monday here, Monday to Saturdays in an attic in London. I discover I shall have to work harder than anyone has ever worked to get my dissertation done in time. That's because so much time ran away at Clifford Bridge! In London I shall sit and write all day; and see you at intervals if you're to be seen and willing. It will be fine. I love working. And I rather like you.

I wonder if your house is fixed yet. And if you've started your University Life. You'll anyhow be in London by the 19th when the first Ring begins. I wrote off and rather vaguely ordered two seats for the whole of it. Will you come to some with me? Two, perhaps – if you can get seats for the other two without getting them for the lot. Which you

---

3 The chorus of which runs:

> With Bill Brewer, Jan Strewer, Peter Gurney,
> Peter Davy, Dan'l Whiddon, Harry Hawk
> Old Uncle Tom Cobleigh and all –
> Old Uncle Tom Cobleigh and all.

4 Sidgwick agreed that the sonnet might remain, on the condition that it was retitled 'Libido'. (Cf. *LRB*, pp. 315–16) In Copies of *Poems 1911* given to friends, Rupert has restored the original name in pencil.

like, – Die Walkure, anyhow. If you can't make it without coming to all with me, or none with me; try the former alternative. Consider all this; and reply.

So Camp's faded from you, has it, "except the smell and the scenery"? What do you mean when you say those things stay with you longer than anything else? I'm jealous again! A little incredulous, though. *Do* they? There are a few things that stay longer. I'll not let you forget some things till you die – But anyhow, I rather vaguely protest, can't I be allowed to be part of the scenery? I so often was. And if I don't smell, I can, you know. I can buy stuff in a bottle and always sprinkle it on me, I mean. Anything, you see, not to be outdone by a rival.

It *is* funny how things fade; sort of fade. Three weeks ago today, I'd only left you a few hours. Three weeks ago yesterday —— But it's in a way remote. The Rupert of then, is almost a third person. I seem to see him capering among rocks or glooming by a fire: and being a most prodigious fool, sometimes.

But it doesn't fade.

It's funny. I've been working here a fortnight and quite happy wildly happy in working and memories. And suddenly tonight I'm rather disconcerted and simply because you're not here. As if something that slept when you aren't present had woken a little. Or as if I'd been stunned three weeks & were slowly coming round, & saying to myself "By Jove yes, I remember – the last thing I was conscious of, I was kicked on the head!" Perhaps I oughtn't to write to you. If it makes me feel suddenly that I'm merely playing, that all this 'working' is trivial pointless irrelevant tiny stuff, because being with you makes everything in the world nothing by comparison. Oh, but it doesn't make unhappy. It's absurd to pretend to oneself it does. Empty and wanting and yearning and uneasy (curse the woman!) but infinitely happy. I feel as if I could live on thinking over what I've had for a thousand years, and not sulk or sigh. – I couldn't, I know. But I can't see *why* I couldn't.

I go on writing; poor stuff. I want to tell you how amazing and real and important some of those moments and things seem. And all I can do is to pour out this vapid stilted dust! The wretchedness of writing! I've immortal wonders to tell you. I could if you were here. But now . . .

Noel, Noel, Noel, Noel . . . . I'll give you the whole world, I love you so. OH, And one of the wonders is that now, after this summer, I somehow know you know what I'm meaning at any moment. I think you always used to. But I never felt certain you did. Oh, you *did*. But I had wretchedly little faith. You were always so far and distant and incomprehensible. You're incomprehensible enough now. But I *also* know in a way. I know you without understanding a great deal: or apart from it. It's not *knowing*: only, – I'm at home in you.

And that's sacrilege.

Oh, 'sacrilege' is a meaningless word now, even. Like Mr Wordsworth's lark you unite the kindred points of heaven and home.[5] It sounds like an advertisement. But I *do* feel more intimacy – knowing – and – known, business: nowadays. All it really means is that I'm improving under your tuition. (God, if you knew how you've altered me, these three years!)

You *are* wonderful. "Ordinary" say you, and "extraordinary Rupert." Fool! Oh, you lovely Noel! The words have no meaning. But if they *did* – if there was anything more than just – Noel – Rupert – what would "ordinary" have to do with you? With the full weight of my extraordinariness & knowledge I tell you: you are amazing, astounding, glorious, unheard of, wonderful Noel.

I have a thousand images of you in an hour; all different and all coming back to the same. Noel, Noel, Noel. And you're so real, sleeping somewhere down South there ⅃ . And we love. And we've got the most amazing secrets and understandings. And I'm so happy. How can I bear it? To *think* of you is Heaven. Noel, whom I love, who is so beautiful and wonderful. I think of you eating omelette on the ground. I think of you once against a sky line: and sitting at Becky Falls: and bathing: and picking dewberries: walking: and on the hill that Sunday morning. And that night that was wonderfullest of all. The light and shadow & quietness & the rain & the wood. And you. You are so beautiful and wonderful that I daren't write to you: And kinder than God. Your arms and lips and hair and shoulders and voice – *you*. A million worlds and ages are smaller than that time. I daren't write. I could only repeat words. Beautiful, beautiful. They're silly. – I love you – There are no words.

Goodnight Noel
Rupert

---

5 Leave to the nightingale her shady wood;
   A privacy of glorious light is thine;
   Whence thou dost pour upon the world a flood
   Of harmony, with instinct more divine;
   Type of the wise who soar, but never roam;
   True to the kindred points of Heaven and Home!
                                    ('To a Skylark')

In a letter to Cathleen Nesbitt in April 1914, Rupert declares that *he* will be like Wordsworth's lark: 'For I'll lie between your face and your heart, . . . and your face is heaven and your heart is home.' (*LRB*, p. 571)

IMPORTANT

24 Bilton Road
Rugby

Friday [6 October 1911]

Noel!

You are lovely as the sunrise – and we have very few more years to live.
    Covent Garden has terrified me by sending, today, tickets for the whole Ring, two of them, in the sixth row of the Amphitheatre. Central I hope. The horror of every one having to get 4 seats – a series – is overwhelming me. Will you save me and take one of these? Otherwise I am ruined: every one I know has got one for the whole series. If you simply couldn't bear going with me for the whole series (or if your family couldn't) you might once swop seats with someone else in the theatre – Bryn, perhaps; or James, who's going with Ka. – We might group differently, once. All I want to prevent is 100 people having 101 tickets and me – consequently – having to sit with a gap at my side. Is all quite clear? Write to me, promptly: and say that you'll come. I'm very rich: & will give you the seat. Explain that our relationship is such that it's possible.
    Yes, yes, Yes, YES!!!
    I will neither talk in the overture nor pretend to understand the music. In a word, I will be good.

with love
Rupert

The thought of you is very comfortable. It walks quite straightly through my mind – Oh, how very difficult. I mean that you are so extraordinary and warm and important: oh, and shining . . . Hush! . . . But I tell you, if any one sees this letter they'll not understand. They'll not see the words I write off the edge, beyond, words only you can read. Noel. Oh!

Write to: The Champions
12, Loudoun Rd.   Limpsfield
St Johns Wood.   Surrey.
N.W.

Saturday. October 7th. [1911]

TWO letters – Rupert!

And *two* seats? O what a coincidence – No, but you are absurde:
tho very good & very eloquent.

Life is short, you say, & the Ring ~~comes off~~ begins on! the 19th &
you love me.

I cant deny any of them, I'll do my best to cope with the situation.

The Ring is the easiest to arrange: I should like to come to two of
them, but I must pay for my seat; If you cant find someone to come for
the other two nights, there's Bryn, she wants to come once & is willing
to pay for it. We neither of us want to see the "Rheingold" much, so you
might go offering that about, preferably to any other. It's a little sad, isn't
it, that you haven't got that box for the season – boxes are so cheap! I
suspect it fell thro', for lack of competence. And is no one going to the
Russian ballet at all? I heard a strange rumour once, a few days ago, that
that great man – the one who leaps – ha: "Nejinsky" – that he had
quarreled & left the troup – did you know?[1]

But London is full of exciting things: I must go to Sumerun[2] & a
new play by Arnold Benett[3] & great deep lectures at my college on The
soul – & all sorts of Art & Ethics; and there are promenade concerts
every evening, & symphony concerts – everything which might foster
& encourage Culture. I *must* leap into it all: come & leap too –
sometimes. Though life is short, its shortness depends on how it is
used, & I'm rather wondering whether, it would prove longest, if I
spent it merely in going daily to College & learning Science by degrees
– giving all my energy thereunto – , or if every evening at five I

---

1 Although Nijinsky did not leave the company at this point, his relationship with his impresario and
lover, Diaghilev, was not without its difficulties, and two years later, after Nijinsky's sudden marriage to
Romola de Pulszky, Diaghilev furiously severed all links with him.
2 *Sumurun* was Friedrich Freska's musical adaptation of *Tales of the Arabian Nights*, produced by Max
Reinhardt (1873–1943), in which Clothilde von Derp was dancing the title role.
3 This was Arnold Bennett's *Honeymoon*, which had opened the previous night at the Royalty Theatre.

discarded all scientific thoughts from my mind & went away to learn about Morals or buy a picture or dance, – or (& please note, that after due consideration, I have given this a separate place) – if I got into the habit of calling on you fairly frequently, when you were genial & not working; & this last, I believe would surely do away with a good deal of the other 2. If I set myself to make your acquaintance (we have just reached a phase when this would be possible), the process of understanding you, would exact hours & more of thought & meditation. I should like to do it; it would be worth doing, I think, but a great work. And is life *wide* enough (mine) to put up with more than one great work?

There's this medicine business, you see. I've always been very vague about it, because I've never had it revealed to me by one of God's messengers, that medicine was my "calling" in Life. Its very unpleasant, however, to have no direction, & because I have a sympathy for all sorts of *persons* – however mean – & medicine is personal, I thought that might do for me. Also I am rather interested in science, tho' not clever at it I'm affraid.

Rupert has been a kind of constant element all this while; like the rain coming down steadyly as one goes along, or something rather firm in the scenery, the horizon or a river; this doesnt explain it, but he was something *there* all the time, a background? Yes that – if it doesn't sound rude. From time to time he has suddenly jumped into focus – quite near, & again – once – threatened to disappear completely; & by these antics has shown, that he wont do permanently as a vague surrounding atmosphere; some day he must be dealt with & re-placed, I feel he ought to come in somewhere, he is important – in fact quite essential; but I dont know what to do with him quite. Therefore I must investigate further, & try & understand him; perhaps, even ask his advice.

Well this jibberish must all be rather tedious: Such thoughts accumulate & must be expressed to someone occasionally: trash to be discharged somehow, at someone's expense: like those poor reproductive husbands you told me of.

Thats what my relationship has been towards you, for the last twelve months. You've been the person most open & wealcoming to any old thing I fell enclined to express, & I've hurled idiocies & stupidness at you – perhaps the very worst things in me – ;

It hasn't been quite inexcusable, I had that distorted idea of honesty which lead me to feel sure you must know, see, hear the worst there was in me – you *must* not make mistakes; & also there was a vague, selfish hope, that you might gradually extract all the meanness &

that I should become a nicer person, at the expense of your comfort; but as a matter of fact, I'm no better, I get worse & worse & you more & more splendid. We must try again, another way. It cant go on – my being so filthy & you so fine – I cant bear the contrast, for one thing.

Please devise a plan. And dont write back & say that I'm all wrong, & soothe me – that wont do.

Your love! Good heaven's, how can it go on so wonderfully, all towards such –

No. that wont help. I must have innumerable conversations with you. At camp (it was all your fault, or all mine) we hardly said a word; of course nothing could have been changed for the better; but what about making a new rule, on the lines of an old & abused one of yours,? "That for the next 10 months, whenever we meet, there must only be talking between us." Or something even stricter – something hard & restraining; awfully good for me! what about you?

See what a lot of good my new work & surrounding have done! I'm all for turning over a new leaf & reforming. Bryn & I are down here for the week-end. Bryn is a very observant person. Margery is going thro' a further crisis, I hear, one more terrible than any there has been.[4] Daphne is alright & we've all got deathly colds. let me know the price of those seats.

Dont wriggle or fail.
Love from Noel.

---

4 Margery was the least emotionally stable of the sisters. Part of her depression now came from her disappointing results in finals – she had been awarded a Third in Economics. Also, unlike her sisters, Margery rarely attracted admirers, and perhaps because of this became devoted to any man who paid her attention. For a brief period in 1907 she believed she was in love with Rupert, and likewise now was in turmoil over Hugh Popham.

As a defence mechanism later, she began to imagine she had many admirers competing for her attention. By 1916 Virginia was reporting to Ka: 'Margery Olivier had not been in the room a minute before she said "I've just refused a proposal of marriage!" . . . Leonard inclines to think that she suffers from a disease of advanced virginity in which one imagines proposals at every tea party.' The Letters of Virginia Woolf, vol. ii, ed. Nigel Nicolson and Joanne Trautmann (London: Hogarth Press, 1976), p. 83.

24 Bilton Road
Rugby

October 9th [1911]

You *are* nice. Despite some fatuity. Oh, Lord, how it cheers my poor old brain, to have your letter.

I must restrain myself from answering – I've a lot I could say – for I've a deal of work to do.

I wish you could come to all the Ring. It's so much better that way. My Swedish friend has agreed to pay me £35 for translating: so I'm *immensely* rich.[1] Can't you only pay for two, and take the others as a favour, because nobody else will? Or bargain with me (on the basis that I shall lose all if you *don't* come)? or pay for seats & not for dinner, if you prefer that way round? Something, I beg. – Oh, it's absurd, you *must* see it all: even if not with me. But anyhow come for the Rhinegold, (I admit it mightn't be thought worth the five shillings) just to oblige by filling a place.

If you come to those, I'll go to the Ballet with Bryn – I want to see something with her. (I'll take you to the Ballet & things anyhow: untutored child. See below.)

If you fairly *won't* come to any one (they're only 5/- each, if you *did* pay) you might settle with Bryn which you'll come to, & which she; I've not time to do your arranging. But, as I said, you come to all. (If Bryn's poor, & if you don't come. I'll equally (being so rich!) give her the thing; rather than sit near a vacancy.)

If we're both in London today week, we might meet to settle details.

I feel elated at being more, at length, than a permanent atmosphere. Awfully good of you . . . You are a Noel. I do love you. I might kick you, of course; for – oh, well! I've no time.

Yes, you may "investigate" me. I'll face it calmly; even with pleasure. And we'll go to theatres & galleries (and concerts!) together: and plunge. But I, like you, have to do it very restrictedly, in time. I'll *make* time: – and you'll have it: – for culture, *and* investigation, & work. The investigations shall be from 5 to 8 on certain days. The culture

---

1 Rupert had been working with Estrid Linder, a Swedish girl at Newnham, helping her translate two plays by Gustave Collijn (1880–1943).

from 8 to 11. We'll mark off times! What fun! And I will *try* to conceal what I'm like. And I will tell you all the truth about Wider Issues. And you shall tell me, something. The details shall be devised when we meet. I shall have (I don't know where) a room or two. No one's to know where they are: because I want to work. When you're inclined you shall drop in. We will eat my remaining crusts and talk.

I will pledge myself to no ordinance. For even though I only wanted to talk for the first three weeks: I might suddenly want to bite your fingers in the fourth. They're very nice. One can't bind oneself to want or not to want. By December I may not want to see you at all. Tra! la! Or the strain may be so great I shan't be able to bear it.

But I'll observe the spirit of the ordinance – You shall get plenty of observation & enlightenment & discussion. I won't worry you. But let it be publicly and definitely certain, that I'm working very hard, and *not* seeing people.

What's wrong with Margery? Another man or the same? Shall we have her to dinner and cheer her?

Love to everyone – I leave here on Saturday.

I suppose you won't be in Birmingham on Wednesday when I go to my dentists. No. How could you? I suppose I shan't be able to help looking.

allerschönste

carissima

χαιρε

amo te[2]

Rupert

"poor reproductive husbands"
DAMN YOU

---

2 Most beautiful of all, dearest, farewell, I love you.

Women's Union Society.
University College,
London, W.C.

Saturday Oct 14th [1911]

Dear Rupert.

      I can have tea with you after 5.0.P.M. on Monday. I cant think of a nice place. There are lots I've heard of; but one mustn't experiment with business meetings. Well – say the Oxford Circus "Appenrodts" at 5.15 or after. Do you know where it is?

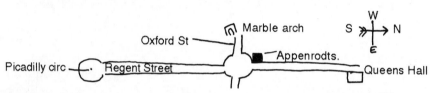

The reason for liking that place, is that I want to be in Oxford St or Regent Street to shop after tea. But if you propose anything better near there, I'll agree.

      If it's alright, you need say no more. I shall have tea there anyway on Monday.

      I'm leading such a funny life now. The fog has penetrated to the marrow of my bones. To day I play hockey. Other days I work till 4.30 & 5. & get up at 7.30.

      Margery's crisis goes on – the same Man.

      Daphne is frightfully ill at Newnham. We're all anxious. Poor – wee James![1]

Love from Noel

---

1 James Strachey, having been in love with Rupert for several years, now also appeared to be falling in love with Noel.

N[ational] L[iberal] C[lub]
[19 October 1911]

I've settled for a time in – you'll jump to hear – Duncan Grant's studio.[1]
He, though, is away. It's the dirtiest place in London, and the
uncomfortablest. It is called 21 Fitzroy Square *second* floor: bell on the
right of the entrance
     I hear . . .

                                                                    Rupert

                                                          [21 Fitzroy Square]
October 19 1911

Memorandum from   Rupert
To   Noel

The Rhinegold was great. (So were you.)
     I think it would be best on Saturday to have food at a decent place
and then drive to Covent Garden. I know a very good empty Italian
Restaurant just round the corner from Gustave's.[1] It is just behind the
Palace Theatre. Several Tubes etc. fairly near. Called *Treviglio*. I will
either show it you, or describe it more exactly. The Walkure begins at 7.
I shall be at this place at 6.5 and order food; risotto perhaps; and by
6.15 you ought to be there. If you can't do this, we must meet at the
theatre, & you eat between Holloway & your home, at home, and on
the way to the theatre: and bring something, if necessary, to eat in the $\frac{1}{2}$
hour pauses. You *must* have a fair amount inside you, after hockey;

---

1 Duncan shared the studio with Maynard Keynes, who was also away at this time, working in
Cambridge. In November they moved into the ground floor of 38 Brunswick Square, sharing the house
with Adrian and Virginia Stephen and Leonard Woolf.

1 Another Soho restaurant, which Rupert frequented.

though we'll sup afterwards, lightly. It will be far the nicer if you *can* manage to come & feed with me. But you're not to arrange that and then find you can't get there till 6.40.

Child, I'll have a chair & a fire and comfort & a tea pot at 4.30 now & then for you, in here. It was so nice to see you here – How extraordinarily commonplace that sounds. But it will be good to talk at ease: I've a deal to tell you yet – about Dudley & the rest of the Universe – You're to sleep.

Rupert

P.S. I *am* here tomorrow afternoon till 4.45
P.P.S. There's going to be a *Third* Ring Nov 8–15 I suppose you won't . . . ?

21 Fitzroy Square
1.a.m. Wednesday [25 October 1911]
(back from the Russians)

Today – in twelve hours – I'm going to see you – aren't I? I just *hoped* I might for a second today: but I didn't. Yesterday and Sunday I was *awfully* ill. Today I'm miraculously all right again: cured by one minute's sight of you with your hair about your face. (In that drawing room I was waiting so, from 5.30 on; for you to come in. And you, devil, didn't.)

At 10 I shall go to the B[ritish] Museum till 12.40. Then, I shall walk up Gower Street past the University back here: and wait till you appear, at 1. If you can be any *earlier*, let me know: and I'll be here to welcome you. Then we'll lunch, & between lunch and 6p.m. we'll
      work
      change (you, at least)
      have food:
      walk about a bit.
or what you like. Will you bring a little work? If you've some to do, I'll like to do mine. Oh, but *anything*: so long as you're here.

You've promised.

So I'll wait in here till you arrive. Unless I get a letter in the morning saying I'm to meet you somewhere at 1 or before. (But I shan't.) I will talk about anything. I will clean up any amount of rooms. I will dance and sing. I will give you champagne. I do (I noticed on Saturday) admire you so <u>immensely</u>. And oh how I love you: every now and then. My former emotions were hatred to what I feel now. I've not seen you for so long: so dreadfully long. But the dreariest date hunting is glorious, because you are alive. Oh, my dearest! In the whole flaming world there's never been anyone like you. Hush -sh. You're asleep; and so wonderful. And today will be so perfect. I kiss you. I daren't write more.

Rupert

Grantchester

Sunday [29 October 1911]

I've not written, and I'm not writing a long letter, because I've work. I'm rather ashamed: – but I won't be. The longest couldn't say much, you know. Oh, how little I can ever say or signal to you! Of all the truth I can only tell you such a little tiny bit – And there's so much to write. I might fill pages saying "I love you, love you, love you . . . " You've become so amazingly more wonderful, lately, towards me. When I think of it – , of you – last Wednesday (so <u>long</u> ago!) and other days. There are no words. There's nothing but the memory of you. It's so real. I know you so well. We've been together at certain moments. – There are things I've given you I can't get back again . . . I can't ever be separate from you. I can hurt you and be cruel and devilish and mean and tear you and destroy you and infect and poison you. But I'll never be free again . . . Nor you free from me. Only when your funny head is quite still, and my mind's stopped; when nothing's any good – (Oh, if you die before I've done loving you, I shall go mad.)

Noel, I keep going aside. I'm trying to get to say that I'm <u>awfully</u> happy. My God, I am happy! I must tell you. I think of you – all round and all over – , what you say and think and are and do and look: and then I'm happier than I thought possible. Noel, Noel, Noel, Noel, Noel. I used to be very happy, often – just thinking of you. But I see now – didn't then – that I *was* a little unhappy – , often – always – because I thought you so often didn't really love me. I didn't know I thought so: but I did. Or I doubted. And now – I'm silly and foolish and babyish enough at times – but I *do* know: I *do*. We're – It still seems blasphemy to write – we're lovers. How dare I pretend I can do it calmly? or look at you and claim anything?

Oh you have such power over me. Now I feel this happiness – and this situation – I feel that if I poured every thought and word and all my love for a million years, it couldn't be enough. What can I give? You could make me do so many things. And I'm so afraid – not *"that"* but *"lest"* they be bad. If you wanted me to become a don, what could I do? Oh, be careful with me, & Be kind! I *don't* want to write this. I want to write a business letter to you, and then work. Noel, let me go, you devil! I'm coming to London again tomorrow, (But for you, I think I *might* stay here.). Where are we to see one another? It's ages since we met, and we've a very few more years to live.

One thing, I demand a Wednesday, sometime. When it's possible and you're agreeable, I want this

Wednesday 1.15   slow quiet lunch
         2.10 – 4.30   Walk at Kew to see the autumn trees.
         4.30 – 5.15   tea
         5.15 – 7.15   Work (in the same room).
         7.15   dinner

and a theatre or a walk to St John's Wood to deposit you – Think! it will be perfect: & so easy! For this week (apart from Wednesday) I'm free always till Friday, when I've to go out to tea & after dinner. So will you kindly arrange a time or two to do what you like with me? At the very least, *two* occasions, please. For I'll be off for the week-end again.

The evenings: you may be taking your mother to something, one day. But you can manage two in a week!

Oh, Noel, *do* give me (I meant to ask) one more chance for Wagner or Covent Garden generally, I <u>will</u> be good. I promise. Smack me. Look here, there's The Ring this week Mon, Tues, Thurs, Sat. Shall we try any of the first three? – I shall keep them open till I hear. Or is there anything else; on any of those days, or Wednesday? The Third Cycle begins in ten days Wed, Thurs, – Mon, Tues. (I think.) Please let me know also about them.

I do bother you. But just reflect: and consider me "at your service". And don't feel yourself bound to "oblige" me. I reach King's X at 5.55 tomorrow Monday and drift to my rooms (which I shortly

change). If you're late at work you can come & meet me & have a meal
and entertainment . . .
  I'm so free & so eager for you – I could talk of a million things.
Work, damn you!
  If I don't see you tomorrow, I expect a note or letter.
  I love you. I love you so, Noel.

Rupert

National Liberal

Thursday evening [2 November 1911]

You're listening, I suppose, to that wild love scene, climbing up to –
what is it –

lachende Liebe
lachendes Tod?[1]

I almost wish I were there.
  I wish, anyhow, I could catch you at the door and whirl you back
to St John's Wood. I want to see you once again – for a quarter of an
hour – tonight. I'd sleep so much better! I'm purely selfish, Noel!
Thursday, Friday, Saturday, Sunday, Monday – oh, it's too terrible. I
keep fingering plans of walking you back across the Park tomorrow –
but I don't know times. And anyhow I'll let you be. Poor Noel!
  and you're with Ka & James watching Siegfried; I wish it was I
with you. And James'll take you home. I wish it was I. How I wish it!
And I'm writing among these fat sleeping Jews. How wonderful you are
– I want, oh my God I so want, to feel your hands on my head again,
before I sleep.
  You're so wonderful – or I know you so well – oh, I love you so, it

---

.1 'leuchtende Liebe, lachender Tod' – 'illuminating love, laughing death'. These are the final words of
Siegfried and Brünnhilde's duet, at the climax of the opera Siegfried, before Brünnhilde throws herself
into Siegfried's arms and the curtain falls.

comes to that – that I can almost feel you here now, *with* me, not very locally, but so strongly: as you are sometimes when you put your head back – But you'll read this in cold morning light. Perhaps you'll barely understand.

I've thought tonight – almost in despair, because the thought was how good you were and how fine, and how impossibly & unworthily mean I. I've thought, even, if its not too disastrous for you. Couldn't you – but that's madness. Only, Noel, don't bother about me. When I spend my whole time trying to make you worry, smile & pass over. Oh, God, I wish I were better for you. I waste things, how I waste! I'm a fool and a rat.

– No we're too near even for whining; I feel that too. It's the amazingest feeling there ever was. And yet I do know, profoundly, that I'm wretched and dirty and a fool, to you, splendid you – I shall never have peace till I'm *with* you, hour after hour and day after day, for a space, *with* you, – not talking or touching, but with that glory round me.

You were vague – & no wonder – to the end. Tuesday at x.y. oclock was driftily mentioned. I'll keep open from Monday noon till Friday noon, next week. You shall let me know at your leisure, and do what you like. On Wednesday my mother's coming to hear a cousin play in Steinway Hall in the afternoon. She offered me dinner & a theatre. I refused the theatre, on the plea – perhaps false – of either dinner or lunch: – it could be either, but would probably be dinner. Bar that, I've got nothing I can't cut, in the week: all's open – I'll show you, my dear, what has been, on and off, in my mind; it may clear my position up! I'd thought of life in general, just now, being, ideally, this. You are about, and I; and we've so much to give and take. Well, we could, I figured, be doing our full work, and yet quite often and unfussily (oh, I know that's where I fail!) be seeing each other. We could have a meal together & find new information and pieces of our minds. We could see things and explore, rarely but delightfully, together; and gain from both each other and the things. Then you could come and talk, more privately and wonderfully, now & again at tea or something in my rooms, – or I in yours, of course, only you don't happen to have any, more than once in a blue moon. And once in a way – a little, even, to show we *can* – you'd come and do work in my room, and I'd work, and after a couple of hours we'd make tea – the whole mutual existence, you see, would be so varying and manysided; and each side would multiply each of the others –

What a Heaven! – I know that in practice I'd be failing continually, snappish, or sulky, or spoiling things – but I would improve. And it would be, (it *is*!) so fine. I've things to give you, Noel, and such things to receive! Your point of view's different from mine, about this, in some ways, I know; and in some particulars sensibler, perhaps, – in, it might be, not thinking half hour lunches Good enough. Oh, I don't know! But you must realise – Ah, I need you so. You could do such things with me. You could make me such things. Don't you *know* how you can alter and make me?

I put it all in a general way. It's the horridest night mare in the world to me that I should worry you into coming when you didn't want to. Do as you like. Only remember how the days fly. Friday tomorrow; a whole long Friday, and we half a mile from each other and never in sight – Isn't it mad?

You see how I'm pleading you should come and work a bit in my rooms on Wednesday and talk, or wander out to Kensington, or even home across the Park – I don't know. I'm only greedy, greedy, greedy, greedy. some Wednesday, anyhow – And, *one* time more, I think I'll go to some theatre with you. Just when you want to see something. For if you don't find me, at theatres, much better than your mother or anyone else, at least you don't find me much worse (I'm talking of the future.) And as *I* find I like that form of being together quite highly, it's worth doing. So we'll try it – during November, I let you have – once more, if you please – (The companionship of it, stealing into some pit – Macbeth perhaps! – together, you (that's the point!) and I – it does seem to me immense and wonderful.) The words are so tame and horrible. It might be two schoolgirls; or an aunt to a nephew ("I hope to see a great deal of you in the near future, dear!") But the words get a bit transfigured, when you're the other end of the sentence. All these protestations and proposals read badly enough. But imagine please that when I write them I'm looking up sometime and saying your name among them, and then the blood comes, I can feel, all around my eyes, & the room seems to reel.

I must finish this. You're in bed, I think: asleep I hope. Noel, take this lightly. – I have got your gloves back. I'm keeping them a day or two. A sleeping draught. Oh, it *is* silly, I'm not ungrateful. I know how good you are to me. I do. I do. I can't write it. I remember; again & again – my dearest good night.

R.

12 Loudoun Rd
[St John's Wood]
9.0.PM. [7 November 1911]

Dear Rupert

    I'm still very weak, but I have been helped by Bryn &
Margery.[1]
    It is clear now, that it would be best that I should not come & see
you among the fleas tomorrow from 3 –7.P.M., but that you should
come back here with me on *Thursday* at 6.P.M. Bryn will be gone out to
supper, & Mother & Margery to the "Walkure"; so the house will be at
our disposal from 6 –11.
    We can have another luxurious meal, & sit in the padded, female
room. Better for me than groaning round the inner circle or frowning in
Bloomsbury.
    So understand, that you wont see me tomorrow, nor I you & that
you can go to the Rheingold & your Mother's concert, & lunch, &
work.
    By Thursday, I may be in a better humour too, tonight it has been
unspeakable, the beastlyness of my state of mind. I will explain as much
as possible, why I go that way occasionally, & what you had better do to
cope with it.
    Another shock tonight was, that they expected you to supper here;
there was a very good vegetarian dish – ; & were grieved & annoyed
that you had even come to the door & not entered. It must have been
my fault.

Love from
Noel

I will fetch you at your house on Thursday *not before 5.30*; Dont wander
in the streets; just work till I come. *No Answer*

---

1 Noel's studies at University College, coupled with Rupert's demands on her time, were taking their
toll, and her sisters had become concerned at her increasing exhaustion.

National Liberal Club
Whitehall Place, S.W.

10.30 [p.m. 7 November 1911]

I suppose you're not in bed. I wish you were . . . But you're fed and at peace. I got into a 'bus & a train, which took me *miles* round. Had finally crawled into Ka's supper party at 8.45 (There's such a good programme at the Russians. Oh!) I wandered out from her just now, &, walking hither, I met a man from San Francisco, who was walking round the world. He came straight up & started talking. Don't you think it's very queer I should have met him? I felt so friendly. But fancy, blundering against you in a taxi at 7.30: & meeting a man called Wellington Something who'd been walking for eight & a half years, at 10.30. I only want, really, to cheer you –

I shall be waiting at three; and on, working. And I shall be able to do nothing till midnight. I daresay I shall hear from you. Come or not as you like. Don't if I should worry you – All's so right: and nothing matters. Please, Noel, if ever I get on your nerves: just send me away. Or take me into some quiet place, & first hit & bite me, & then put your head on my hands and sleep.

I'm so gauche and irritating: and foolish I know it. And it hurts so. When I think you dislike me, it so too horrible. But even that doesn't matter. Absolutely not at all. It's an hour's folly on Tuesday evening. But Monday and Wednesday – the Best goes on.

We'll be so peaceful and happy tomorrow, if you come. Or anyhow.

I'll ask you things & take answers, as coolly as if it's to myself: I won't nag. And you won't hate me – It's absurd, pretending one's talking to someone else, when one's talking to you – But that's how the trouble rises –

I'm a mean thing, full of smallness and jealousies and dirt. But I won't let you go; yet. And I won't give in, either, and admit I'm so poor that I can't love & work. I *will* stay in London: and see you, when you like: and work undisturbed.

You're a tired thing. I love you so – tomorrow – And that coming Sunday. You *are* good (Dudley's here. I'm going to inform him I've "told" you.[1]) Oh, faith, and love . . . I'm a poor creature. But I love you. Goodnight: most holy, dearest.

R.

---

1 In September, while walking on Hampstead Heath, Dudley Ward had told Rupert of his engagement to Annemarie von der Planitz. (Cf. *LRB*, pp. 317–18)

[76, Charlotte Street[1]]
Wed. night – [8 November 1911]

all right: tomorrow. I'll be waiting – inside – Ring the top left hand bell:
& if nothing happens, knock.
  I don't see what Margery & Bryn have to do with it –
  All's right. You can explain away. I'll be intelligent. Don't worry.

                                                                    R

                                                        The Old Vicarage
Sunday. [12 November 1911]

Noel,

        You made me think, rather. I'm a fool, and keep taking it for
granted things have changed – more than they have.
  It comes off all right sometimes, at Camp, perhaps, and at certain
meetings. Not in London in Autumn . . .
  I think the position is this. You're working in London, more, in a
way, than you've worked before. It takes up more time, I mean. It leaves
you rather tired.
  I'm working in London, rather hard. And though I can generally
make time, work takes up most of my energy and perhaps leaves me
rather stupid.
  In such conditions and under the present circumstances you find
you occasionally hate me when we meet and (which is much more
important) that you pretty well always don't find anything more in it
than in meeting anyone else. Less: for I'm not behaving very pleasantly,
and what I talk about is either *why* didn't you see me yesterday or *when*
are you going to see me tomorrow, which isn't very interesting

---

1 Rupert had just moved to these inexpensive lodgings, found for him by Ka.

conversation, and also, I think, it subconsciously irritates and displeases you to feel that I'm taking it all more hungrily than you – it makes it all different; I mean, from talking to somebody you liked as little but who also merely liked you as an acquaintance – I don't know: I'm never very good at guessing your feelings. Only the truth stands. I haven't (or we haven't?) carried it off, just now.

I do feel humiliated; and angry. But that's not important – I give in. Poor Noel, I'll release you from your persecution and your conscience! I'll give up worrying you. I'll leave you to the people you like being with, – Bryn & Harold Hobson & whoever they are. You've really got a fairly serene future in front of you. I shall be much more in Cambridge the rest of this term, only occasionally – after this week – in London: two days at a time and so on. And next term I guess I'll be mostly abroad. For the time I am in London, this term, I'll not be nuisance. I shall let you know roughly when it is, and if ever you want to see me or to talk rationally or to go to anything, you can let me know. I can always fit it in. You must take any steps there are, that's the point. I shall be always willing, but I shan't make any proposals. There's a weight off your mind.

There was one thing I wanted to talk about. The Christmas holidays. I'm going to get some house somewhere for a bit – on some downs or by the sea, & work talk & walk there. I wish you would come, a bit of the time. It'll be better than London.

I'll, anyhow, see you here, probably, in a fortnight. You can come for five minutes, or for a day, or you can stay here. (I wish you would do that.)

I believe you've got my text of the Ring. I rather want it for Siegfried & the Götterdämmerung. I suppose this won't get you in time on Monday morning. If so, if you could bring it along & slip it in my door (addressed) in some interval, I'd be thankful. But it'll do if you send it off to get to me by Wednesday morning.

This week I'm going to be in London Monday morning till Saturday: because of *Tristan*, on *Friday*, I think. Would you like to come to that? I'd be quite good. I'd let you read the German –

I find I'm taking – great heavens! – Alfred[1] to the Russians on Tuesday –

Lord, Lord! I'm afraid you see through me too much. But I'm better than you think.

---

1 Rupert's younger brother, Alfred, followed him to King's. Like Rupert, he was killed in the First World War.

I've a lot of things to give you, someday, when you'll take them. Truth, and knowledge of some things, – oh, and other things. I'd like to make you quite perfect. You're very wonderful and I love you very much. I don't know what you want – I wish I did. Perhaps you'll tell me, one day.

Goodnight, child. I kiss you –
Rupert

The Old Vicarage

Sunday evening. [19 November 1911]

I saw you long ago.

I shall stay here till anyhow Wednesday. I shall probably come up to Charlotte Street Wednesday to Friday or Saturday. For I've still stuff to dig in the B[ritish].M[useum].

This is a bloody pen.

Dickinson[1] asked me to lunch next Sunday, because [John] Masefield'll be staying with him. I replied evasively. I shall have to let him know. Next week-end I shall have to be in Cambridge from ten to 2 on Saturday night (don't say so.), and *possibly* 9 till 11 on Sunday morning. I have no other engagement. But I *may* fit in a meal with Dickinson if its convenient – on, say, Sautrday night: for I'll make him change it.

Well, I want to know what you're going to do. I rather left it to you to decide about where & with whom you were coming. I want all the time you can, and want to, give. No more: and no less. It's all very simple, and true. Of course I <u>want</u> to see Bryn. But I'm very busy, and I want to see her, mostly, after Dec. 9. I shouldn't be bothered if she came: & if you think you could dispatch her so that you could give me as much time as you wanted to, and as you would by the other plan.

---

1 Goldsworthy Lowes Dickinson (1862 –1932), Fellow of King's and member of The Apostles. While an undergraduate, he had become a close friend of J.H. Badley, and had taken an active and helpful interest in Bedales ever since its foundation.

That's my *advice* – *my*, selfish, advice. But do what you like. It'll be so
nice, whichever you do, that – I'll be civil! But I'd like to know: both
which plan, and what times. I don't insist on knowing immediately. But
an early answer *would* oblige. If there's anything to be *said* – , you can
say it. (Of course, now I come to think of it, if you both came here, &
Bryn went out to supper on Sunday, it would be rather delightful . . .)
(You *don't* have to return on Sunday evening, do you?) In either case, if
you're wanting quiet *and* able to come for a good chunk of time, you
can bring your "work" & I'll sit & write & on Webster. And at the end
of two hours I'll look up and say "liebe dich". And go on working. And
in any case I'm always open all week-ends to entertaining, – *especially*
(when I should be *delightful*) on the 9–11. Did I say it'd be best of all if
you put up here, alone? Anything: anything. Don't worry! I remember
the appearance of your mouth so well. Noel. – You're wonderful: and I
feel so full of love towards you.

> with love
> Rupert

> The Union
> [Cambridge]

Monday evening [20 November 1911]

I'm writing in a room you've never been in. Queer.

I was so plain and clever about proposals when I wrote yesterday,
that I quite forgot the second thing I was wanting to consult you about.
Poor Noel! another thing to put your mind to! It's this.

On Boxing Day

I go away

from home, to take a cottage in the country and walk and talk and
eat and read. Before I go abroad. That's anyhow, my idea. For a
fortnight, or even more, with people coming and going, perhaps. Well,
will you be able to live a healthy and rational life in December or
January? You may be going to the Lakes or Wales. But isn't there other
time? If so, I want to arrange it with a view to you: if you'll come for a

week, I mean, we'll then work out what other people are to be there, and how long, and so forth. There are relations of yours I want at some period. But you're most important. If you want to bring a sister with you, you can – If —— But there are inumerable delightful "ifs". Just give me your views. And things'll begin to settle. (I suppose you'll refuse if I suggest you walked there with me? –)

Oh, and where do you advise me to go? Bryn's Midhurst place sounds too far from the sea: Lulworth, one knows to be superb. Dartmoor's too far, probably? The New Forest too lugubre. –

Oh, oh!
Rupert

Women's Union Society.
University College,
London, W.C.

Wednesday. 2.0.P.M. [22 November 1911]

Heres a go!

I dont think I can come this week end at all. If I came it could only be from late Saturday evening to some time Sunday evening; for I have – always – to get home & sleep there Sunday nights. And I cant come earlier on Saturday, because of a hockey match (I wonder, how much that will insult you?)

Bryn will be going to stay with Daphne on the 2nd, & perhaps Margery too; so there wont be room for me at Newnham. And the alternatives – (1) Staying with one of them at your house, & (2) staying alone with you – wont do either.

(1). Because I shouldnt like to persuade either of them to come & stay with you, when you had much rather they didn't come, & would only be glad of them as of usefull padding.

(2). It would be difficult & painful to deliberately act in opposition to my Wala's [mother's] advice. And she hasn't yet reached the stage when she thinks it isn't rash & inadvisable for me to spend solitary week ends (or walking tours for that matter) with you.

I'm affraid this will all make you very angry. You will rage & snarl & blaspheme – I see it vaguely; but I'm not going to mind it, over here – safe in University College.

I think it will be easy enough to come to your house in the holidays; and, appart from whats seemly, I should certainly like best to come with Bryn or Margery – or the other one (if you are having her). This is because I like them better than other people. Also, you mustn't have James – when I'm there; but youve probably thought of that.

I'm affraid I dont know of any actual house or village which wd do for you. But I know Midhurst is too far from the sea.

Is'nt it farther east, that the downs come close to the coast. Why not try & get a house not far from some quite popular summer sea-side resort; where there will be no one in winter, & houses will be cheap?

I haven't got a map; but isn't there some likely place South of Lewis, or even more east?

Look on a map, & then trot down to the place & inspect it.

Well I suppose I shall hear how you are from M[argery] or B[ryn], whom you'r sure to be seeing today, tomorrow or the next day. Thank you for writing two letters.

If you post them too late (by the way) to reach 12 Loudoun Rd in the early morning; address them here; then I shall see them before night. A general rule.

Love from
Noel

B[ritish] M[useum]

Thursday. [23 November 1911]

"Rash and inadvisable" . . .
My God, you are a worm.
Well, the offers stand.

R.

POST OFFICE TELEGRAPHS

CAMBRIDGE
NO.29.11

Office of Origin and Service Instructions

West Strand   Handed } 2.37 P.M.   Received } 3.13 P.M.
in at   here at

TO {   Rupert Brooke   Reading Room
British Museum

Waiting after 4.15 Illuminated Manuscripts Noel.

King's Cross waiting room.
and in the Train.
5.55. [29 November 1911]

She – Celesta, la bells – is ready to start; wrong side up, indeed, but happy, and rather quieter.[1] And I may pay for it the other end! Joy! (I apologise for having been agitated, that moment, about it all. I saw your horror and your flight. I sit comforting myself – you can't answer – that it's ultimately all your fault, my nerves being so ragged, – even if it's ultimately all *my* fault, that yours are so . . .)

"Celesta?" said the official. "Celesta", I said: relying on my soft hat and long hair "my good fellow, have you never played a celesta?" "Kind of 'armonium, I daresay," said the official. And let it go, at that.

---

1 This keyboard instrument, which had been invented in 1886, consists of metal plates suspended over resonating boxes and then struck with hammers. Rupert had offered to transport the instrument to Cambridge for Dent's production of *The Magic Flute*. Dent had decided that its ethereal bell sound would be perfect for Papageno's magic bells.

Armoniums may travel, it appears, with human beings. Other kinds of instruments, – organs, perhaps? – are classed as machinery or dogs. If, however, I'm not met the other end, the celesta and I are hand cuffed and put in the Parcels Office together, till paid for.

I don't suppose that at any moment of your life any one's wanted to hurt you so much as I have for the past week. If only you could have been there and I could have talked, or if only I could have written it well enough! But there was no one to hurt but myself. I was glad to think I'd said some atom of what I felt on a post-card.

I told you I hated Békássy when I saw your letter to him (not as much as I hated you, & me.²) I did, but not through "jealousy". (That's ready enough, oh yes, if you want it.) Not that, – or not mainly that. Not even only because of the old thing, that you and he had things to talk about and interests and knowledge together I could never share. But because you wanted to see him more than you wanted to see me (I thought.). You liked him more. He was one of the two or three hundred people you preferred to me. – *Me*, damn you, the person you pretended you, vaguely, in a way, "loved".

Silly, isn't it? I won't go on. When you appear, I feel as if I'd been silly as a naughty child; not wrong, exactly, just silly, irrelevant. And anyhow I know I'm sleepless and tired, and therefore probably unable to judge things. But my God! I hate you sometimes – not loathing as you feel to me, hatred, quite different. Hatred because you're indifferent to me.

Cure me! Let me see you for two seconds on Sunday, or I'll think even five minute's bicycling is more trouble than I'm worth, and I'll go mad and not ever see you again. It's about Sunday I'm writing. Come for one second, and for more if you're wanting & find me amiable enough. I shall be there, I've said, alone from 9 onwards; working; till midnight. Drift in when you like. I *will* try to entertain you! It'll be a week to my dissertation, (I've scarcely done anything for days.): so I shan't be able to see people with a free conscience. (Except you.) That's why I daren't see Bryn: & hesitated over Békássy. Also because I don't want to curtail my time with only you. However,

2 While Noel was camping at Clifford Bridge, she had received a letter from her school friend Ferenc Békássy, in which he told her: 'Wherever I am and whatever I do, from writing poetry to flirting on various occasions, – I always begin thinking about you. And really, there is no one else I care to be with so much . . . there is no one else I can talk with!'

He was now studying at King's, and in a letter dated 28 November, he says that he has just received Noel's reply to his August letter: 'You can't imagine how glad I am you weren't annoyed & accepted the flattery "cum grano salis".' Rupert had met him for breakfast that week and it was presumably then that he saw Noel's letter. (Olivier family papers)

if it gives you pleasure to bring the creature out, I shall certainly enjoy it (if it doesn't curtail *you*) and I'll try to lull my conscience. The only thing is, can we get him away again after an hour? I won't spare more.

Oh, I leave everything to you; everything.

I don't really believe he likes your handiwork even though he is, being not-English, the only decent person in Cambridge. They all loathe me. It's impossible he should escape the infection. England, culminating in you! I pray God daily for the German triumph.

(I wonder if the Signior (= Békássy) has been acute enough to perceive James . . . I doubted it . . . Perhaps you'll illuminate him. – Don't give us away, by the way.)

I'll be able to work now I've seen you. Oh, good-night Child: sleep, sleep, sleep! I'm sorry I'm so filthy. If you take the least notice of my silliness, I'll kill you. If you don't, I'll kill myself. Forgive! At least I dare take off all my clothes before you!

I'll be cheery
Rupert

College.

Thursday Morning [30 November 1911]

Rupert

This is awful!

You mustnt go on like this, angry & wakeful & not working. I'm sure its all my fault. I know it is: because I never seem to be able to make it clear – in words – when things are alright.

I havn't the *least* idea what has put you in this state. From your postcard I didn't even guess that you *were* in a state: But yesterday seemed to prove it; because you looked worn out.

When I saw you the time before, I thought we had cleared the (old) difficulty a little; you seemed contented (more or less), & I

immagined you would go & work peacefully & gaily until the end of
your dissertation.

Then suddenly, that little snappy post-card – followed by the
calming arrival of the poems; & close on them the uneasy letter to Bryn,
the telegram & your miserable looking self.

It cant all have been provoked by my dutiful (& quite usual) little
letter about my mother & my wish not to allarm her; you've heard all
that times & times before.

What is it? Were you affraid I wasn't coming to see you in
Cambridge (*did* I say that?). Because, any rate you know now that I *am*
coming & want to come (or else I shouldn't) in the morning until time
to get to Cambridge for tea. What else can I do?

You mustn't be so dotty & queer. If you'r grey & stern on Sunday
I shall be affraid. – & its that fear (if anything) which makes me hate
you; its when I feel that your going to say horrors, & that you are
thinking them, & that I can only shudder or squeak – I've been quite
truthful for months now, so there shouldn't be any misunderstanding.

I'm not bringing Bekassy on Sunday.

Love from Noel.

Grantchester

[Postmark 1 December 1911]

Noel dear,

I'm sorry.

I'm all twisted and tired; and I think I see that I've broken our
arrangement. I'm sorry. I'm a devil to treat you so. Oh, I've so little faith,
and also I'm so hungry, sometimes, for seeing you, – but it's mostly that
I've so little faith; so that (even after everything,) when it seems as if
you didn't care a bit, I get mad. It's not *all* my fault. You did write as if
you didn't care to take any trouble ever – I get so desperate – Next term
– the term after – the year after – always the ten-minutes-a-fortnight
game. It's all so unfair. Some decision you make in five minutes – where

the fear of "alarming your mother" decides you – costs me a week of horrors. Of course I get into "this state". But I am a beast. And I have broken the arrangement. – But I'll look at it all when I'm better and clearer. And, as I say, when I see you, I know I'm wrong.

I'll be placid on Sunday. The prospect keeps me up through these three performances.[1] – the first begins in three hours, and I'm almost dead now. I won't be "grey and stern". Poor old Noel! Anyhow, you're not to be "afraid". It doesn't do. I may lose my temper for five minutes. It won't be much.

Come to breakfast & stay to tea if you like: consonantly with your Cambridge arrangements, I mean. I'll take you a walk to Haslingfield, if it's a decent autumn day – Bicycle –

Goodnight, poor thing; and don't imagine I'm in extremis. I've turned the corner. And I'm so happy you're coming.

I wonder how often you'll recognize me on Saturday. Anyhow, you won't see if I'm pale. I wish I were more satisfactory. I wish I could give you something to make up. I think I do, though: if you knew; – a bit.

I love you more than anyone ever will. Damn you!

Rupert

If you do come in the afternoon to the Flute, & let me know, you can come round to the Stage door after it & see over the stage. It would be an experience for you!

Grantchester

[4 December 1911]

Dearest Noel

I'm sorry I gave you a bad time again yesterday.

---

1 Rupert, who had been taking singing lessons with the baritone Clive Carey, had agreed to play one of the seven slaves in Dent's production of The Magic Flute at the New Theatre, Cambridge.

I've decided to shelve questions for six days as far as I can. I've attained a measure of calmness, and started work, in a way. I shan't be able to finish my dissertation, but I shall send in an incomplete one, on the chance. I don't think it's much good.

Next week I'll decide about coming to you, and things like that. I should like in any case to see you next week two or three times in a quite ordinary way: in the way we might have done and didn't do during the term. I shall be free the whole week, and you said you were always free enough. Haven't we the strength to wander about together for a bit just as two very intimate people, as we perhaps are? I want, you see, to take you (and you me) to tea at Virginia's. And I'd also suggest that you ought to take me to the Cezanne-Gauguin exhibition,[1] and to the Maxim Gorki play.[2] You're in a so uncultured home, you see, – I have to look after these things. These two last depend on your other movements: for you're not to stay up more than two nights in a week. You can let me know at your leisure: for none is a thing that requires much arranging. I'd like *fairly* early information if you're going to empty your house and give me supper, as you threatened. The "tea" with me, if you want it, can be any day. But are you able to have *purely business tea*, in a shop, on Monday? I shall pay for your food, be curt but gentle and amusing, and behave as if I've been married to you for *years*. I may even bring James for ¼ hour, to help. For it's only to talk about permutations and combinations. – Which you can, if you'll kindly use a quiet strength, be thinking out, quite cursorily and without worry. I'm *determined* to have my friends at my country house in December, for all your bloodiness. I'm going to *The Stage Society*[3] on Monday with James. I ought to be out by 5. or 5.10. Then I should take a taxi to what shop you ordained. Our last one if you like (*de Bri* or something.)

with love
Rupert

---

1 Since Roger Fry's 'Manet and the Post-Impressionists' Exhibition, the previous autumn, there had been tentative shows by other galleries, of which this must be one, to test the public reaction to the shocking new artists Fry had introduced.
2 *The Lower Depths* had begun a three-week run on 2 December at Kingsway Theatre.
3 The Stage Society had been founded in 1899, by Frederick Whelan, with both Sydney Olivier and George Bernard Shaw on the committee of management. It ran for forty years, performing plays of artistic merit but which were of no interest to the commercial theatre. Thus they gave the first London performances of, amongst others, Chekhov's *The Cherry Orchard*, R.C. Sherriff's *Journey's End* and Lorca's *Blood Wedding*. The Stage Society's matinée production, which Rupert and James planned to see, was an adaptation of the novel *Esther Waters* by George Moore.

Your face has changed from strength to beauty so suddenly – not that I ever missed beauty, or shall ever miss strength. It's so frightening suddenly talking to a stranger.

Oh, my dear, my dear, I wish I could say how important it is that I love you, and *how* I love you, and how it weighs against everything else.

You're very fine. Goodnight

Women's Union Society.
University College,
London, W.C.

Wednesday. 11.30 [6 December 1911]

Wehe, wehe!

I seem to be responsible for all disasters; & worst of all – now your Dissertation wont be finished. *Do almost* finish it: work like a river & dont forget to sleep; none of us can do without it.

I'll meet you for the business tea at 5.30 on Monday – Oh where? *I dont know London – or its tea shops*; but I know, that I want to be near Picadilly Circus or Oxford Circus after that tea on monday. I'll go home soon & ask Margery to tell me of a good place – She's had tea in every shop in London – with every man – by now; then I'll write the Name & address of it on a Post card & send you (if you know of just the thing, let me know).

I can come with you to any place in the world, as long as you send me home for supper (at 7.0). But I *must always* be in by then; Its a new reform. Perhaps also a time table would be usefull to you:

On	Mondays	I get off at		5 . 0 P.M.
"	Tuesdays	"	"	5 . 0 . P.M.
"	Wednesdays	"	"	4 . 0 . P.M. (or before)
"	Thursdays	"	"	4 . 30 P.M.
"	Fridays	"	"	4 30. P.M.
"	Saturdays	I get off at 12.30; but generally play hockey.		

Because of my not ever going out in the evening; I suppose we cant go to the Maxim Gorki play. But does the Cezanne Gauguin business go on at night too? *Surely!*

You didn't succeed, poor thing! in giving me a "bad time" on Sunday. I find that I was happy all day; & it made me gay to last for weeks.

Yet you seemed sad & worried enough to make me weep; I must have lost the power.

It *was* lovely.

Your house party looks to be difficult to arrange; but it must be done.

I'll think about that – you work.

till Monday.
Love from Noel.

12 Loudoun Rd.
tomorrow: at Limpsfield

December 20th [1911]

If you can think; could you consider the suggestion that there was one point we didn't take into account in making our rather deffinite arrangement.[1]

Its about your feelings – the cause of all. Weren't they perhaps gloomy & continually irritated because, for about two months you have been working so hard & London is so awful & the last week you nearly killed yourself. Surely all that must have had some effect on your power to "*bear*" the relationship as it then stood. Perhaps you forgot to feel that the scarce moments (when I rejoiced in you) did make our strange & jerky life worth wile, even to you. If you cant immagine & remember the worth of such times, would'nt it be well to give them a chance to happen again, before all is settled?

This is no personal plea. Only I see, that as we thought so wisely

---

1 On Friday 15 December they had met at the Moulin d'Or and then walked along the Embankment, trying to decide their future. At last Rupert declared he could not continue their relationship, until Noel was prepared to make more of a commitment.

& hurriedly in the Restaurant & by the river, we rather neglected this; & . . . may have made a mistake. *We must not make such a mistake.* thats the point. So please try & be sure, whether or not most of our incapacity to get on as we were, wasn't due to tiredness (of both of us perhaps). If you cant think it out. I invite you to spend a day in the country with me alone to make sure of what we feel.

Love. from.
Noel.

If you feel sure that we have arranged correctly; then no more need be said.

24 Bilton Road

December 23 [1911]

Dearest,

I dare hardly write, for this reason: that I'm in a whirl of changing decisions and beliefs. One minute I feel how relieving it is, to have cut across that tangle, and how certainly I must go away for a year; till we can begin clean and lovely again. The next minute I'm collapsed into saying "I'll talk to Noel once more – I *must* see her once more – and all will straighten itself out and be clear then: one way or the other". And then that seems cowardice. And a moment later I'm aching to throw pride and resolution to the winds & to fly by the swiftest expresses to get five minutes as soon as possible with you to tell you that I was an utter fool, tired and cantankerous and unworthy, and that all's good and anything's worth while, so I see you now and then –

I'll try to present some more or less coherent attitude.

I've been almost asleep, these days. Sometimes, I find on looking back, I'm quite attractive and garrulous in my sleep. I suspect I cannot have been interesting, though. But I haven't been considering things, at all. I vaguely feel I ought to have some very clear and deeply-thought-out conclusions to offer you. I haven't. You've been a dull cloud on the horizon, occasionally. I've dozed. After the first day, I've felt no sort of

Angst: except when I've looked forward "January . . . February . . . March . . . – then it began to hurt. But it all appears not only incredible; but uninteresting. But that's sleepiness, I know.

Oh, I waver. Sometimes I stick so to what I said that Friday. Sometimes I want to chuck it all away, and go back – but to what? That's when I begin to know I was probably right. I'd only go back to a Noel who barely wanted to see me – might welcome me then, for some hours, and be wonderful, and kind, – and then accept – grasp at – a month's absence. And it would all begin again.

My dear, you've tired me so. You don't know how you've tired me, worn me out. It's faultiness in me, but there it is; I can't stand the strain.

Yet there are moments – I've just been sorting papers preparatory to going abroad. I've come on photographs of last year's camp, and of Bank (you on a horse!). They brought so suddenly back the things that are between us. It seemed incredibly stupid and wicked that we should mess it between us: or lose anything. Oh, Noel, Noel, who's wrong and a fool – you? or I? or both?

This has taken me longer than I'd foreseen. And I want it to get to you not later than the first post on Wednesday. So I must write briefly – one or two things it's easier to make clear in writing than on the edge of some speech. There'll be a great deal left, for writing elsewhere, or saying.

If I don't go away for very long – there are two alternatives before us. (1) To go on as we have been doing: or (2) To change the position towards more freedom for you and frequenter meetings, – or infrequent, longer periods together – and a greater intimacy. This latter you couldn't or wouldn't do – we've argued it over. The former I couldn't face. *Hinc illae lacrimae, nicht wahr?*[1]

You've rather suggested there's an additional overlooked consideration in connection with (1), which may make me change my mind. Viz. that I've been tired; & that the normal I may both be able to "face" it, and be able to see I can.

(I write like the prig and journalist I am.)

It may be; especially if it's backed up my suddenly remembering – realising – how good it all *is*. But (I'm still tired & fractious, may be) I'm inclined not to think so.

You see, I should still go on being tired, every now & then. And

---

1 Hence those tears, no? 'Hinc illae lacrimae' was first used by Terence in *Andria*, I: i: 99, when Simo is describing his son's grief at the death of their neighbour. The phrase was also later used by Horace and Cicero.

then all this past horror would return! (And it's sometimes to be found when I'm *not* tired; I'm an unhealthy creature.)

And I'll never be able (so I think, now) to enjoy its goodness fully, for long. The thought would always steal back, that its goodness was nothing, being so far less than the good it might be. The occasional teaparty with you, dutiful daughter and respectable young lady, would continue to have its sweetness taken by the thought that if you were a little less of a daughter, or less dutiful & respectable, or if you loved me more, – we'd be away together, over some hills, talking and laughing, saying everything, alone in the world. It's queer you can't see it, you know. Put it on a lower level. My mother would be greatly relieved if I neither mentioned nor saw any of your family (including you.). Supposing (as by all your ideas I'm bound to do) I obeyed and humoured the good lady ("abstained from giving her "unnecessary" pain"), and we sat apart, you and I, some twenty or thirty years, till she died, sustained by the consciousness that we loved one another and the comforts of our respective home-circles. *Can't* you see that what's gone on in the last three years is about a million times better than that?

A : B : : B : C.

What, after all, *do* you contemplate? We'd "go on" in the way we have done, you keeping all the life that's so pleasant to you, till . . . till your mother said we might go further – that is to say till our going further didn't risk causing her Ladyship's callers and suburban friends to say or feel things that (though she knew them to be silly) would hurt her feelings a little. Have you worked out, by the way, just *when* the Surrey and St John's Wood upper middle classes will permit you & me to go a walk together? "Going on". I can see you all, sliding from the advanced but utterly respectable home where you've none of you ever done anything outside the ordinary routine for fear of hurting the feelings of people you are fond of, into the equally respectable if less advanced homes which you will severally run with the gentlemanly civil servants your Mother will permit you to marry (oh, you'll most modernly marry whom you like, – but you'd never like to marry anyone such that other, respectable peoples' opinion of him would hurt your mother, whom you're so fond of.)

The picture, the prospect, – my sentences – would seem to all of you neither funny nor unpleasant. That's because you do not admire yourselves. You may be – collectively – proud – that is quite different. Anyone who has ever admired you – all of you, and especially, damn you, *you* – could see the mad horror of it. My God! if I could only

make you see your degradation – consisting only in this – the heights
you might be on. One's brought to (2.). And I've no time or ability
(on your birthday, with those damned children singing, as a year ago,
the carol incessantly, outside "No–o-el-l! No-o-ell-l! – " to persuade
you – I never have – that it would be better if you were freer. I vaguely
hint – wave my hands – "splendours" . . . You refuse to admit
anything or anybody more splendid than your life and your family.
And I'm too dumb to tell you, if you knew sometimes how you
clumped down on my dreams. We *are* superb, and great – what we
live and do. But if you'd only see, for a second, what we *could* be. I'm
not meaning in our *love*; but in the way we took life. We could be such
you & I, that thousands of people, afterwards and now, would make
us names for the heights they knew the best. "Rupert & Noel," – I'm
solemn and serious. Don't you guess, even now, what people like
Geoffrey think about us? – Oh, I'm not meaning that peoples' *opinion*
or praise is the thing to go for. I'm only using it in the hope it's some
use as a mirror, to blaze to you, what we *might* be. – Only you can't be
bothered. You don't know what you are. You can't see. I can. I know –
I've told you, in a way, sometimes. You could do anything, shine out
anywhere, if you wanted it. Haven't I seen you filling a thousand
rooms and fields with a light and wonder. You've got intelligence,
damn you, and everything else. And, Good God, you're only nineteen.
And you and I, now, (for other years – anything may happen: we'll
hàve them too, perhaps: but anyhow, this) could be so splendid. We
could shine out to the world. And to each other we'd be saying and
discussing such things. To go a walking with you – oh, I can *see* it.
You fool, why do you give it all up? Why don't you – when I <u>tell</u> you –
believe it's possible for instance, to go to call on Virginia? With me,
and alone, you could do all sorts of things – in the way of being
something yourself, not (not *only*) a member of a family! You sit at
home . . .
      It's all incoherent – as it comes to me. I'm sorry. But it keeps
falling, you'll notice into a queer form, the whole question: the ideal I
stick up in my heart as in every direction spoilt by your family-life. Oh
yes, it's absurd! It *needn't* be so: only, is it? I'm slowly being convinced
(psychologically, the dangerous way!) that you must be choosing
between slackness & your mamma, and me & right. If you do have to
choose; I suppose I know which way it'll come out. And that's why I'll
funk pressing the choice ninety-nine times. But at length, out of shame, if I
do? –
      I pour it out for what it's worth. I haven't time to read it over. I

shall say something clearer, perhaps, if I see you: if not, I shall write once, again.

See here: my plans. I go to London Wednesday morning for 24 hours. If I'm to see you on *Thursday*, wire on Wednesday to the National Liberal (or write if there's time.) If I hear nothing, I go to Lulworth: Thurs. morning.

c/o Mrs Carter

Churchfield House

W. Lulworth

Dorest.

And thence I can come up at any moment.

My dear, Good night. Construe sense out of this whirl. It's there. I love you: anyhow. I love you. I love you. I wish you were here. I touch your head and shoulders with my hands: and kiss you once –

Do what's right. Goodnight Noel –

with love

Rupert

The Champions

Limpsfield

Thursday [28 December 1911]
in the morning.

Wa – wa – wa – wa – wa ! !

I want to scream:
Because I cant bear your being so wrong//

Its only because you still – even now (& I cant get at you to hit you; as I could coming back from Becky Falls to camp) will drag in your old mean grievance against – oh! – the "respectable" & the "middle class". *Leave*, <u>leave</u> it alone; dont muddle up our question – tangled enough already – with your old spite; it doesn't concearn us, it doesn't have influence with either of us & it cant help – it only irritates.

That's rather harsh; but its best to leave it at the beginning of the letter.

And go on.

I think its all rather clear by now. Because we *did* get through a good deal on the Embankment, although it seemed at the time that all was confusion & that we could never regulate what happened by reason. But now the main points stand out.

It was decided then that you couldn't bear the life of short meetings & long absences; my perpetual contentment & callousness in the life away from you, my pleasure in other people; my occasional hating you; with only a very unensured possibility of some camps & days & walks together – the only real satisfaction to you.

You couldn't bear it, it made you wretched & feel hopeless, gave you sleepless nights & spoilt your work – oh – infinitely horrible. It couldn't go on.

No it couldn't – only one thing: perhaps living in London & working so hard was the cause of all? I asked you. And you answered that perhaps it was; or partly; & then, you thought not on the whole.

So we've settled *that*; – you cant bear the old way. (*Why* you cant bear it needn't affect the case; only you might like to know, that I see why & can accept it without blame)

Next. What shall we do? Here I settle it, by my refusal to go a walking tour with you. to stay a week end with you to call on Virginia with you; These three being examples of a greater freedom you would like us to have.

Rupert mein, I do refuse, & will try & explain. (I did explain over the Thames)

Not because Mother wouldn't like it (God knows that that hasn't been a reason strong enough to stop me from doing things I liked, before now)

Not because I want to be snug & safe & respectable, & wish no disapproval from the fools.

Not because I dont see the glories we two might create by living to our utmost & splendidly.

I see that & want it (almost strongly – poor dear!)

But we cant, its the old misery – how can we live like that when I shall be wanting, sometimes, to scream at you & run away; when you will be gnawed wicked by your jealousies & be wretched at times because you notice in me the meanness, & thin evil feelings I have – about you – the hatred.

You think that that would all disappear with more freedom? Oh, I dont. If it is true that the more we meet, the more you will want, then the contrast, the awful difference between our loves – mine the poor, stolid, best-that-I-can-do and yours – oh heights – would grow & weigh us down again – beat us down.

For isn't it that, that has done us all along? It is obvious – there at the bottom of everything.

Once in a wood in Devonshire after those bilberries, you said you could bear the difference; And that seemed so titanic & superbly brave, that I fell down & worshipped (or almost did); but you couldn't, you were not & will never be strong enough; & I was right to fret.//

So, as before the conclusion is we must give it up; until we can carry it through; until you love less, or I love more, or until we're both stronger & can bear anything. The last is what I most hope for.

Oh Rupert! what would be the good of three days alone in a wood – & both of us fretting away? Its that, that mus*tn't* happen, it would be the worst,; & *its* the alternative, that you uphold.

I've just read your letter, its very eloquent & seems to have said all this – well. Still I probably write, more to get the situation into my own head, than to point it out to you.

We only disagree about the one thing now: –

You say: "Glories!" "now!" I say: "fretting & wretchedness now. Perhaps Glories later!" are possible.

I think we had better agree, anyhow intellectually before we settle. So you must write again & say whether you still hold out for the more-freedom plan; or what you think.

Then if we still disagree, in letters, we must argue it out face to face; though I rather suspect, that we had better not meet, if it comes to your having to go away for long; it would be harder, for you I'm affraid.

For me it would just be a pleasure, to see you again & be assured that you are still there, & recognise how you are – oh & say good bye. Slight, little pleasures, just because I'm fond of you. It could all be done, by your coming here for a day; or my meeting you somewhere between London & Lulworth. The first is easiest for me, only we might meet everyone in Limpsfield walking in the woods. But we can arrange all that if necessary.

I wish I could send you some account of what I am doing that would please you; but at all you will only snarl. Perhaps one thing will console:

I have a slight cold in the head & a back-ache – & it rains every other day.//

My dear, you can put your thundering conviction to me: that I must chose, between "slackness & mamma" & "you & right" ("right?") It will bring you no harm – never fear. I chose gaily: *you* my dear man – & that other thing; but what next? we still have the same problem before us.

Love from
Noel.

I'm sorry this letter's so snappy.

Rupert had expected to find a group of his close friends at Lulworth, and had looked to it as a haven of peace after his miserable autumn. When he arrived, he discovered not only James Strachey, but also Ferenc Békássy, two of his rivals for Noel's love.

His relationship with Ka, who had always provided caring support, had developed during the past year, and Rupert felt ready to transfer his love from Noel to her. However, she had asked Lytton to invite the painter Henry Lamb to join the group, whom she was greatly attracted to. On Saturday 30 December, Lytton drove over to collect Henry from where he was lodging with Augustus John, and returned with him to Churchfield House. As Rupert saw it:

The creature slimed down to Lulworth; knowing about women, knowing he could possibly get you if he got a few hours alone with you (his knowledge turned out to be justified.)

I was ill. Influenza (or poison in the house) frustrated me that Sunday. I was in the depths, leaning utterly on you. Oh my God! how kind and wonderful you were then; the one thing in the world I had.[1]

For, while Rupert was ill in bed on Sunday, Ka and Henry disappeared for a long walk together, along the sea shore. When they returned she announced to Rupert that she was in love with Henry, adding that he had the same Christian name as her father and that he was older and more mature than Rupert. Rupert was inflamed with jealousy, furious and distraught at the idea of losing another woman he loved. He demanded that Ka relinquish her love for his rival and agree to marry him. Naturally, she refused, saying that she had no intention of no longer seeing Henry. There was a violent scene, Rupert by now convinced that she had somehow betrayed him and that to save herself she must become his wife. Ka, alarmed by his tirade, eventually agreed to go out to Munich and live with him there.

---

1 To Ka Cox [?29 February 1912] (KCA).

Churchfield House
W. Lulworth

Saturday [6 January 1912]

Dear Noel,

I've been trying to answer your letter. I'm very sorry I haven't.

I have been ill and feeling very tired: and as the days go by I get worse. Also, I can't get my plans settled even for the nearest future, and I don't know what I shall be feeling in even two or three days. It isn't your "fault" this time! In addition to all the other horrors, there's now a horrible business between me & Ka, – we're hurting each other, clumsily, as one does. I'm worn out by it. I'm telling you this to show you why I've been so beastly in not writing. Only please don't say *anything* to anyone about it.

So I don't think there's any good as things are in meeting, just now. You'd only find me a stupid ill limp, impossible to handle. I could say or do nothing. I *must* go away and rest and change. I'm at the end of my strength and even now I don't know how I shall be able to get out to the South of France to join my mother. I want to go on Wednesday, or so. (After Tuesday my address will be National Liberal Club for a day or two. Then through Rugby.) I shall write later on; & perhaps we'll meet then. I don't think there's anything for the moment to add to your letter. It was very fine: in its clearness and strength. It was so much clearer and stronger than all I've written or said: I felt ashamed. I knew once more what you were really like.

I can't write more now. I'm very sorry I've been such a nuisance, – to you & everybody. Please forget me entirely till I'm decent & well

again if ever I am. Be – be Noel: which means such good & greatness.
Good bye.

   You'll see from my dates when you can get hold of me if it's very
immediate – Tuesday & Wednesday. Good bye.

Rupert

Jacques and Gwen, warned of Rupert's condition, came to collect him and took him to the famous London neurologist Dr Maurice Craig, who diagnosed that he was 'obviously in a state of severe breakdown'. He was to go abroad immediately and relax completely under his mother's care.

Rupert left for Cannes, and began writing almost daily letters to Ka. They met in Verona at the end of January and then travelled to Munich. They had little chance to be alone, as Hugh Popham arrived to visit, but on 17 February they left for Starnbergersee, and managed at last to sleep together. However, Ka admitted that she had seen Henry again before leaving England, and Rupert collapsed once more into a jealous rage. Ka realized that Rupert was in a dreadful state, and four days later they returned to England.

Rupert, who had been eager to have a physical relationship with Ka, now found himself disgusted that she had agreed to it. The puritan streak in him became obsessed by the idea that she was no longer chaste, and that, having slept with him, she would be easily seduced by any other man that tried.

24 Bilton Road
Rugby

March 15 (The Ides) 1912

Dearest Noel,

I've treated you badly. Illness pain madness & the horrors must excuse me.

You wrote me an amazing letter at the end of December. I only answered it with a short excuse a fortnight later: and since then I've written nothing.

I must write now, even if it's (as it must be at present) a futile letter. – I feel I've been so beastly to you.

I don't know what to write.

Child, I can't tell you all I want to, yet; because it isn't mine to tell – till it's finished with. You see that?

We were, probably, going to meet once before I went abroad, & thrash out a detail or two more, and say good bye – probably. You remember? (Why should you?) { (But of course you do.) }

Then I went to Lulworth. I was rather at the end of things (I see now) – my health & nerves and things. Not your "fault"! The specialist said I must have been heading towards it for a year or two, perhaps more. And for the last six months or so my progress downhill had been rapid. Momentum. Work & fussing & things. – Half mad & ill & collapsible I was at the end of December. And with the beginning of the new year, horrible things happened to me. Concerned with Ka, as I told you. They'd have half-killed me. anytime. But then – I had six days in the most horrible state you can think. I couldn't eat or sleep or do anything but torture myself. It was the most ghastly pain imaginable, worse than any physical pain, dragging on, unending – Everything seemed to go. If I thought I had to go through that again, I should shoot myself. It was madness – I can't describe it. It was multiplied – the pain & horror – because I was almost mad before – You see, after the six days, I was so physically weak I practically couldn't walk. I tottered up to London & then abroad. I wasn't I. There was obviously no point in my seeing you. It wouldn't have helped anything or meant anything. We'd fairly well decided I was going away anyhow for a bit –

I was a few weeks at Cannes: then at Munich with Ka: then three weeks here. I've got much better – My weight, which had gone down stones & stones, is now immense. I am very fat.

I'm not clear yet, though. I've not begun to work at all. I shall go abroad again, sometime, between 10 days & four weeks hence, & start working. At present my mind seems still dead. I don't see that I shall ever be able to write things again. I don't know. It depends how things turn out. I feel dead. I shall write again, fairly soon. I shall probably want to see you & tell you things. Perhaps you won't want to see me. You may be hating me by now.

Noel, I've been very ill, & I'm not yet through. I want to know, though, how you are – what you're feeling. I *suppose* the "serenity" we bicker about to be bearing you as tranquilly as ever through London life. Only – some one (we have a mutual acquaintance or two) said you were looking tired . . .

I see how beastly I was to you all the autumn. I'm ashamed of myself. You, in your letter, were, of course, entirely right. It *was* my tiredness – nerves – that precipitated things. I must have been unbearable. (I did most of the paying, which is something.). I still think I was right in most of what I said. After all, if it's Rupert-on-edge who's so unbearable a lover, Rupert-on-edge is probably all you'll generally get in *that* direction (i.e. in the direction of Rupert) So decisions have still to be made on that basis . . .

Your letter at the end of the year . . . it was superb. About four times a year you wake up & think. When you *do*, it fairly obliterates anyone else's endeavours. I wish I had a mind like yours: but awake continually. I had been muddled enough, jerking out disconnected things to you. You straightened everything out in that letter. I even see that it largely *was* two different questions, your family-atmosphere & your relation to me!

But I'll write or talk later in Time, sometime. I merely mention that I admire you infinitely. Even if we never saw touched or *heard* of each other again – you're about the most colossal person I've ever known.

I'm only writing this, after all, to say that I'm not silent through beastliness; & that in many ways I'm pretty well again; and that I'll write again, & say more, both about the past and the future.

If I died before I ever wrote or saw you again, those last years 'ld stay a thing I was infinitely proud of and glad of.

love from
Rupert

I'd like to give my love to Margery & to Bryn & to Daphne if she's back: but dare I?

Oh God, it's a rotten letter. You're amazingly fine.

12 Loudoun Road,
St John's Wood. N.W.

March 18th. Monday [1912]

Mon pauvre Rupert!

But I *was* glad to get your letter, and I'm answering it although I almost believe you didn't mean me to. Because you mustnt imagine that you ought to have written or that you've been mean in any way; I never expcted you would write till you were much better – we arranged that – and your last letter explained quite clearly why we had not better meet before you went to France.

I've been hearing from time to time how you got on, and had got a right idea – more or less – of you at present. I'm sorry you suddenly worried about me.

I am very happy, because there is lots to do on every hand & I'm busy trying to learn to work. The most exhausting thing is laziness perhaps that makes me look tired rarely. Or I may have been seen one day indulging in a chill. But these little things of London are as charming in their way as all the rest of it here. Fogs, frost, spring, birds, buds & all. They combine to engross & delight one up & down the day.

It must be dark in Rugby & I'm glad you mean to go abroad again – but let it be Paris or some place not Munich! *Its* such a place of emerald green & cheques & novelty; I almost hate it for its swiftness. Go to Italy or Spain; Some good place where the people have tough brown skins, & you'll get saturated with light & warmth (no, Paris wont do.) But you have probably decided, & anyhow we never had the same taste in places.

I cant understand what happened at Lulworth; only vague pictures of it, a kind of night mare, drift up. That must have been worse than we either of us feared could happen, even when in the midst of the waste of last Autumn; I'm affraid it *did* prove nothing but waste to you, & there can be no pride in it, tho' it was the upshot of some fine things.

I'm here, not at Limpsfield, (perhaps you thought there for the week end). And ready to write or see you when you want it. My term ends on the 29th. And then I shall go to Limpsfield for the holidays; & then back here to live with Bill & Eva [Hubback] for the summer term, & so on.

I havn't thought much about our position, or plans for you & me; because it must all depend so on our feelings, & I dont know what either of us will feel when (when?) next we talk.

Yes I can wait & wait – thinking of chemistry & shoes & capital punishment – the power (which we believe is dormant) hasnt left me, by which I could peel potatoes into infinity. And it isnt even a power; its a knack for lifelessness, despicable, but useful today, tomorrow & until you'r well & prancing into the herds of the playwrites.

———

Was it very wrong? I wouldn't let Bryn offer to call on you at Rugby. She wanted to so much, & still does. But I feared that you still felt that you would see none of us. You wanted complete separation once. Is it still the same? She is not very irritating, anyhow when one's not feeling too clever. But never mind, it is a light-hearted wish – & perhaps tiresome. And she's very good.

We all got your message of love brought by Ka the other day. And today I told M[argery] & B[ryn] how friendly you sounded – Daphne has just run thro' from Cambridge on her way to a reading party in the South, & she left before your letter came.

All's well. The country is full of good people, whatever you say. The beasts are funny.

Thank you, thank you for writing. And oh I would weep – if ever I could – for your poor lost fellowship.

Love from
Noel.

Rugby

Monday [25 March 1912]

Your letter cheered me a deal.

It was indeed as well to have prevented Bryn from coming. Not that I don't want to see her. I want to see her *immensely*. (It suddenly struck me the other day.). I must see her. But I couldn't have stood the strain of her and my poor mother in the house together!

I shall see you. Either on Thursday or Friday in London or else, (perhaps anyhow) come down to Limpsfield in the next fortnight (?) I'll let you know as soon as I can. It's so difficult arranging when one's disconsolate & listless.

For I'm going to leave here soon. I want to be in Germany in (say) a fortnight. Between Thursday & then, I want to spend a week or so somewhere – by the sea, perhaps, – with James part of the time, may be: & to see you.

I'm extraordinarily tired this evening. I scarcely slept last night. So my letter's dull. Oh my dear Noel, I shall be glad to see you again! I shall be beastly – be gentle with me! You'll find me a lot changed.

I've been alone so much – in my mind – nearly the whole time, in pain, alone. It will be nice to see you all. I do love you all so much.

Lulworth, & all this since, wasn't your fault – wasn't about you. It's so hard to say things. I'll tell you. Oh, my God!

You're not going anywhere, after your term's over? I heard vaguely of Wales for Margery? Bryn? & you & I must also, you see, at least just see them, if I can, before I go abroad. So can I know by when they'll be out of reach, as well as about your movements –

Oh, my fellowship. That's all right. It lay between me (with one more shot) & a Scientist (with none). So they gave it him.[1] They've practically promised me one next year: if I'm alive, which is improbable.

Child, I'm so terrified of meeting you. You'll find me so queer – everything's so extraordinarily different (And I'm *very* fat.) You'll do me good: though – I'm very grey. I almost *daren't* meet you –[2]

Your letter was so incredibly nice & so very you – I saw you so clearly – it makes me cry.

love from
Rupert

---

1 The fellowship was given to Hamilton Hartridge (1886–1976), who went on to become, in 1927, Professor of Physiology at London University.
2 Writing to Ka the following day, Rupert declares: 'I'm going to see Noel. I can stand it (it won't, I mean, wipe you out! I'm strong: & I'm only going to see her twice) . . . I'm sick with a sort of fear . . . She – you don't know what she stands for – stood for to me – Do you I wonder understand about love, Ka?' (KCA)

Mermaid Club,
Rye, Sussex.[1]
!

Sunday [31 March 1912]

I mean to be among you tomorrow evening, in time for dinner: if I dare.
    I start from here at 1.40: get to London at 5.6: & get next train from Victoria – (I *may* cut across country Tonbridge – Edenbridge: if so – or in any case – I'll wire)
    If you want to stop me, wire here before 1.40: I sort of feel your mother mayn't like me . . . If you're too late to put me off, you can meet me at the station & send me back . . . I thought of coming till Wednesday midday or afternoon . . . I'll come Tuesday morning if you like you may turn me out, of course, – Oh, I've said all this.
    There is no doubt that you're the finest person in the world.
    How *dare* I see you?

with love
Rupert

Beech Shade
Bank

The Saturday [6 April 1912]

I *say*, being here, you know; – and precisely three years – Easter time – Oh, Lord!
    Mrs Primmer is well. The trees are there. The black hut stands. Also the holly-bush – And the room. Oh!
    Dearest Noel, you *were* good. It's incredible – I didn't *know* there were such things as you in the world.

---

1 Rupert spent a restful three days here with James.

You – & I deserved nothing – less – gave me immense strength (compared to the weakness I've been in). And you confused me, too. I thought, before I saw you, I was settled in my mind. It seemed impossible (within one's limited view) anything should alter it – my certainty about the various possibilities. And now you – your presence for hours – its madness to kill oneself when you're in the world. So I'm vacillating again . . .

I do worship you so.

I found Ka pretty bad. We had rather a rough time. This is by way of being a Collins.[1] Limpsfield made me incredibly better. Could you let it get round to your Mother how nice I found it?

I'm going through with all this business: & I don't know where I shall come out. I've got (I was ashamed; but you gave it) though I'm vile, *you* somewhere at the back of my mind. It helps: oh God! Don't think me silly or weak – one gets reduced by months of what's been happening. I wrote to Bryn in Wales. It may have crossed her. If she appears, send her on here, if she likes, promptly – I shall write again

with love
Rupert

The Champions
Limpsfield

April 10th [1912]
(Margery knows, because its her birthday & she's 26. I am going to give her a present – poor old thing)

Wednesday

Rupert.

Bryns gone at last: I had one day of anxiety about a letter she sent here to be forwarded, & there were no posts out – it being Easter

---

1 A 'Collins' is a letter of thanks sent for hospitality, from the notable example of Mr Collins in Chapter 22 of Jane Austen's *Pride and Prejudice*.

Monday. Then I was rather allarmed when she suddenly arrived last night; I thought it would mean at least a 3 days before she got off again. But no: this morning she caught that very good train of ours, & altho' Mother said "what does all this mean?" she is probably well on the way to Brockenhurst or near it.

I'm sorry you have met so many of the trains she was *not* in these last few days. James sent me a touching account of it.

That journey down from Waterloo must have been miserable. After what happened in the station, & with the prospect of a late lunch when you at last got there. The thought made London a gloomy place. It was too hot & the wind was strong & blew the dust over one. All the joys – the smartly-dressed people – had gone & only the men in a hurry & women with last Autumn's clothes straggled in the streets. Like Paris in September.

Lowes Dickinson – by the way – *also* thinks that you had better go to Paris – not Germany – when you go abroad. Because the people there are more penetrating & they wont so cherish you. And French, Rupert, is *lovely*.

But you wont listen.

Oh the lovely days, after you had gone! The plum trees suddenly turned white in front of the house – & more of that Black-thorn (which we picked) came out all along the lane. Except for these, the three next days were heartlessly like your two days.

All the good old friends of the kind you dispise suddenly sprouted up – & came dashing in with invitations to tea & hints for supper. Bunny & Harold & Hugh Morgan slept up in the woods & in the afternoons we played tip & run in the Hobson's garden. There were also teas & a baby.

Adrian & Duncan called on Sunday, & went thro' it all; but they were very nice & even seemed happy.[1]

I havnt worked at all yet. But Hugh went yesterday, so perhaps there will be less tip & run in future. He, still adopts a very injured atitude, as if he will never forgive us, for your brutality at camp. "So silly of him!" But he succeeds in being very pathetic – he'd be best dead.

You will write & say when you'r coming? I suppose it depends

---

1 Adrian Stephen had come to Limpsfield with Duncan Grant to pursue his courtship of Noel. The two visitors had arrived in the middle of a tennis match, as Bunny recalls: 'Noel and I were busy retrieving the balls for our betters out of the vegetable garden and the herbaceous borders, when suddenly two strange figures marched round the corner of the house.' Duncan had then held Bunny's attention, 'knowing that [Adrian] wanted to talk to Noel'. (*GE*, pp. 210–11) Duncan was later to fall passionately in love with Bunny, so perhaps his behaviour was not as selfless as it sounds.

only upon when you go to Germany. Or do you want to get in another week-end with James. Fergus[2] will probably go on Saturday – & that evening there is a party at the Garnetts. Bunny seemed to think it wd be splendid if you came to it. But anyhow, you could go to bed early.

You must stay long enough to say something, I understood so little last time. And I've probably even distorted the facts by now; anyhow the future seems a jungle.

Oh your great telegram suddenly arrived here, after having spun right down to Wales & back.

I hope you'r having tea with Bryn now.

Love from Noel.

Thursday night – May 2. [1912]

Not tears: nor Blood: But cocoa spilt by the maid bringing breakfast

bei D. *Ward*
Kant strasse 14/G.H.
Charlottenburg
Berlin
is my address for another fortnight: or through Rugby.
I want to know your London flat's name.

Du, Noel wie geht's dir?[1]

I'd got so far with a letter to you, Noel, when yours came. The one you wrote to the National Liberal the Saturday I left England.[2] You've still, I'm touched to see, that unlimited confidence in the N[ational] L[iberal] C[lub] as my perennial abode. They kept the thing a week & then sent it to Cambridge. At length its' got here. I rather wish I'd had it all the time. I'd meant to write a general letter about Berlin: all the

2 Fergus McCleary was a first cousin of Noel's, who would often visit The Champions.

1 How are you, Noel?
2 This letter is missing.

stories – Tonight, for instance, I went to a play called *Der Artzt am
Scheideweg*, by a man called Shaw[3] . . . But I won't, for the moment.

Damn you. I only slept four hours last night, & used the whole of
them in dreaming about you. It was an infinite long & detailed dream: I
was staying with your damned family – even The Governor had come
home. We had private theatricals. The dentist figures rose again –
Colgate, *zum Beispiel*.[4]

Noel, in your judicial investigation into my conduct, don't pay too
much attention to my accounts to Margery & Bryn. I couldn't tell them
much of the truth. Could I? I love them very much, & I'm grateful to
them, & I don't like deceiving them – concealing (I don't mind very
much, though.) But you're the only person (in Surrey) who knows the
whole story (you know it more wholly, if not more in detail, perhaps,
than anyone else at all.) And, by the way, you're not telling them –
letting them see – anything important, I mean? You promised, you
know. I know you aren't – only it's not *my* affair, exactly. Moreover,
you're only a bloody woman.

The finger of God, you see, has to play rather a larger part to them
than in reality.

Your letter. Damn you! Damn you! DAMN You!

You come into the thing at this point, fresh from your world
where nothing happens, & want us – me – to pretend nothing's
happened in mine. Damn you! It's like an archangel coming to
Napoleon before Waterloo & saying "You know, where *you* made a
mistake was in that march to Moscow . . . And, as for the present, I
don't think you ought to go on with this horrid war at all!" And your
satirical attack! You fool, you *know* I'm low. The whole thing's low. One
has to meet people like Ka on their own ground. It isn't yours, or mine
– it wasn't mine, it is now. Oh, you're right enough about some of the
things, & especially about trying to control things with one's
judgement. – You from your heights where little happens & nothing
at all matters.

But I'll tell you. I see clearer now. And there's several things you're
wrong about. It wasn't much The Finger of God – only a little . . . It was
more . . . that determinations *aren't* (especially if you're in a rotten
state) and *mustn't* be, things of a moment. One makes one's mind up
slowly, averaging over a period. And then one keeps to it, in spite of

---

3 *The Doctor's Dilemma* by George Bernard Shaw had been translated into German by Siegfried
Trebitsch in 1909.
4 For example.

doubts or deadnesses. Oh, and of course it's all a-groping. One wants one thing now & one thing later, and most of the time one doesn't know *what* one wants. One can't tell, in oneself, whether things are causes or reasons or excuses.

Seeing you, all of you & *you*, & other things, perhaps, had brought me up with a cold water shock. And in any case my emotions to anyone by then, were pretty dead.

No: that's not clear.

Before, you see, it was very simple. I was reduced to the lowest. I could see two outcomes. Either I won or I lost & killed everybody. So, at least, Evil did not wholly triumph.

But then, I tell you, two or three things happened in me. I got harder & stronger from you: & strength & hardness meant the refusal to submit meekly to degradation & torture, & it meant the desire for punishment & for "vengeance" among other things. And I began to realise that the world which contained you wasn't to be left in such a hurry (It's not necessarily a noble thought, my Noel. Look at it this way. Suppose I came on a negro trying to rape a woman on the edge of a precipice, & the situation was such that either (1) I could run away or (2) we could all fall over the precipice together; if I thought I'd rather *not* leave so nice a world, & turned away, – what'd you think of me?). And also my feelings, to Ka or anyone else, seemed to be dead for the moment.

And then I began to wonder – to feel rather than think – that there might be a third possibility in front of me, – if Ka *did* prove to be poisoned too far, – i.e. to cut the whole thing off & stand free. I mightn't be able to do it when the time came. But it might be worth aiming at – as a possibility & in an eventuality.

Well, to do that, I had to make myself as hard & strong as possible in order to be able to stand with my head above water. If I went all under again – when the time of being with Ka came – it'd be going back to the old simple alternative again. That's what I meant by "madness", the old state of utter abandonment. It was to save myself from that – & from infinite pain & then killing everyone if the worst came – that I wanted to be able to think of you. The present thought of you, & of all these other things, hardened & strengthened & also gave a horizon – reminded that there was more than the mud at hand & around.

And the more I thought & felt, the more doubtful I got: But the more it stood out that I must have two things to fight the thing through: strength & meanness. Strength I got from you, meanness from myself.

You see, it's no good going into it either weak or good. Either puts

one into the power of the other side. And it's fatal to be in the power of
that sort of woman. I know this sounds beastly to you, you little fool.
But there it is. I tell you, I've done with the other business – the nobility
& suffering business. It's not good for one, & I haven't got enough
decency, left to try it. Also, it's damned bad tactics. You don't
understand. It doesn't *matter* about hurting Ka. You're not to talk about
it. In the first place she's not fit for you to talk about. In the second place
you don't understand. Ka's saved, it doesn't matter if she has suffered in
the process. She's deserved a lot more than she has suffered and will
suffer. If she's lost, the more broken up & spoilt she is, the better.

Ka's done the most evil things in the world. She has – or she's on
the way to have – dirtied good & honour & all high things, & betrayed
& degraded love. Think of the filthiest image you can for the fouling of
the best things by the worst. Ka is doing that. For the sake of all those
things, & for the sake of the Ka I used to know, & for the sake of the
good love there was between us, I'd not care if I saw Ka *dying* of some
torture I could inflict on her, slowly.

Understand all this; realise it. It's not hypothetical romance, nor
somebody else's case. It's what I've been in, for months; it's what I'm
meaning, and doing: real – to *me*. It's ignoble enough – oh, I know all
about that. I often remember about the nobility & the other words, – in
my spare minutes, or when I want to think about something else, to get
my mind off the real things. Bless you, I *know* – I can imagine how a
high-souled person ought to feel: – no, not a high-souled person, but a
real decent fine person; just as I can imagine how a person in good
health & energy would feel. But *I'm* just a scuffling dirtied hurt maimed
human soul; myself & I don't happen to feel like that.

But I conceal that I don't from everybody except you. Oh, I don't
know very clearly how I *do* feel – as this letter makes very obvious. Most
of the time certainly since I've been here, I don't feel anything at all.
"Getting my own back" & all that you're so scornful of. Well, I *do* feel
that, sometimes, in my shamed shameful heart. One does, you know. I
feel a lot of other things too. And I know, – you'll be surprised to hear, –
to a certain extent, whether they're good or bad. And, knowing that, yet I
don't stop feeling them! And your threats, that if I come ignobly
triumphant a ridiculous & unpleasant figure, out of this – you'll so hate
me! Well, being dead, I can afford not to be moved much by even that.
And, after all, if I were alive – should I much care? Why should you – I
almost wrote, how *dare* you – demand that I should? As you pointed out
with your unfailing charm, you've so far, on a balance, found that my
existence works out at about zero for you – that you've liked & disliked

me in about equal quantities. Well, the change from that to a minus balance, from a sum of indifference to actual hate – you know, it doesn't matter much, does it? Oh, Noel, you mayn't use weapons you've discovered. The cartridge is confusedly blank. I could think of a lot of images. You can't eat your cake & have it: – or rather, you can't refuse your cake & vomit it. All this is small enough: – on my level.

You may be saying, (I fancy), – *why*, when I came to the conclusion that there was this third way conceivable – of getting out of it – & that I must harden, & also that I was pretty dead towards Ka & everything else – *why* didn't I give up & not come to Germany?

Well, it wasn't, I've said, wholly the will of God that brought me! It was the desire to go through with things; not to funk; & the knowledge that the deadness might pass; & the idea that when one's made up one's mind, with hard work & pain in the process, one mustn't be shaken by other considerations suddenly appearing vivid, on this day or that. I was confused enough & perplexed. But it seemed I'd better keep to my plan. And anyhow, would you have me leave Ka to her fate, & not fight? How *could* I? Especially in mid-career, like that. Think, Noel, please. Do imagine it. I tell you, I *am* the champion of good, in a way, here – even if I'm not good. I can't help thinking that. I know it. And I may be the instrument of punishing Evil: if it comes to that. Do you think this sounds silly? Nothing's quite silly: if people believe it painfully enough.

And finally, what was there to gain by my funking the thing, or to lose if all turned out for the worst – & my "madness" even came again? Only me, you see; & a rotten rather broken me. Damn you, why *should* I stay in England or anywhere? What had I to get out of it? I couldn't work or write decently. Pottering about, with nothing ahead. "There was Noel", some of my friends might have told me. But *you* can't, you see. I wasn't fit for Noel. I'd myself made unfit for her. And in any case Noel is – a person who can't at all, she says make out if even the last four years are + or – , . . . whether she likes or dislikes me more. It's scarcely *that* that could hold one fast enough to make one shirk things, is it?

[. . .]

You don't, of course, understand about Ka: and about her being hurt. I've written about it. I've been in love with Ka: & I am in love with her, in a way, & I shall be, I suppose; & I know her better than anyone does. She's better than you, than any of you, in many ways. She's, in most ways, unusually brave. You're all rather cowardly. She has feelings. None of you has any. But, I tell you, she's infinitely below any of you: and *you* Noel, she's not fit – it's sacrilege & shame if she ever touches you. That's *truth*, you little fool. I may marry her. I may kill myself for love of her – but I <u>know</u> that's true.

For the rest; I'm sorry I was "cold & gloomy" that last afternoon. But what could I? Oh, it was ungrateful; yes. I daresay after the next few times I shall get used to parting with you for ever. It happens, roughly, every quarter. But the novelty's not worn off.

You, you, oh, you! I see, in some ways, so very clearly: packed up against my pillows in this quiet room (it's now Tuesday night/ Wednesday morning: but you see I never, nowadays, get to sleep before 3, and rarely before 4.30. So one may as well write, as lie & think?)

I'm frightened: as one used to be before a football match. Not knowing what will happen. I've been in a sort of stupor this fortnight. Ka comes in two days. I shall write again, if I may. About what, I don't know. I daren't, I can't, write then about anything but slight things – theatres or weather. But I shall want very much to do that. It seems – to put one in touch – oh, one daren't be in touch. But, – in sight, or something. To remind one – I don't know. To prevent madness. You see, it's all got to work out, what my feelings are. Oh, if you loved me, I couldn't write to you or be anything but dead to you. And if you cared not at all, I couldn't bother you. But as it is, you're rather luckily between – interested in me, aren't you. "fond" & a little sollicitous, as one might be for a favourite horse or dog. Damn you. So you'd want to know how I'm going on, & to be of assistance if you can. Is that right? If so, all the objection to my writing a letter to you, comes from within me. The lines when something in *me* cries out "You mustn't! you can't! *You*, as you are & with what you've done, can't write to NOEL now – to Noel, who has loved you – whom you've loved: (whom you love)".

Oh, what I have said & asked for has been, I see, the grotesquest insolence. But you were so amazing – and I've always had the theory of you not feeling things! So I talked to you, & asked for things, as if – I were clean, & for you. I kept forgetting what I was. You block out things so. How can one behave decently to *you*? It doesn't apply. You're too extraordinary: too great. I nearly asked other things, but very shame held me at length: – What you prospected, *had* thought, & *did*, of the future – Ah; but one *couldn't*. Only, you see, I did, and do, see some things with such extraordinary clarity. When I came back to you lately, & saw you again & felt much calmer to you, – &, in addition to that, unemotional to everything, dead; then the fact I was so calm made what I saw easier to see & much more certain. It wasn't anything born of excitement or heat –

I see, you know, how entirely you're the greatest thing for me. I see it almost unemotionally: as a fact. I see all sorts of alternatives and hypothesis, quite impersonally & unprejudicedly. I may marry Ka; or get rid (somehow) of all this & go off, in the end, elsewhere, & marry – anybody. And, in either case, I believe, my life can be extraordinarily splendid and very happy, full of fineness. But, in any such case, it seems to me to miss it's greatest possibility. Do you see how a thing can be wonderfully good, immensely worth while, and yet not its best possible self? If Milton had written all his works except *Paradise Lost*, – Comus, Samson, the sonnets & so on, – he'd have been an astoundingly good poet, our best, *but* – he'd have missed the central thing, he'd have been infinitely smaller than he is, he'd not, you know, have been Milton.

Noel, Noel, Noel; Noel with whom I've been through – all that these years have held – & to whom I can say anything; this is what, I sometimes know, you are to me. Soberly, greyly, clearly, as the dead see. I *see* that you're – that *you & I* is – the greatest potentiality for me – & for you, I think. Life together, somewhere and how, & for some period, the whole thing: being one. You, Noel, & I. It may be impossible: it very certainly may never come off; we may have missed it; and certainly if we never heard of each other again we might easily entirely forget each other in a few years; & I may have been, or may be spoilt, & you may be, I see, in a different way. But – it's, I know, the greatest thing conceivable.

It's a queer thing to be writing this, when I'm just going to live with – perhaps marry – someone else. It's unfair & insolent to you, & unfair & treacherous to Ka (if anything can be unfair & treacherous to Ka.) . . . But it's not either, really. Anyhow, it's true.

Oh, my dear, my dear, my dear, you must see it and know it.

I don't know what's going to happen. I only know this; and that the past *has* (it becomes clearer every day) been unspeakably, unbearably, good & fine; and, I think, that I shall, somehow, see you again, in no very long time.

I think I've in some ways rather muffed things with you. You've been rather stupid, sometimes; & I've been worse. I mean that, especially lately, I've tended to appear before your mind as – in ordinary life – a not very pleasant figure; rather disturbing, rather clumsy, rather damping. Irritating, in a way. Not fitting in with the good things of life – "Bryn & Bunny & me dancing in the woods." Fretting, wanting deferable things: impatient; not altogether to be trusted. Nicer, in your absence than in your presence. I think I see it. I'm sorry. I have been a nuisance, I see now. Adroitly managed, though, I'm capable of being quite sociable & friendly – if I lend a hand in the managing – But it's all too long – to go into that.

There's one other thing, I see about myself. That waiting wouldn't ever quite have done. For other people, perhaps; but not for me. I've too much burning inside. You scorn males for it, & dislike it. But it's there. I need marriage or some equivalent: & I should only rage till I get it. Don't curl your maiden lip. It's you that are unpleasant: not me. (You aren't really.). You, you're a funny Noel.

It's almost broad daylight, & I've just spilt most of the ink on the pillow. I can't go on writing. I'm tired, & my head still aches. I'll have a try at sleep.

The smell of the spilt ink suddenly reminds me of the ants at camp – & how they make one's hands smell.

The world *must* be curious, through your eyes: like a ball of worsted. You've a lot of faults, & I quite clearly see all about you, at this hour o' the morning. You are the finest & most glorious thing by far I have come across in all my life. (But you don't see it!) Good bye. Be very happy. Care for me, care for me, Noel. I'm not fit to write

love from
Rupert

From None of your family have I heard since I left England. Alas! Alas!

44, Greycoat Gardens,
Westminster, S.W.

Tuesday. May 13th [1912]

I am affraid I have been keeping these documents rather too long;[1] Bryn tells me that you lie awake of nights for need of them: so here they are,

---

1 Noel refers to the instructions King's had sent to Rupert, about the procedure for applying for the Augustus Austen Leigh Studentship.

sleep now and R.I.P. – as they say in the Westminster Cathedral round the corner.

I cant see my way to becoming a catholic just yet. I went there last night and saw the curiousest & gayest ladies bringing flowers to Mary and kissing the feet of the Christ, and in a place set apart there were candels burning, & great numbers of dusty & practical-looking people at prayer. Has everyone of us the right to go & pray like that or does baptism & confirmation have to come first, as it does when one wants to communion or confess? Before I decide about the christening, I shall go again once or twice, & see if I like the smell of incense for long – (buying a little); Bunny is coming to Mass too soon.

Strange that my hasty note – excited by Bryn's earnestness – should have so turned yours to strife & anger & argument. It was meant but as a poor thing, a vague persuasion or suggestion; I am really sorry it stung so, perhaps it sounded more bitter to you than I meant, because you were so sick of thinking of it all.

Now, I'm very hopeful, perhaps unreasonably, feeling that, leaving things to slow dicisions by the – instinct (or what?) Character, rather than to quick reasoning, you will still go well. I cant believe that Milton could have failed to write Paradise Lost ((even tho' I never read it)). Neither is it possible that I might not have been born. And you – I expect – will achieve the best for you even tho' you cant see yet (or ever) what it is.

Oh its just optimism. And I cant help feeling that things would go better still if you would sleep. You mustn't get used to lying awake or having night mares; they have a poorer chance of being abolished if you expect them so regularly & resignedly. I saw a lobster being hypnotised just now. They stood him on his head on a piece of glass over water and rubbed him up & down all along his back until he became languorous & finally slept, letting his pincers droop & his long red feelers lie flat. It looked dilicous for him. Get some one to treat you the same way – they'd better rub up & down the back of you – standing on the head would probably not be convenient – in a hot bath – oh there are lots of tricks if you'd only be sensible & try.

I'm glad you'll be writing me pleasant letters about Berlin & the country. I'm really writing now, to encourage you; you must say if you want to hear more answers from me, because I'm not sure whether I'm not being a nuisance writing this. But I hoped, as I was in such a good temper, it might be alright.

Your friends here are very pleasant to me. I had tea with Gwen &

Jaques last week, and now poor Gwen wants to go on with a painting
she started at Limpsfield and I'm to go and sit on Friday. Its rather nice
to be stuck up & staring for about an hour, while Jaques makes strange
noises of displeasure at his work, and Gwen makes sudden remarks in
her good real voice. They are the best of people.

James is still very bounteous and patient; I never can really believe
that he's quite a wicked worm, even if he does snarl sometimes (at old
friends) its a weak little noise, and altho' he has coil upon coil of
incomprehensible parts – one can reckon on their all being grey &
feeble & melancholy. He has offered to conduct me to Earls' Court to
Shoot the Chute – can he swim?

Virginia is coming to see us here the day after tomorrow. And I'm
going down to her new house at Asheham² next week-end. It'll be a
great thing, even tho it do prove that I'm too common & much of a
dunce to associate with these folks.

But anyhow they're all paying you tribute.

Love from Noel.

A Later Date.

And after all, neither I nor my mother nor Bryn nor Margery can find
your scolarship papers again. Your right in saying you left them at
Limpsfield, because I saw them & took charge of them – & apparently
lost them (in Norfolk probably). Oh dear – Its bad to be incompetent
with someone elses business! I *am* penitent & sorry. What shall you do?
Can you write about it again – or will they be angry? Perhaps I could
find some other man to pretend he wanted to enter for it & to ask for
particulars – wd that be any help?
[. . .]

Life is rather a doubtful affair just now. Margery still seems to be
terribly mad. I'm affraid, that nearly killing her in the bath room did no
good. She seems to have faith in nothing nor anybody. Bryn's very
splendid.

Bill & Eva are as nice as I could wish, they exact nothing & are a
pleasure to come across in the flat. They're stimulating too, because so
different.

Its sultry in england & there's dust again blowing about. I'm going

---

2 Virginia and her sister, the painter Vanessa Bell (1879–1961), had taken out the lease on Asheham
House near Firle in Sussex.

to fail in my exam; but I shall probably go to the seventh symphony next week. One cant live properly without good sound from time to time.

Go on living, Rupert, whatever you do. (Never mind whether I have the *"right"* to say it)

Noel.

Destroy this envelope with this postmark[1]

Ende Mai

(precisely 5–7pm May 30) [1912]

My address is bei Dudley
Spichern strasse 16/G.H.
Charlottenburg
Berlin–

I was awfully happy to get your letter. I'd meant to write a hundred times before now: but time slips so deadly along. There's no occasion to write at one moment rather than another . . . The last letter was that great long definitive one from bed that I sat up most of one night to write. Oh, I didn't mean it to sound full of strife & argument. Yours (to the N[ational] L[iberal] C[lub]) had stung only because it ought to. I only answered so earnestly & guiltily because you seemed so important & what you said so possibly true.

I was so dead in Berlin all those weeks. I suddenly found I was dead. And I'm still dead. That's what's happened, all that's happened. For I find I must tell you what's happening: unless you don't want to hear.

I just care about nobody & nothing in the world – least of all Ka. I

---

1 Noel did not destroy the envelope, but she did remove the German stamps and postmark. Rupert was now north of Berlin with Ka, a fact he wished to keep secret from his friends and family in England. They had left Berlin on 20 May and travelled first to Neu Strelitz, then to Felberg, and were now in Müritz. Throughout the visit both had remained calm, avoiding painful questions about the past and postponing any decision about their future together. In a frank letter Rupert described his feelings for Ka and Noel in a letter to Dudley: 'I remain dead. I care practically nothing for any person in the world. I've anxiety, and a sort of affection, for Ka – But I don't really care. I've no feeling for anybody at all – except the uneasy ghosts of the immense reverence and rather steadfast love for Noel, and a knowledge that Noel is the finest thing I've ever seen in the world, and Ka – isn't.' (*LRB*, p. 378)

was afraid I might be going to fall into that wildness of passion again (I told you.). That's why I wanted to keep – things in mind: some good things. Well, that's all right. That danger's as far away as anything in the world. It's more unlikely than anything in the Universe that I should kill myself! It'd even be supererogatory.

I feel nothing for Ka except a great pity for her that she's so weak, and a dull uneasiness because she's unclean. But I can't stand this very long. I shall go off very soon – I don't know where. I saw her a lot for ten days in Berlin. Since then we've been a week in the country: but we've only just found rooms. We're *not* going to live for a month together.

(Ostensibly, I remember. I'm in Berlin: & she's up here in the North.)

For everybody I feel just blank. There's a man called Dudley – I remember, intellectually, that I like him very much – but actually I don't care twopence if he drowns in a gondola in Venice[2] – There's you. I've remembered – half dully things of these years. Grantchester and a Camp at Penshurst and quite insignificant things (like Victorias) – & once we even had a mediocre tea in Knightsbridge. Oh, God! They've been *so* good, everyway. One only sees it now. But I'll not go on. But even the dead feel – gratitude, or some such emotion. These nights, sometimes, I've lain awake and called for you & prayed to you, so hard, because you're so fine – you're you. I suppose you don't understand –

Your letter made you out pretty happy. But I mistrust London: a sweltery place. Your term'll end in a fortnight? And you'll be at Limpsfield? Good.

I want to hear about the week end at Virginia's. You're a lot less practised, & so slower, than that lot: but if you go on saying you're "less clever" & all that stuff, I shall burn you in effigy here & twist your arm nine times when I come to England.

It's fun, isn't it, sitting in that circle – the intellectual windiness. And Virginia has lovely stately ways about her. Are you strong? Because it's a rotten atmosphere in all that circle (ask Jacques.). And it does one a lot of insidious harm if one isn't strong. They're mostly very amusing people as acquaintances, but not worth making one's friends: because they're treacherous & wicked. So take care: & take care of Margery. I suppose you *are* fairly strong. But less, possibly, than you think.

---

2 Dudley and Annemarie had married in Munich on 11 May and then gone to Venice for their honeymoon.

(Funny, isn't it, last autumn I was urging you to frequent Virginia – & you were a little pigheadedly, refusing. And now you're going there: & I, in Germany, am . . . nervously unhappy.)

About Margery. I know what would be best for her. To go to France with Jacques & Gwen, & then to Berlin to Dudley, & see me if I'm on the Continent; & generally make a Welt-reise.[3] It *would* be good for her. She ought to get away from all you – especially now the ultimate cure of death in the bathroom has failed. Do press it on her.

You write rather beastlily about James – rather anyhow, as if the position was that one had to make out he wasn't altogether a worm. I suppose Gwen's been telling you he's a worm. It's not true. Lytton is filthy, & for God's sake don't touch him. The rest of the family are pretty slippery. But James is all right. He's unlike you in being sensitive. But he's a very fine person extraordinarily honest and trustworthy, very intelligent, and meaning well (which is important.). He has been spoilt in some ways by association with, & admiration for, Lytton – But they're not fundamental. Use him well.

It's nice to hear of Gwen & Jacques going on. They're good people. I'm finding out how important goodness is: and how dreary mere cleverness. Oh, I'm coming round to you bucolics: a little shamefacedly.

This isn't much of a letter. I'm sorry. There's really not much to chronicle: except cold & rain in the weather, & fever & headaches in my health. I've a dim idea of roaming up through Denmark & getting a boat across to England & settling somewhere – Grantchester? – for the summer. But term'd be over. Should I ever see anybody? Bryn (her letter came today: held up in Berlin some days) foreshadowed a quiet summer for you all. I suppose Sir Syd.'ll do something sudden and desperate. I've a feeling I'd like to hear a lot of rather good people laughing a good deal. Some time I should come where you are (unless your distaste had grown too strong) & sit & watch you reading Paradise Lost, &, maybe, occasionally help by telling you the meanings of the harder words. But if there's any sudden cataclysmic plan involving all your family, you might tell me of it promptly. Supposing Sir S. took a House in the Hebrides . . . . . . Taking all of you, all round, I find you rather an essential part of my English cure. So if you were all inaccessible, I might just wander down to Italy —— I'd not find, anyhow, much point in returning . .

But don't *say* I may be coming back soon. I don't know . .

You might write. This way (for I know you're busy). Scribble a

---

3 A world tour.

note or two about Current Affairs on a bit of paper. And, after a while, collect the bits & send them off. Quite easy, eh?

I'll write again: better. I heard you & Ka had lunch together. It gave me rather a turn. I felt sorry.[4]

Your letter was so nice (with lobsters & the rest) that I feel bound to tell you I'm sleeping better. I nearly died with rage when Dudley got a letter before me – Tell me with infinite detail your present actions & movements.

I enclose my latest poem.[5] I walked alone two days beyond Potsdam (S.W. of Berlin) down the lakes. Hence this. (All that's a lie: but it explains.) I'm afraid you won't like the poem – Keep fine.

with love (& other things)
Rupert

[. . .]

---

4 Before leaving England, Ka wrote to Noel, asking if they could meet: 'But if you'd rather not I shall understand . . . I can't look very far ahead – I think you are very marvellous & very generous . . . if you hadn't been as you are, I might have been sad last year & I wasn't. This is a sort of clumsy affection I'm trying to express.' (Olivier family papers)

5 The poem was published with the title 'By the Lake. A Music for three voices' in The Eye Witness, 10 October 1912. See p. 179.

Die Natur.

A lake . . . and then a wood . . .
– That's good, you know, that's good!

The blossom in the trees,
– *Distinctly* Japanese!

White bloom against the sky,
– A perfect Hokusai!

Blue waves and one white spot,
– Sheer Hiroshige, what?

The blue behind the white,
– Oh, delicate! oh, quite!

The white against the blue,
– Artistic, *through and through!*

The plum tree, nicely-placed,
– *That's* what I call good taste.

The rushed bend and bow,
– What price a wood-cut *now?*

The petals on the lake . . .
– That's fony, *no* mistake!

The petals drift apart –
– Real, high-class, cultured Art!

The petals fade and sink . . .
– Fetches yer, I *don't* think!

R

N.B. bei Dudley Ward
Spichern strasse 16/G.H.
Charlottenburg.
Berlin.

[Postmark 11 June 1912]

Dear Noel,

     I suppose I'd just better report to you. I feel, vaguely, like a ticket-of-leave man: – though I don't know what a ticket-of-leave man is.
     I am well: sleeping better: brown: and so on. Oh, Lord!
     I seem to remember writing you a rather dreary letter. This'll be dreary too.
     I suppose you're absurdly fumbling away over exams. Noel, you're not to let London & the heat make you tired or ill. I forbid it.
     Tell me where you're going to be all the summer. I sail so well & so *gern*[1] now, that I'm going to spend the first part on the Zuyder Zee & spend the second on the Broads. Will you join me?
     I sit here (wondering what on earth I want to say, though knowing well enough *how* I want to say it) with Dudley round the corner of this double room, clicking away on a type writer, and Annemarie on the other side of this little table, attentively studying a German History of England. ("I am English now", she will confide to you, in that funny accent of her,). She *says* she is looking up something in an old school-book. But she has been reading it for an hour, with her tiny brow puckered. So I know that it is a wistful, shy attempt to get a

---

1 Readily.

little more intimate with her adopted country. She & I have just drunk our Ovaltine – she's so tiny & thin that I convinced Dudley & her that she must take it. I have a tiny bedroom here I can retire into. Sometimes we have meals out: mostly Annemarie skilfully cooks them. Conversation is the oddest mixture of English & German. A sentence slips from one to the other in the middle. "Hast du *Reynolds* heute gesehen? He was asking for you. 'war ein bischen traurig, I thought . . .'² and so on. Dudley reads innumerable papers, and occasionally, picking something out of one of them, clatters off an article about it. A.M. attends to the flat, reads, & writes. Sometimes they trot down the street together. Occasionally I'm between them, a gigantic nurse with two children. Dudley spends most of his time in proving to Annemarie, with a kind of testy logic, that the German language is a bad one. She replies with little spurts of incoherent & entirely momentary patriotism. It ends with a grunt from Dudley, & a flashed amusement from her eyes to me – a spiritual wink. She takes me, most tacitly, and most captivatingly, because most shyly, into her confidence over Dudley. "We two see" is the attitude, "how funny he is; and how lovable." One always capitulates to the tacit-confidence-trick. It flatters so.

Tuesday morning)
German's such a silly language. What do you think "Er ist nichts weniger als ein Dummkopf" means? You'll say "He is nothing less than a fool." Wrong! It means precisely the opposite. "He is anything but a fool." If you want to test anyone's knowledge of German, put this to them.
   I get fond of these two Dudley & Annemarie. Which is good: for I'm rather empty & dry in my heart, & I want to like somebody or something. A.M. doesn't understand English people, & is anyhow infinitely shy, and she's practically a child of 12; so her advance is infinitely slow. And I, of course, am apparently self possessed & immense; & actually more immovably shy than she. So her advances are slight & timid, like a child's. She has a vague feeling I'm rather ill & unhappy*: & she likes me. So she, last night, – for instance – as she crept away to bed, ventured a transient hand on my shoulder – scarcely perceptible – with her *Gut Nacht!*: & so fled. Leaving me

2 'Have you seen Reynolds today? . . . he was a little sad . . . ' Alfred Rothay Reynolds was Dudley and Annemarie's flatmate, who was working in Germany as a foreign correspondent for the *Daily Mail*. He had read History at Pembroke and was busy finishing his first novel, *The Gondola*, which was published in 1913.

feeling old as the hills; and wondering if all old people were, under that granite exterior, as fussily shy as I am (they *are*, I know). For I spend hours a day wondering if I ought to say *du* to Annemarie. (I know I ought, of course) Oh, I *am* old. I find I'm so incredibly paternal to these two – to everybody I know. I have a constant anxiety lest they come to any harm. I hover about, fluttering elderly wings of solicitude. I plan secretly that Dudley may get good & regular meals, & manoeuvre most complicatedly that he may not strum on the piano when she has a headache, or that she may get enough sleep. I feel an extraordinary responsibility. *Isn't* that the clearest, final, sign of definite old age – to feel so responsible for one's friends? Or is it only the instinct of paternity, perverted to other objects? For I've a theory that one is ruled by psychological laws in such things in much the same way as women are by physical. When you, I mean, conceive a child, it very quickly sets up a series of mechanical, physical reactions that end in your breasts becoming milky. So "nature" provides for the child when it appears. I support that, a year or two after men fall in love (1908!) a series of psychological reactions is produced that results in the paternal emotion – ready for the child when its passed the mere infant stage . . .

I've got to go out now. I shall write to you again: soon. I'm going to work very hard for a bit: if I can. I'm not going to see Ka anyhow for two or three months. Perhaps for ever. I shall know I suppose, when I get alive again. I'm so dead, child.

I do wish more than all things in the world, that youre fine & happy.

> with love
> Rupert

A letter from Bryn! – I shall answer it.
* Not that I *am*, you know.

Berlin
Thursday morning [20 June 1912]

I am disturbed, because two hours ago I woke, and I cannot get to sleep again, although it is very early morning. That is rare, being unable to sleep in the morning.

I have been to Dudley. He was asleep with his mouth open, & that made me sad. It is seven oclock, he says. So I shall lie here an hour or two more. I only went to sleep at two. Damn! I shall be irritable this evening. We start for Cologne at 3, & get in at 11. I've been reading a book by M. Gide for the last half hour.[1] He says every book is a collaboration: between God & oneself. And that the greater God's part & the smaller one's own, the better the book. That seems to me amusing. But I suppose that the opposite – the *less* God's part . . . the better – would be amusing, too. It's going to be so hot today.

I daresay its an open secret by now that James is coming to Cologne for the week end.[2] It'll be funny to see an Englishman again. – Dudley, after all, is only a foreigner; and any-how married people have "invisible glass shades" all round them . . . They ponder, & knit their brows, & have long silences, & do not tell, & do not go to *cafés* of an evening. Oh, dear! But I cry over them for children. I am so old that I know everything; and I'm infinitely sorry for everybody. I'm sorry for everybody in the world because they're playing about and laughing under the shadow of enormous catastrophes. And anyhow they're such attractive pathetic little figures, these human beings; they wind themselves into one's affections so.

Last night, for instance, I said Good bye to little Reynolds. – But I haven't told you about Reynolds. I shall.

There's no news, except that the *English Seminar* in the University here has an awfully good collection of modern English Literature: – Shaw, Yeats, etc.

6.0.pm
At that point I lay back and groaned for an hour and then slept uneasily, till Dudley woke me at 9. We are now in a second class carriage between Berlin & Köln. Dudley & I & a fat man who is travelling from

---

1 André Gide (1869–1951), French novelist. Gide became a close friend of the Raverats, who introduced him to Rupert in June 1914.
2 Rupert and Dudley were going to stay in the Hotel Kölner Hof, Cologne, where James was to join them, and accompany Rupert home.

Russia or Poland to England. So fat, & perhaps 55. He has a double
chin & queer whiskers, greater at the bottom than at the a top.
— Even in a train I can't draw — He is like a drawing by Mr
Chesterton. Oh, he is so unhappy in the heat — unhappy that he's fat: &
very helpless. Alternately he goes to sleep, & drinks. He drinks
innumerable bottles of aerated water, in a grim
endeavour to stave of apoplexy. And always he
groans. For three hours he has been fighting death.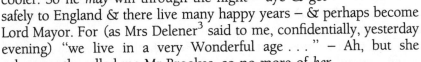
At first death gained steadily. But lately he made a rally
& drunk a very great deal, & then groaned enormously,
and turned a little less grey-green, and panted less. It is
cooler. So he *may* win through the night — aye & get
safely to England & there live many happy years — & perhaps become
Lord Mayor. For (as Mrs Delener[3] said to me, confidentially, yesterday
evening) "we live in a very Wonderful age . . ." — Ah, but she
subsequently called me Mr Brookes, so no more of *her.*

Dudley & I watch the old man, nervously. Each time he groans,
Dudley shudders a little. And he groans very often. We have a little bet on
it — Dudley & I. Dudley thinks he will die. Often I see Dudley's eyes fill
with softness, & then I know he is thinking that somewhere in Poland (or
Russia) there is a mountain of a wife, soon to be widow, and some lovely
chubby little children, all but fatherless. But *I* think his wife died long ago,
& that his children are all grown up, & rather dislike him.

So. So. I cannot give you much news. I am probably going to write
four articles a year on English literature (modern) for a German
magazine & receive some £2-2-0 for each. But they are short.[4] Also, I
am — despite your almost criminal negligence — elected to that
Scholarship in Kings. So *there's* £70 to the good (less what my mother
deducts from my income) — [A.W.] Verrall is dead. That doesn't mean
much to you. It gave me rather a jerk. His mind was so *particularly*
lively — It'll give the mediums & the S[ociety for].P[sychical].R[esearch].
a good time when he gets going, the other side. He was an Apostle*, of
course: rather a good one.[5] *Sh!

---

3 Unidentified.
4 Rupert had two articles published in the German periodical *Internationale Monats-Schrift für
Wissenschaft, Kunst und Technik*, one entitled 'Robert Brownings Jahrhundertfeiern' (February 1913)
and one 'Das Wiedererwachen der Dichtkunst in England' (April 1914).
5 A.W. Verrall died on 18 June 1912. He was married to Margaret de Gaudrion Merrifield of
Newnham, who was keenly interested in the work of the Society for Psychical Research. She encouraged
both him and their daughter Helen to develop an interest in the whole field of psychic research. Verrall
was, as Rupert suggests, incredibly devoted to The Apostles, 'the best thing that ever happened to me in
my life'. Quoted in *The Cambridge Apostles* by Richard Deacon (London: Robert Royce, 1985), p. 49.

I am writing an American revivalist hymn, entitled "Going Home to Godville". – But I think I told you that.

We're just correcting & sending off a thing to the *Morning Post*, a letter. It's a Plot of Dudley's & mine. A fellow made a speech, saying this, that, & the other, about Germany; all wrong. So I'm writing, very meekly, disguised as a Retired Colonel, to know what authority he has . . . He'll reply. Then Dudley, from Germany, & I from the Old Vicarage, disguised as the Old Vicar, will severally Sit on him. It's all part of Dudley's career. But that's all *if* the *Post* prints the letter.

If I ever see you again, may I take you to (a) The Russians in Petrouschka (b) a Test match?

I'm so sorry for you, my Noel: going through life & not knowing what you are. You don't know, for instance, what you've been, what things you've done, lately. *I* know. Ha!

I wish I knew what you were doing, & what thinking. I'm too tired & too rotten to write a decent letter. Don't read this one. But read – do you ever? – the letter I haven't written. Do you know what's in the letters I just can't write? . . .

Even that rings stupid. I'm longing to see you. I'm nearly ripe for England. I love you so.

Rupert

The Train

Sunday [23 June 1912]

Holland's a flat country: James is very amusing: – what shall I tell you? I don't know. I know nothing except this one thing, that I'm coming home, – I'm going to see you – I suppose. I'm coming home. I'm going to see you: you.

I think I shall cross with James on Monday night/Tuesday morning. I've got to be in London on Wednesday night; after that – irgendwo[1] – I soon drift to Grantchester. I wonder if I shall see you.

---

1 anywhere.

Perhaps you're still at exams. If you'd like it, write me a note to the National Liberal. Any time except from 7–11 on Wednesday; & any place.

I don't really know the locality of your family – I mean if they're situate in Limpsfield or London, I daresay I'll pick one or two up somehow.

I've got a feeling I'd like to be with them – with you (euch) – for an hour or two. It's one of the few things that *really* invigorates – I'm curiously dull & dreary. I've even a sort of shame at drinking in life from you all, & giving nothing – Oh especially *you* (du) invigorate – Oh I say, I *won't* be *too* dreary, child: I promise. Only I'm so thirsty to see people & just to sit & talk to you.

Oh, it's so queer, the world. You do seem to me so very really good & lovely – it's like coming home to lovely familiar things, back out of deserts & starvation & fighting & wandering, – coming back from one's own horrible company to see you. I seem to have known you such a very long time, Noel. We seem so frightfully mixed up –

It's inconceivable, it's inconceivable, how you've helped me & made me continue –

I wish more than anything else in the world to do you good – to help you or give you something – Oh, that sound's so stupid – And I expect it's not true for long; – I'll often want far more to do myself good – only, it's true just for this moment. –

Oh, damn you: it'll just be good to see you. That's all. You can accept that? I'm a dead thing – but I'll get alive again having seen you.

Cheer up. You've not written to me. Perhaps you hate me. I don't care. But you don't – Oh, help me –

Noel, Noel, Noel, Noel, Noel, Noel, I'm coming home. I'm coming near you. I'm coming home.

                                                                      Rupert

44 Grey Coat Gardens
Westminster
Monday [24 June 1912]

Dear funny Rupert

Its a nice night this night; and you'll be thinking
London looks lovely. I came up just before supper from Limpsfield – it
was rather grievous there; we were all trying so hard to fit plans
together, Mother is going to Jamaica in September & wants me to go to
Switzerland before it with her & Daphne. I dont want to go very much
& it saddens her; and in that family just now there is a great movement
– against anybody hurting anyone's feelings. Its a rotten movement –
makes them worried & nervous & makes me feel desperately
disagreable. Coming back here is a heavenly thing. Westminster is a
kindly district. The exam, which I've been having for a week, ends on
Wednesday. That night we're all going to the Russian Ballet – in various
seats. Will you be coming. do you think? May be the Governor will treat
all his family to the grand circle – would you come there?
Then I go to Limpsfield for about a month – & after that, go to all
sorts of places.
Oh, I've been very mean, in not writing more. You were splendid.
[. . .]
But I cant write now, all the strange & varied news there is to tell
you.
If your in London on Thursday – I shall still be up – are we on
speaking terms; or are you a nervous wreck?

Love from
Noel

Riversdale,
Goring,
Oxon.

Saturday [29 June 1912]

Dearest Dearest Dearest Noel

I found I had to see you yesterday afternoon, just to satisfy myself that all was well. I was so happy it on the whole was – or seemed to be. It's incredible – how one *aches* that you shouldn't be unduly worried or distressed or hurt in any way. But it's also incredible, to me, how comparatively happy I've become, for the moment, – in the discovery that there's anyhow one thing in the universe that can give me pleasure and not give me shame – the endeavour to be of help – any how potentially – to you – Oh God, I suppose you feel this very sentimental & rather silly? Couldn't you translate it into your own queer language? . . . Perhaps this is only rationalising the emotion which is merely at seeing you again – you, so twinedly part of my mind – as I keep finding – (I'll explain about the human mind one day: it's very simple) – you, who are, anyhow, you – I shall see you on Monday or so . . . & again later in July, probably.

It's funny – I feel as if I understood so much in the world: even so much of that lovely absurdity known to an indignant universe as Noel's mind – I feel as if I was at last beginning – it's always so infernally hard – to synthesise the appearance of Noel & what Noel feels like – Oh, even separate they're (though both just perceptibly comic at moments) amazing – (By the way, there was a moment in Herr Epstein's Studio,[1] when you looked incredibly beautiful. Never mind!).

You don't *believe* me, I know, but I do feel frightfully flat. Oh God! you don't *know*. I want, plainly, to sit & smile for a month & feel for that month – in heaven – Oh, you'll never see how one needs that. So I shan't worry you: I shan't violently propose to you: I shan't suddenly weep upon you: I shan't haul you into a wood & make a scene because you're so extremely bloody. In fact, I'll be far less beastly, if less amusing, than the Rupert you used to know. I only want to be about sometimes. Because your presence is so amazing. Will that do – for a

---

1 Rupert and Noel had met the previous day at the studio of sculptor Jacob Epstein (1880–1959), at 72 Cheyne Walk. During June the public were invited there to view his latest work, a monumental carved tomb for Oscar Wilde, which was soon to take its place in the Parisian cemetery Père Lachaise. However, the French authorities took exception to the work, which depicted a naked winged male, and kept it covered with a tarpaulin, despite angry protests by many artists and writers, until 1914.

month? You give so much – perhaps you'll even give life again – or belief or whatever it is –

Oh I *do* believe now, that you're fine & wonderful & what you seem – & *not* a woman. – You're Noel: you *must* be: it overwhelms me that it's true, when one sees you . . .

What's absurd is that you can tolerate me. But I'm going astonishedly to assume you *can* – till you tell me you can't: for you *do* – it seems –

Nonsense again, you'll think. – But I'm not certain what you think about me. I only know what you are worth to me . . .

Isn't there *anything* I give you or can give you? I long so to be some good to you –

Oh, perhaps it's feeble to look at it that way. It's much sensibler just to batten on you, selfishly.

But how can one cure shame, self-contempt?

Noel, Noel, Noel, anyhow understand that, that I'm able to understand a lot, and ready to do anything in the world for you – & that I'm resting for a month –

You're amazing & incredible. It must be a dream that you exist – or anyhow that you can behave towards me as you do – Perhaps not – I suppose you can't properly understand my shame before you: Not so much because you don't know what I'm like as because you don't know what you're like – Glorious Noel! –

Do you object to my fussiness? Poor old Noel! But, after all, we're living & it's all very important. But I won't worry you – child.

I'm tired, after the excitement of coming back: but frightfully contenteder than I've been for so long. I play tennis, very badly: & lie about . . . I like being here – the smells & feelings of summer bring things back – oh God. England's so nice: & the summer. Norton[2] & Gerald Shove[3] are here . . . There's just a touch of the atmosphere I don't like about them – You know? But I'm coming to Limpsfield –

with love
Rupert

---

2 Henry T.J. Norton (1886–1937), mathematician, who had been elected to The Apostles in 1906. At Cambridge, 'Harry' became one of Lytton Strachey's closest friends and in 1918 Strachey dedicated *Eminent Victorians* 'to H.T.J.N.'. He later became one of the fictitious admirers that Margery convinced herself she had.

3 Gerald Frank Shove (1887–1947), an economist from King's, in whose house Rupert and a small group of fellow Apostles were staying, including G. Lowes Dickinson and Eddie Marsh. He had been a member of the Cambridge Fabian Society Committee, together with Rupert, Ka, Margery and Francis Cornford. In 1915 he married the poet Fredegond Maitland (1889–1949), who was a cousin of the Stephens, and in 1945 was appointed Reader in Economics at Cambridge.

                                                    Grantchester.

July [Postmark 12 July 1912]

Monday night.

The shock came when, having paced wonderingly through the garden
& round my room, recognizing, nothing, remembering, I mounted to
my attic bedroom, & there were the two chairs, the table, the feather-
bed, and, alone on the mantel piece largely framed, serene as if we
hadn't parted even for six hours, – you!
    I fairly broke down.
    It's so queer. All the books are here, you know. And I didn't know
they *really* existed. – It suddenly joins on, July & December. When I
went away from here, it was rather cold, but fine. There'd been a week's
feverish work at the dissertation. Oh, and before that *The Magic Flute*, &
the Sunday you were here – a hundred complications with you, & after
you'd gone I flung myself on the floor of that bathing-hovel & cried for
an hour. I couldn't quite make out why, then; though I discovered a
fortnight later by the Thames & in the Moulin D'or.
    But when I left here, I didn't know I was going to slash at all these
ties, – with such incredible pain. I didn't foresee Ka & all the horror; &
illness; & Germany – I was that Rupert. And now I'm this – July &
December *don't* really link up. There's a discontinuity.
    So I struggle about, trying to get in touch with myself.
    When I arrived, I wandered out onto the lawn, waiting for supper.
On the lawn, in the still light of the evening, I saw a figure in a chair,
writing, at the little table. He had bare feet. His hair was fair & long &
he kept putting his hand through it. What he was writing was not a
letter: for there were several sheets, & he wrote on at an even pace – it
must be Literature. He was dressed in grey.
    It slowly came upon me that it was *I* at the table. I'd probably been
here all the year, writing & wandering about. But who, or what had
been in London & Lulworth & Cannes & Munich & Rugby & Berlin?
Who was it watching myself from the window, then? Was it again I?
Which was the chief I? Was there to be a fight? – At that moment the
figure looked round. It was – he'd always modelled himself on me so
much, – of course, Antony.[1]

---

1 Cyril Anthony Neeve, the son of Henry and Florence Neeve, Rupert's landlords at the Old Vicarage.

I've bathed. It seemed to wash off a good deal. I do no work. And I'm terrified of being alone long. But I rest.

I've made a vow *some* when to bathe again in that clean rocky place in Devonshire. It was cleaner than elsewhere in the world, & it is made holy because your naked body has been in it. Perhaps I can get clean, if I bathe there again.

[. . .]

My mother has written me a financial letter, limiting me to £100 a year, & making out I've had £72 already. So I live on £28 till January.

I'm so eager for a moment's Camp – in August if you're back: or in September. *Do* keep it in mind, child.

Denham Russell-Smith is dead. That doesn't mean anything to you? It makes me gloomy[2] –

Limpsfield is the only thing that does me good. I hope Bryn's inside is all right.

"with love"

Rupert

Be good.

[The Champions,
Limpsfield.]

In bed.
Saturday evening [13 July 1912]

Dear Rupert

I've been wanting to write, but I expected a letter from you, and couldn't risk their crossing – that is always so "tedious". So I tried

---

2 Denham Russell-Smith had been a friend of Rupert's at Rugby. It was with him that Rupert had his first, and probably only, homosexual sex. They slept together on 31 October 1909, in Rupert's room at The Orchard, mainly, Rupert later admitted to James Strachey, 'to see what it was *like*, and to do away with the shame (as I thought it was) of being a virgin'. He goes on to describe the experience in detail, concluding that, since then, 'I felt a curious private tie with Denham himself. So you'll understand it was . . . with a sort of dreary wonder and dizzy discomfort – that I heard Mr Benians inform me, after we'd greeted, that Denham died at one o'clock on Wednesday morning – just twenty-four hours ago.' Letter to James Strachey, 10 July 1912, quoted in *The Neo-Pagans* by Paul Delany, pp. 78–80.

to be reasonable, & wrote a confused letter to that Adrian, a blunt thing, mostly a muddle, and I *cant* tell whether it will do him any good, or whether its an awful mistake; its so difficult to do the right thing in cold blood, I almost thought I oughtn't to meddle with him at all, with my silly *sorryness* & absurd *pity*, I ought to simply hate him passionately & let that direct the whole thing; these wise reasonings are insane.[1]

Then I wrote to James; which was more fun; he is at any rate, not a loony. Bryn & I are trying very hard to contrive a ten days with him in Scotland – he'll have a wee house up there in Septembre, & it might be very nice. It wouldn't, I think, do away with chances for camp: – there'd sure to be some one week-end left to rush off in a boat on a river, or the sea. My Wa [Mother] will be gone by then and it would be a pleasant thing to have a final breezer before turning in with Ethel for the winter.

Well, well, I dont know what I'm going to write about; 't'll be a chatty letter, I guess, if we're not careful.

You poor Rupert, looking about in Grantchester! I read Bryn how you met Mr Neves on your arrival, and she was very much touched: she said you always did make her so sorry for you, your unhappiness was so convincing. Mudie[2] & I sneered (perhaps Mudie didnt). But even I am begining to recognise some of your life. I find I've a very clear idea of how its been going along for the last two or three years, it may be a totally mistaken idea; but it arose out of your letters & what you sometimes tell; and it seems to hang together so well that I'm actually begining to believe in a little of it. May sound daft – never mind, its a great change, I tell you; because I've probably been going since birth just *not* believing in peoples' existences (you gave that atitude a philosophic title once; in a train on the way from the New Forest, to Somerset for us & Swanage for you.)

Monday Morning (Yea, even before breakfast!)
At last, it appears, I am adopting your scrap method of writing.

You mustn't take on so about our having hooked in Hugh [Popham]. They say you had Lowes Dickinson, surely he was a pleasure – & not difficult to entertain; he cant have fallen through too? We had to have him, Margery was determined. She exclaimed vehemently the

---

1 Leonard Woolf writes this account of how Adrian Stephen behaved when they lived together at 38 Brunswick Square: 'Adrian was extremely lethargic and critical. Unless pushed into it by Virginia or me, he rarely did anything but sit in a large armchair reading . . . Then he fell in love with Noel and became still more passive, inert, depressed, and aloof when he was rejected by her.' *Letters of Leonard Woolf*, ed. Frederic Spotts (London: Weidenfeld & Nicolson, 1990), p. 531.
2 This was Margery's nickname in the family.

other day "I do wish Bryn wd marry Hugh!" & then there was no diverting her, but he must come here at once, & it was carried through, tho' we all objected a little, and mother quite deffinitely. He's just gone off, with Bryn accompanying him to the station, and one of my cigars to cheer him in the train. He's been very agreeable; you'd better have him next week end.

Gracious! how can you talk so of darkness & no hope – you ridiculous thing; you go on too long. Life cant still be all against you, and its not fair to pretend & bemoan. If Grantchester is a better place than Limpsfield, just now; wa! it should be pleasant to be there. No, but I do see (as I was saying) that youve had a very trying time (you smile – & bow graciously?)

I think I never shall understand what you mean by "horrors", nor how you can feel such strong things (or say them) against Ka. Oh I didnt dare talk about her to you, incase you should get furious; but still I cant understand *a bit* what you – not only you, but Gwen & Jaques – can find so wrong in her. Your words are all vague and so tempestuous that they bewilder. You'll think me mad, (& its in case I am that I'm confessing (you might help – and anyhow you should know)) but its the same old difficulty; to begin with I cant see that she's done anything wicked – all this about awful things – what is it? And secondly, of course, since whatever she's done doesn't seem to have spoiled her – why should you all disapprove so? If its made her wretched, one just feels sorry that she is; or if its made you wretched – one feels sorry for you. La! this is not supposed to be an explanation of righteous feelings; I dont know whether they're good or bad, perhaps they are pernicious. Its only to show how far away I am from understanding what seems so clear to all of you. Perhaps I oughtn't to bother you about it? But I cant bear blank misunderstanding; & I want to grasp that part of you too.

I'm a fiend to tease so. Dont be worried by it. I'm sorry for having so dull a sympathy.

Did His Excellency show how pleased he was to meet you in the N[ational] L[iberal] C[lub]? He said you were the only fresh & pleasant-looking person there, & he seemed really to have been touched by the sight of James too, he admires his phisique so! Theres a little beast, found in Australia, a kind of Lemure or a cross between that & a degenerate monkey, with silky fur & small round face: its eyes are very large for seing in the dark and it goes about by night; the people call it the "Night Walker". All this Father compares to James. I expect that its quite a little beast with a rare, shrill cry. (Now *you*, be silent! This is for *your* amusement *only*.)

I shall soon have to go & finish my riding breeches – which I make – (I've had breakfast) We're all living together again, that Ursula [Cox] has come back, and its a womanly household.[3]

Lord! Margery is pale as tallow and her eyes still look suspicious & desperate & affraid; she has quarreled again *furiously* with Bryn (B was furious too) and she & her Ladyship are on – au fond – rotten bad terms; for three days there was open hostility between them, now its better, as they sometimes rag. Bryn I – of course – still find very pleasant; but its true she isnt the best thing in the world for Mudie; Besides the above *furious* encounter, there are constant slight bouts, which Topsy (Ursula) keeps from becoming serious by determined & impartial humour. Most of these things go on in their bath-room, so I only hear echos. Margery's got your way of looking at people on the brain; all that about the hards & softs (ridiculous!) unfortunately she carries it even further than you, and goes about smelling out people, who say things on purpose to hurt other peoples feelings, and when she's found them, she determinedly dislikes them (which again, is going further than you). If such atitudes constitute softness (was she an example?) Bryn is certainly not – soft – & softness is not deffinitely good, as opposed to deffinitely bad hardness (which I was affraid of). Well, I'm still a beast. But I do *disapprove* of the old Mudie, I could bear all, if only she would *behave*, but no – and disapproval will out. Better when were all away.

                    Write, injured Rupert!
                    (love from)   (why "with love"?)
                         Noel.

You're *very* nice!

---

3 Noel's cousin Ursula, known as Topsy, had been staying in Moscow with the Ertel family, who were friends of the Garnetts.

[Grantchester]

Friday morning [19 July 1912]

Dear one,
[. . .]
Your great letter improves, even, on acquaintance. I've read it over innumerable times. It seems extraordinarily nice. Oh Lord, it lures one into all the old illusions about you – your character, mental power, & God knows what nonsense – that I thought I'd grown out of. Perhaps they're true. –

Anyway, contemplation of you (from here) makes me extraordinarily happy. I've such a lot to say to you – about general & about particular things – I could talk for a week: – all quite happily.

(I'm not going to pretend I approve of your attitude to Margery –)

– Oh, one thing. I'll not have you think a moment longer that I've been miserable these last three years – (you say you at length see what my state of mind has been.) I know now. I've been happy, & splendid. I'll expand that one day. Let it stand summed now: that I've been happy & splendid.

Justin's going to Maynard's tomorrow for a week: & James thinks of next week-end. I wonder if you & Bryn'll be sick at Justin's appearing? I'm doubtful about James. Will he be waiting for the slightest sign of intimacy between you & me, to make himself wretched with? Ought he to come?

I hope you're thinking out a scheme for including a decent camp, early as possible. I'm going to hold you like a Jew to your word (or beyond it –) I guess you'll have to go to James during the end of August. I'll leave him earlier than I meant: to oblige you –

I'm so undecided about Adrian. I hover & fret & flinch about your affairs most awfully. (Oh, I insist on doing so!) It seems *remarkably* important about you. I expect your letter to him was, as a matter of fact, extraordinarily nice. –

Oh dear. Perhaps you were right to begin with. Right by chance. You see, Noel, my dear, what I – desiring you to be perfect – found amiss, was that your action wasn't *dictated* by the best admixture of reason, instinct, & desire for good. You may have chosen the right course. But I wanted you also to choose it for the right *reasons* – I expect your instinct (of hatred, you say) ought to decide the main course. But your humanity ought to decide the way it's to be carried out. Isn't that right? – I think, indeed, that there's more chance of you harming James than Adrian. – But I'd have you, in putting Adrian away, do it as fairly & decently as possible –

Oh damn it, you *are* extraordinarily "decent" (as Dudley'ld say). Only – you're ignorant, aren't you?, of some things. And human – Don't, that's the main thing, have the Adrian business hanging on, & over you, & a permanent irritation. Frankly, but oh! *kindly*, cut the rope. – That's it, what I'm tediously wanting (what impudence!) to preach to you. You talk of your "pity", & "sympathy" (& dislike them) as sources of action – No, don't do it out of *pity*: do it out of *kindness*. And have done with it. There's such a difference – sympathy & pity are bad when you hate, aren't they? I'm very confused about it all. I'm only clear that I painfully want your good.

I've sympathy with you – you can't think how! & less kindness – that only in so far as its part of my love for you – Sympathy with you is all right: & so lovely – Oh my dear, I'm muddled, I'm afraid. I'd get clearer, verbally, perhaps –

"With love" – did I explain? – was my idea of a joke. It might have meant almost anything. A quotation, perhaps. From my letters last year? Or, – "that's what's being put in letters, these days," Or that I'm too feeble a creature for my feelings to have such a name, except in joke. Or – almost anything you like.

[. . .]

Dearest, I'll write about Ka, or talk. You *mustn't* be afraid to ask me, because of my perhaps being stormy or absurd . . . It's such an insult to me. It's incredible how it hurts.

> with, you know, love
> Rupert

I enclose Mr Max Beerbohm's ballade on their Majesties. It may amuse you – [1]

---

1 Rupert had been introduced to the caricaturist and writer Max Beerbohm (1872–1956) by Frances Darwin on 24 May 1908, and thought him 'a quaint little person'. (*LRB*, p. 130) 'The Ballade Tragique a Double Refrain', in which a lady and gentleman of the court argue over who is duller, the King or the Queen, is said to have delayed Beerbohm's knighthood for twenty years.

Dudley and Rupert on the Cam.

Ethel Pye and Noel, at Buckler's Hard, 1910.

Rupert at Buckler's Hard.

Jacques Raverat in 1910.

Clifford Bridge, Devon, 1911.

Noel, Maitland Radford, Virginia Stephen and Rupert.

Geoffrey Keynes and Daphne.

Bryn and Justin Brooke.

Ka, drawn by Henry Lamb at Lulworth, January, 1912.

Bryn after her engagement to Hugh Popham, 1912.

James Strachey with Loge
(above) and Lytton Strachey
(below), in Scotland,
1913.

Canoeing expedition on the Severn, July 1913. Paul Montague, Bryn
and Hugh Popham, Daphne, Harold Hobson and Bunny.

Camp at Brandon near the River Ouse, August 1913.

Vanessa Bell

Adrian Stephen and Daphne.

Noel.

Duncan Grant.

Maynard Keynes.

Noel with her first child, Benedict, in 1924.

[Crown Hotel]
Everleigh[1]

Monday evening [29 July 1912]

I had tea, sat a little, walked four miles alone, changed – I don't know what the time is, or where anybody is. There seems nothing to do but write to you. I'm deadly tired.

At one time I swore not to write to you for six weeks. But I can't do that. I must write.

It's so damned full of you, this place. There are spots where we walked, the lawn where I saw you in so many attitudes, all you, – there's this room – why shouldn't you swing round the door now? – you did yesterday, this morning, the day before yesterday.

It's come down on me again a little – the horrible feeling that I *must* be in a dream – that I've only got to say or do something – if I only knew *what!* – to wake & find the world good. I had it yesterday & this morning. It must be some grim nightmare – all the pain. It cleared off while you were in the summer house – then there was only the knowledge that you *were* present, & the greediness of snatching at the moments.

Oh Noel if you knew the sick dread with which I face tonight – that bed, & those dragging hours – And the pointlessness of tomorrow, the horror that it might just as well be this evening, or Wednesday, for all the pleasure, or relief from pain, I get out of it.

The procession of hopeless hours – That's what's so difficult to face; – that's why one wants to kill oneself.

It's all swept over me. These last few days: & so much stronger & more certain than before – and rather different, too. It seems deeper & better – oh, I can't explain it all.

I thought I was empty forever, – though even from Berlin, in early May, I knew & wrote that you were, in the end, the most important thing in the world for me – but now, it has come back, clear. Into a battered & ill me, – perhaps that's why I'm worse to you than I need be.

Oh, Noel, Noel, Noel, my dearest; think! Remember all that has been! It's more than four years since that evening in Ben Keeling's rooms, & the days on the river – when we were so swiftly in love.

---

1 Maynard Keynes had organized a house party at this small hotel by Salisbury Plain. His guests included Rupert, Noel, Bryn, Daphne, James, Justin and Gerald Shove. During the day there was horse riding and croquet tournaments, and the evenings were passed with readings from Jane Austen.

Remember those days on the river; and the little camp at Penshurst, next year, – moments then; & Klosters; and the Beaulieu camp; & one evening by that great elm clump at Grantchester; & bathing in early morning by Oxford; & the heights above Clifford Bridge camp; & a thousand times when we've gone hand in hand – as no other two people could; – & twice this year I felt your tears, Noel's tears, on my hand. There are such things, such things that bind us. Half what you have grown to be, is my making: half of what I am is yours. It's in the meeting of our hands, & lips, child. You *must* know it –

I cannot live without you. I cannot indeed. You can make anything of me – For you I'll do anything, or make myself anything – anything in the world. – Oh god, but it's killing work, waiting alone all these agonizing hours & days & weeks –

You must see what we are, child – I cannot live without you. – But remember, I'm not only in love with you; I'm very fond of you –

Goodnight, child – in the name of our love

Rupert

Send your Swiss Hotel's name

SONG

All suddenly the wind comes soft,
   And Spring is here again;
And the hawthorn quickens with buds of green,
   And my heart with buds of pain.

My heart all Winter lay so numb,
   The earth so dead and frore,
That I never thought the Spring would come,
   Or my heart wake any more.

But Winter's broken and earth has woken,
   And the small birds cry again;
And the hawthorn hedge puts forth its buds,
   And my heart puts forth its pain.

[Everleigh]

Thursday night. [1 August 1912] In Bed.

O child, I'm so miserable.

Tomorrow Justin (who has his car here) is going to drive me to Ka's. I'm going to walk out, lunch somewhere with her, talk; & take a train on to Rugby.

You see, it's no good putting it off. One can't go on waiting & waiting. It's a horrible strain on her. We decided, when she left Berlin, to wait a month or two, till we – especially I – were better & healthy & sane, & then see – see if I loved her, if we should marry. Well, its's no good going on. I don't & can't love her. Things have begun to come back into that numb dank place that is the abode of my feelings: but not love for her. I couldn't ever live with her, I know – from experience even. I should go mad, or kill her, in a few months. And – I love someone else.

We've got to part. I suppose she really knows that by now. But I've got to tell her, tomorrow.

It's the terror & pain of this – of ending all that was between Ka & me, & of hurting her so much – that I find unbearable just now. I can't think of anything else.

Noel, Noel, there's love between you & me, & you've given me such kindness & such sympathy – in your own Noel way – I'm wanting your presence so much – I'm leaning on you, at this moment, – stretching towards you. You don't know how. I do suck help from you, child; your hands & face, & mind.

I'll give you everything in the world, when you want it – Give me sympathy & love & understanding now (These words are hollow bloody damned dreary pompous things – but read them right) – Understand – you can – Don't, for God's sake, take it all wrong, & pick out things to hate me for –

Oh, even that's evil – I know I'm safe – on things I can't express . . . four years. It's Noel I'm resting on – telling all this to, now.

You see, child – Noel – there's been so much between Ka & me. We've been so close to one another, naked to each other in our good parts & bad. She knows me better than anyone in the world, – better than you let yourself know me – than you care to know me. And we've given each other great love & infinite pain – and that's a terrible, unbreakable bond. And I've had her.

It's agony, *agony* tearing out part of one's life like that – You see, I have an ocean of love & pity for her. You don't understand that, you talked of my "steeling" myself towards her . . . I don't. I don't hate & despise her – By God, I'm infinitely far from it. She did once what I, you know, thought & think a mixture of a filthy ghastly mistake & an evil crime. I've "forgiven" that ages ago – the word "forgiven" sounds, I swear, as ridiculous to me as it does to you. It doesn't exist – I'd give anything to do Ka good. Only . . . she killed somethings in me. I can't love her, or marry her –

She's been astonishingly, breakingly, good to me. And she's the bravest person I ever knew or imagined – And tomorrow I've got to tell her – to say goodbye. It's almost impossible – Oh, I'm so sick at heart.

I wish to God you were here –

Noel child, I wish to God, too, you could either understand, or trust me. I *didn't* make the whole fuss out of "horridness" – One doesn't break oneself up & suffer weeks & months of ceaseless torture merely to be 'horrid' – to show one's grumpy nature. I've been in Hell. Nothing can ever happen nearly so bad again. I might kill myself for you – but it'd all be clean pain. – Oh isn't it anything, even, that I saved Ka – as she said – from such utter shame that she would have killed herself – saved her by my pain & love. You may disagree with us – but can't you admit of our point of view being right – & see that I've bewilderedly acted & suffered at least as an ordinary decent person, judged by decent standards. Oh, Noel, I wish I hadn't been through all these seven bloody months, merely to result in you thinking me a little more 'horrid' as a result – Trust, Trust, if you *can't* see everything –

Hush! I must go to sleep now. And then, horrible tomorrow. Will you believe that I'm going to be as kind to Ka, as possible? Your last letter to me ended "You're *very* nice" – so you *may* believe it

Let me know, sometime, what you're doing.

Goodnight, I love you so. I'm better for having written to you –

I love you –

Rupert

Hotel Blumlisalp
Griesalp
Kiental
Berner Oberland.

[2 August 1912]

Mon pauvre Vieux!

You'll be twenty five before this reaches you, and that will make you more forlorne than ever. When they read my character in childhood (it was old Garnett, of course; so perhaps it doesn't count) they said: "Heart – hard. Hard as nails!" I grinned with pride, and never forgot. and people sans heart – or hard – they also say (the world – not E[dward].G[arnett].) can never really understand the other people. But we can see something, a little, even we with atrophied feelings & peu de cervel.[1] I see this much: – But la! what help a list of

---

1 Peu de cervelle – little brains.

what I see. It is so much of what you feel, that when I am absorbed in it, when I happen to drop into your position – as remembering your voice expressing it, or reading your letter, I become as hope-less as you, seing no chance of any good, unless you marry me, see that it is grey and a horrible waste, the ghastliest thing: a mistake, if that vague thing – the *chance* that we should once be together & confidant – should suddenly, quite deffinitely be abolished. If all these times that we have known one another have helped build up such possibility and have depended on it, then they help now to make dreariness, becuase you were depending on them, & they turn out to be – what? (But here I cant see any more from you – my own very deffinite belief in the good of the times we've had sways you). But I think you are stranded somehow – quite what did it, I dont know; there has been a hope disappointed, & a certainty of clear good outraged. So you can say nothing but arguments & complaints, and do nothing but bemoan. And clearly you can take no joy in the other things which still go on. O, I hope they dont irritate you beyond endurance. I'm sure that you must keep up, plunge a bit & then get another footing. I know you will ultimately be strong to deal with all this nonsense: la Vie – pah!

I'm wretched & perplexed (tho' I still eat well – go about with cheerful mien) that it should be me who has failed you so horribly. I could curse & bully any other person & so get some satisfaction. But I see that I am right too; and that there should be any inevitable cause for this horror – oh so intensifies it. My dear I would be tortured in revenge for it, but I could not prevent it. It is so strong, the feeling that I mustn't marry you. It has grown up for years; side by side with the things that bind us (which you wrote of) other moments came, making me more & more sure that I didnt love. I saw nothing to hate, which you could possibly change, it was the mean in me, which picked out bit by bit, parts of you – deffinitely & unalterably yours – to find fault with & ultimately to hate. If you knew the littleness of these components of dislike, you couldnt understand that they should count so, they are things which ought not to be noticed – not allowed consideration – You would be right, because you are bigger than I am. But I cant put aside the nigglyness in myself, it has the greatest power over me, to ruin any good I could have to do with, & to cause the utterest misery, since I should know it was meanness winning: It could defile all the splendour you brought near me. That would be the worst. That shalnt ever be allowed to happen.

Rupert you mustnt die or go mad, or be dreary, just because Noel is romantic & petty – surely *now* you see how petty. You pass it, dispise it and go on. Its too miserable to be allowed to hurt you. I am so ashamed and so sorry that you thought I was at all tolerable. I know that my existence is shocking. I am too disgusting to go about at all, to be capable of hurting good people.

I muttered about it before. Tie pins & a profession are all I'm fit for. Tie pins for affection (Lord, it has led me astray!) and medicine for raison d'etre. With those I shall achieve all the happiness I am capable of. The better things need passion: and passion is not latent in me, it never grew there – at best I mourn it.

Bless me! what stuff that is that I wrote yesterday. You may as well see it all, it probably signifies something. Today it didn't rain & rain & rain & the mist didnt come filtering in through the thin walls of the pension to make everything cold & pale. But we went sweating up the hills to the top cow shed, where the woman who makes cheese sold us milk. Daphne & Mother were very jolly & wallowed in a rain puddle they found settled out of sight on a mound; we slept a little & got sunstrokes & then came back. All day the incoherentest thoughts about you went in & out, and now its evening, you've become a more important thing. I dont know *what* to write; I want to explain & talk to you, to try & make you dispise me yet not hurt you & make you angry or wretched. If only my letter could send you to sleep soundly for a week, so that when you got up you would be so vigorous that you could do anything alone, and live in the finest way, never wanting anyone to help you.

But that, I imagine, wont sound ideal to you.

It's a sad thing that I cant suggest anything which you could use. You are so unwilling to face away the pain – you refuse to subdue anything in you harshly & doggedly, and you despise the knack of putting aside & deliberately forgetting (even tho' you cant do any of those things). Once you can see through this nightmare you'll see what infinite good is left for you, worth your living to be a hundred for. I'll leave you alone. It probably wont do me much harm, for you to stop pandering to my flat affection – it should never have counted.

I cant be coherent.

You *must* wake up.

from. Noel.

August. 3rd.

In the train.

Saturday – [3 August 1912]

Today I'm twenty-five.

It was Hell yesterday.
I wish to God you were in England; that I might talk to you.
It is inconceivable that two people should be able to hurt each other so much as Ka & I. I've left her in such agony. It is terrible. Ka was fine. She might have been bitter – one is, after a strain. But she wasn't.
And she's an amazingly honest person – I hope she'll gradually get better. She talks wildly, now. But everything passes. She's unfortunately going to live in London all the autumn – But with luck we shan't meet – I may have to write again, to clear up points. Otherwise, it's all over –
Wednesday. I just let this slide for four days, in a stupor. – Also, I thought I might hear of your address. I suppose I'll send it to Limpsfield. Will it get any further? I'm in Birmingham again, for the dentist in the station where I once sat for hours, trying to meet your train. Of course, it never passed through Birmingham. What a woman!
I go tomorrow to the Gilbert Murrays at
        Beckhythe Manor
            Overstrand
                Norfolk
Ka keeps insisting that we must marry. But it won't do. She wavers, at present at one moment she said I must marry somebody soon, – if not her, I must marry you. At another, she wanted me not to see you for some time, so that I might relove her . . . She's in a bad way. It half kills me every time I think of her – I'm extraordinarily miserable. I'm going to see Frances Cornford tomorrow. She's the only person who can help Ka. I – that's the bloody horror of it – can't. And the sort of friends she has – James, or Virginia, – are useless: mere takers.
Oh but I sometimes wish I could see you, child. I think I've become a coward. I think I'm a coward about life. And I've noticed it today at the dentists. Last year I had a tooth out – it took hours & inflicted incredible pain – & I fairly tumbled the poor man over by my courage. This year I found myself shivering & wincing before he touched me – It's bloody having all one's nerve gone. –
That's dreary soliloquy.

I sometimes wonder if, being so romantic, you despise & dislike me for being whining, despondent, uneasy, glum, silly – miserable, for – oh, a year perhaps: & a year's all that children's memories can reach back. I'll be more competent when I get out of this bog . . . You don't, or won't, understand me though. You can't imagine how infinitely more I feel pains & pleasures than ordinary people. It's despicable: I'm rather proud of it. I feel a million times more than – so & so. Yet I'm really far stronger. One day you'll quite suddenly see – Never mind – Oh God, I wish I could get straight –

Write, child, once. In your letters you sometimes seem to like me. You did last time you wrote . . .

with love
Rupert

I love you so.

c/o Gilbert Murray
Beckhythe Manor
Overstrand
Norfolk

Friday night – [9 August 1912]

Child,

It's so hard writing to you.

And if I spill ink on Lady Murray's sheets, what'll she say to me?

Your letter, found here today – yes, it's incoherent, but, I understand some. And it's very you.

It's rather hard luck getting a letter like that one's first day on a visit to strange people. It's fairly harrowed me all day. They must think me horrible. I'm tired anyway.

I spent most of yesterday talking to Frances. She's Ka's only decent real friend: she's good, &, not being a virgin, she understands things. She wants me to go abroad for a year – to Australia or somewhere, & work manually. It'd be better for Ka, she thinks. For Ka's very desperate just now: & a year's wait'd mean strength & calmness to her. Of course, my answer'd be the same – But she'd be able to stand it then –

It'd be better for me: because I might get well again, she thinks.
And, of course, I could assure her it wouldn't matter a damn to *you*.
I might do that. Or I might merely go off till January – or I might
stay – I don't know what to do. One thing is, I'm frightened of leaving
you in that bloody place London. I'm afraid of evil coming to you. Your
friends are a bloody useless & poisonous lot – your friends & mine. I'd
rather be where I can help.[1]

Sunday
You've different ways of dealing with love, you & Ka. They're both
pretty deadly. It seems to me a bit of hard luck, knowing you both. Your
letter does make it hard to go on existing. I'm not doing any work or
making any plans. I seem to have got beyond it.

Noel, you have done me wrong. You owe me something. Oh,
Child, how could a person like you sit down & pick out little
things ——

The following Sunday
You'll see, I find it hard to write this letter. I've tried several times: but
always been too tired, or something.

I've got you to acknowledge "splendour", now. That's something!
– for an unimaginative & forgetful person like you. Oh God; they could
be doubled & multiplied & perpetuated & other things wiped away, –
if you but would. It's such madness – you <u>do</u> like me so. I've – oh, quite
recent letters! – to prove it!

Oh, child, Noel, what *do* you want of me? What would you have
me? I can be anything with your desire & demand: & so wastingly
nothing without you. Do you want eminence or money? They're the
easiest things in the world. So you want liberty? You should have utter
liberty. Are you tired of decency & do you want brutality? I could give it
you, as much as you could swallow & more. Or strength? or
kindliness? Or, being a woman, is it filth you're pining for? I assure you,
there's no lack in me.

Oh, what *is* it, Noel! You must tell me. Is it that you want, before
you retire from modern virginity, to enjoy flirting & having James &
Adrian & the rest dangling dolefully round . . . ? You can get all that,
married if you wish.

---

1 Writing later to Dudley, Rupert says: 'I daren't leave Noel for a year . . . Females are fools – virgin
females. And the ideas about "sex" in all these circles are, as you know, monstrously false.' He adds that
if she were ever seduced, 'That would kill me.' (*KCA*, 27 August 1912)

"Petty". Oh, my dear, you see, I know you so well. And I know you're not petty. "Affection for tie-pins" may be your line. But then you do it – or so one madly fancies – so supremely. One desires, above all else in the world, to be recognized as chief tie-pin. We have different ways, it may be true, you & I. But I don't want you to love my way. God forbid! I know what you're like; & it's that I want: "pettiness" & all.

You must. You must. We may not end & mar everything here. It's so easy to see what's happened. What generally happens is that people fall, romantically, in love. On the impetus of that they get over the difficulties, & marry. And then that goes, & changes, & marriage produces a different sort of love, which supports it. We were in love, & we didn't marry. And with knowledge & long companionship that love changed & ceased; & as we've not married the other hasn't come. What a bungle to have made; when you think what's at stake! But it would come, you see.

Oh child, there's too much binding us together. If it tears, it drags away everything from me –

I could do & be anything, everything, with you. – Oh God the things I could write & make & do. I know it.

But now I can do nothing, nothing. All my vitality turns in on itself, & wastes me.

I must see you: whether I go away or not. But certainly if I go away. Oh Noel, how could I leave you in this bloody place for a year? I'm rather desperate.

Will you come somewhere in September? I'll get myself under control, & behave decently! And it may be good. Camping – with fires & the open – has been good, hasn't it. It would be fine to get that again –

Answer about this.

I go on Tuesday to c/o   Justin
                              Leylands
                              Wotton
                              Dorking
                              Surrey
for a few days.

You could say, if we met, what you thought about my retiring to California. And how much you'd welcome the respite –

yours as you left him,

Rupert

Auf der Multhornhütte
Berner Oberland.

August 19th. [1912]

Dear Rupert

I'm so affraid of letters crossing; but of course they will and I shouldn't have been such a donkey as to write to you at Grantchester. When you get it I shall probably have regretted all thats in it; – every day I wish something more of it unwritten. All your letters, one two three came after it had gone and they made it clear that such grim argumentation had not been what you would like best. If you can disregard the stupid feeling-lessness of it, it may be some use, for at any rate its true as far as it goes. But I'm ashamed that it wasn't more amiable for you going about England so sad.

I wish I could help now, but what can I do for you from here? I think, that in England I would be miraculously kind and could talk to you so well and so long that you would accept everything & rejoice in it. But I cant persuade you in a letter that you *are* strong & that you *can* prevent these incomprehensible feelings of yours from torturing you. You mustn't put it down to week nerves & just slide into unresisting agony. You must know, as well as anyone, that nerves wont harden through inexertion. Lord! I could shake you, and stroke you for your folornness, because you're wrong and pathetic.

Ka's probably right: that you ought to marry someone, she understands you. But if you cant, if there's no one that you can or will marry now, dont become dotty, like Margery is supposed to be, you *must* be able to do something to keep alive; without that. Be fine again, & dont spoil whats left by fury.

I was so sorry when I heard that you'd let James anoy you and had discarded his holiday; he should be the last person to be taken offence with.

In the train to France. *Thursday.*
And then I couldn't struggle on any more. Daphne & I were making a last effort at a Hochtur[1] before we left the wretched drizzling place. We telephoned for a guide and he came at a great speed from Kanderstey over the mountains: the next morning he led us off early up the valley

---

1 An alpine tour.

to a glacier at its head, there we were roped & went up it partly in deep snow; at the top it ended sharp like the crest of a wave and we could see over onto the huge rolling plateau of snow where we had got to find our hut. There were ridges of rock and one or two peaks sticking up out of the white, and at two corners, the ground sloped away as glaciers & broke into the valleys.

Before we had trudged as far as the hut, it began to snow, and that lasted all the rest of the day all night & all next day. We established ourselves inside & never ventured out, except once to try & see a view from the highest ridge of snow – we saw nothing but mist, until we left to come home.

A man & wife & their little boy were living in the place. He cooked for us and she did nothing except hug her son occasionally and grin a good deal: they were a healthy lot. The small boy played dominoes or farming among the mountains on the lower bunk with toy cows & tobacco bushes and he let anyone who liked play too. It was an agreable life, as long as it lasted. Very soon the feeling of being established there crept on, and we could feel almost hospitable to the other parties of people, twos & threes, who staggered in cold & drenched from time to time. Two Englishmen were dragged in almost fainting by their hardened old guide; they could talk no German, & were feverish because so weak, so they shouted at him & nudged him to attract his attention. The Germans came in parties of four or five and seemed happier; they brought with them soup & meat & wine, and made a great spread on the long table and ate & laughed at it a great while. There were more hardy people too: Members of the Alpine Club or Swiss guides passing over from one valley to another: these went away in the snow storm soon after they had come, only stopping a little while to get warm. And all the while D[aphne] & I sat there watching people, talking to some of them, trying to write or playing on the floor with the little boy. When the crowd got too great, we slunk into the other colder room, reserved for ladies to sleep in, and without a stove. Our guide Johann Ogi brought us food every 2 hours. We got to love him fondly, he was young but very much bent under innumerable ruck-sacs; his chest was hollowed & he coughed very often and spat – please God he wont die of consumption – he had a forehead & eyebrows like Nijinsky's, and as good a smile.

So, we were engrossed and I couldnt find words to write properly. When I got back to Kiental, your letter came, the one in answer to my horror. I must try and answer *it*.

I must send this off quickly, because I want to hear from you, again. I was pleased with Frances Cornford's suggestion, if only you will be able to carry it out! Could manual labour charm you enough, to keep you away a year, far away where you wont see any of the usual friends, nor enter into their ways? But if you go, let it be proper & complete: dont just skip across the chanel and have friends over for week ends and every facility for coming back as soon as you feel enclined. Go so far that there will be a great & dreadful journey between you & England, & bind yourself to some engagement by time so that you must, to keep it, stay away – a year say. And then when you are there let there be hard work, so hard that even if its not very interesting, it must absorbe all the energy you have everyday. I've never succeeded in working – but as far as I got it did seem to hearten one up; & all the other people, the old ones with habits, say its the only supporting thing, like a skeleton; and you havnt proved that theyre wrong – you never worked, except when you worked too hard & died.

You'll think it disagreable of me to so encourage youre going away. But, apart from all the old truths, it would actually be *best* for both this time. I cant help you now, by seing you often, I cant even merely please, I make it more difficult. And I am deadly decided & firm for at least a year to come. You must go and be alone till your feet have grown again, you have toppled from love to love and from circles of friends into other circles too much. Yes you *want* marriage and you almost need it; but you shouldnt have it till you can do without it.

I'm affraid I still keep cold; I dont quite feel enclined to believe you, when you say you feel more strongly than anyone else – you declare it, thats all I have to go by (you may be prejudiced), and even if its true, it makes you a poorer thing than most people if your controlling strength isnt proportionally great; the best one can say for you on that score, is that you're unbalanced!

But I'll come back & talk to you before you go. Do you still want a camp? I'll try & be as nice as possible – yet hope to make you hate me. I could bear that very well. I wish I could change places with Ka, in your feelings; I wish you could see how lowly & meanly I creep compared to her.

But most, I wish you would be happy; you *must* be, quickly. Run away & get well & be happy go among happy people, away from filthy

London & folk with indigestion, go where they'll kick you if you sulk.

O I mustnt write any more. Each time I try to be soothing it turns harsh – not even cheery. Please dont mind it; there is really only one feeling (one or two): the old sluggish affection for you, and now a dull sorrow that I help to hurt you and a wish that I could mend everything. There is bitterness too, but that I cant explain – it means nothing & is ridiculous, it mustnt be noticed when it comes out in writing.

It is better at Prunoy than in Switzerland, with those two very nervous people. Jacques & Gwen must really be far more sensitive, but they dont fuss so. Margery is again having a spell of fine spirits – she has been entranced by kind Radfords & sailing in Cornwal. We get on very well together here; but when I think, I believe we always got on well – it was libel that I was brutal to her – even when fighting (which only happened once) we spoke very friendly words. She never knew all the disapproving disgusts which I expressed to you. When she is nice she is very nice; there is nothing to be jealous of here, and she is happy. She seems triumphant in a quiet way about Bryn & Hugh. She planned it a little, but is suprised at the success I think.

How do you like Bryn to be a married lady in a month?[2] Will you join the feast & riots, which such as Bunny & I are going to insist on?

Recover, recover, recover

Be gentle, be gentle with yourself and be sure to forgive me, if I must make you angry.

from. Noel.

---

2 Bryn had told Rupert when they were staying with Maynard at Everleigh that she was in love with Hugh Popham and intended to marry him that year. Rupert, who had always found Bryn attractive, was seized with jealousy and attempted to lure her away with him for an affair, an offer which she seems to have had no difficulty in turning down. (Cf. *The Neo-Pagans*, Paul Delany, pp. 188–91)

London – Rugby Train.
Wednesday [28 August 1912]

My dear Noel,

The letter which you in collaboration with some clergyman, wrote, reached me chez Geoffrey last night, & hurt a great deal.

It was good of you to write, and (cutting out a lot of stuff about a hut) there was a good deal of it. So, at least I can pride myself on still being a lot of trouble to you.

I have deserved a good deal from you; but I don't think I have ever deserved cleverness, moral cleverness, as in a modern play. "You want marriage and you almost need it; but you shouldn't have it till you can do without it." Do you remember writing that? It must have been very easy, so perhaps you don't. I hope you're ashamed of yourself.

Rugby)
My walking trip with Bryn fell through, owing to her disease.[1] I was left with the alternatives of waiting to see her in London, going on for two days or so to [G. Lowes] Dickinson, & proceeding straight to Scotland where my walking party starts today. But, feeling very ill, I came here. I've had a splitting headache for 30 hours, & in general I feel in far dissolution. I may go on up North in a day or two. I don't know.

I feel it very probable that I shall smash up altogether this autumn. I think a great deal & very eagerly of killing myself, if my present state goes on. I spend an intolerable time in every kind of agony, day after day. I can do no sort of work, reading or writing. If I'm like this, I don't see how I can face camp, – though otherwise I want it very much, & I must certainly see & talk with you sometime.

It's the *waste* that makes me so sick & angry. You are enabled, by initial stupidity and by years of careful & laborious practice, to despise me. There is the extraordinary spectacle of a silly little worm like you thinking me "unbalanced" and "pathetic". So you'll not understand the waste. But I know, & a few more, what I am & can be like. I know how superb my body is, & how great my bodily strength. I know that with my mind I could do anything. I know that I can be the greatest poet and writer in England. Many know it. All these things are there, & ruining

---

1 Bryn had a summer cold.

themselves – tearing themselves away, useless. I could be anything in the world I wanted, with you. And nothing without you.

Camp. I collected the following places.

(1)   The lower Ouse, near Denver, Norfolk; it's broad & one sails. One could sail right out onto the Wash – Flat rather lovely land.

(2)   Porlock, N. Devonshire. Sea sailing.

(3)   The Dart. ditto. Both these lovely places.

(4)   Broads.

(5)   Swaledale, Yorkshire. Moors, a river, waterfalls & great pools (also a tarn.). Wild. (Justin knows it)

If I think I can summon enough power to put illness & pain away & behave at Camp, I will let you know, & then will you say if you will go & where & *when*? – And with whom. My one hope is that, as Camp is always queerly out of the world, wonderful, out of the train of events, I may be able to slide out of this train of agony for it, & live as of old – for those days. Will you let me know when you get back & what you intend to do? I may stay here & go to bed. Or I may go up North to Norton & his aunt. In any case I am prepared for anything, at any time. I will let you know my address, perhaps. But this address is a safe one.

You are rather mistaken about James I didn't "take offence with" him. It had been coming inevitably to this, for months & months. It's complicated & bound up with things you can't understand – . It's part of my new view of things, that I find creatures like that, Stracheys & so forth, not only no good but actually dangerous, spots of decay, menaces to all good. Even if one doesn't mind rats <u>qua</u> rats, one has to stamp out carriers of typhoid – All that conflicts so violently with my personal affection for James, that being with them for long produces great unrest & explosions. It's impossible. I don't mind seeing him occasionally for short periods. But he doesn't want that – I have been very fond of him. And I miss him more than you'd think.

This isn't much of a love letter: but I rather disdain to offer you love, now. And if I wrote of my sufferings, it'd waste time. Besides, you'd reply again that you only had my word for it . . . You have a generous & magnificent way with you that disarms one!

I've loitered & dragged & torn through August. It has been horrible. I suppose I shall see you again, and something may happen – you may, even, 'sooth' me as you say – you can be at moments, (one's startled to remember) great, when you care to.

But I can't go on like this, now I've got through this month. September – October – November – Es geht nicht. That's the one thing I know for certain. I can't go on like this.

You needn't *tell* me I've "fallen from love to love" I know. I'm
ashamed, & sorry. Oh God! I deserve reproaches. But I've paid enough,
haven't I? for being unfaithful to you. I was evil. I'm sorry. I'll pay &
pay. I've come back, child. I committed adultery. But what you threaten
is divorce. It may not be. We've gone too far. We must marry. Not
immediately, if you will. But we must. I'll give you everything in the
world – You mustn't kill me. I must marry you.

                                                                    Rupert

Please give my love to Margery: and to Gwen & Jacques

                                                      Chateau de Vienne
                                                              Prunoy
August 31st [1912]

Oh Rupert

        I *am* ashamed; but its because I've hurt you again and made
you angry. Please burn it all & forget it. It was clumsiness – I really
wanted to offer suggestions & help you, if you wanted help. But my
suggestions were probably absurd and the talk, I know, was rubbish.
Make an image of me & put pins into it; that's what I've been trying to
do so much lately, but I slipped & some of the pins went into you by
mistake. I *will* try again.
        We must begin to repent now, and I must especially. It was stupid
of me ever to have showed the little bit of love I had for you, and wicked
of me to let you express your love for me. Because its you, who are
suffering, who must know, and you say I've done you wrong and that
"we've gone too far". I could feel sure, sometimes, that it was good; but
only good as it stood out alone & not balanced against consequences.
Now, if it brings you all this horror, you must curse it & I must regret it.
        Dont, dont add to it all, the idea that your going away with Ka has
hardened me. I will never reproach you for that, you must have
mistaken me (I was probably giving an example of your dependence).

You know, that in the whole of that business, the only thing I loathed & couldn't find sympathy with, was your final atitude to Ka. But even that now, I will not blame you for, I will agree that I cant understand and its my fault. You were free to do what you liked then; hadn't we just dicided to give up our tormenting connection & for you to go away.

It was last November that I decided & you found out I didn't love you – the idea of marriage & lots of thought about it has just strengthened my knowledge.

But you, you *mustnt* be nothing. I'm *sure* you are full of big strong things, which will count, when you're mind isn't too exhausted to express them. Please, *please* rest and see only the best people there are. Leave the old horrors: James & Ka & me & your mother, all of them. There are still people who are nothing but good. There is Dudley & Jacques.

Jaques & Gwen are so good for me: I came here all contracted & affraid & bitter about everything; but they have helped, by talking a little and mostly by just being about & being so nice. They are wise too, sometimes. Perhaps Frances Cornford was like that for you.

I suppose you were right about James – if you saw that he really *did* transport evil. I could never define the harm he brought, but I sometimes felt a horror of something there with him – some blackness & shinyness: – it used to grow as a meamory, when he was away; generally I didn't feel it when I saw him. Perhaps it was the same you were affraid of. Anyhow you didn't need him now.

I'll camp, if you like. But I don't much believe in it this time. I had rather talk with you for a day somewhere, than try & live with several other people there – try & talk to you & live with them at the same time: – it seems too difficult. I shalnt be back in England till the 6th at earliest. Once I am there, there are only two plans I have.

(1) to arrange with the Provost of the U[niversity].C[ollege]. about my career for the next year.

(2) To camp with Bunny & James & Daphne for a few days. Dont be horrified by that. James counts on it, and he will be alright with Bunny there, who only invites the best of him. It will be for a very short time too. We are going to put a tent up somewhere quite near Limpsfield and admire the autumn season, make jam & listen to Bunny reading aloud. I promise you, James wont be hurt – he shall be soothed; & he wont be allowed to do any one any harm. He will be subservient to our Limpsfield atmosphere.

In the winter I shall see only Bryn & Hugh & Margery & Ethel Pye & some old Bedalians, and Jacques & Gwen, when they come back. If I go to Limpsfield for week ends, I shall see Bunny & more Pyes – but that will be all. You need have no fear of slug-like influences from the people Jacques calls "the Jews". (they comprise the Bloomsbury household & the Stracheys, I believe). Especially, I shalnt see James, nor Adrian: – that I have decided for my own good. If I ever meet Virginia (please God, I do!) it will be about once in three months, what more is there to fear? Bearing in mind that I'm *very tough*, and no one has ever succeeded in doing me an injury, but myself.

So you mustn't be affraid to go away because of me. It *is* a waste your staying where you get more & more worn out; there can be nowhere so hopeless for you as England. I hope Norton's tour will come off, & you wont go to bed in Rugby.

Oh yes, I see the waste, well enough. I see that you could go on wasting & wasting till there'd be no more hope of recovery. And I do believe – you've made me (even "your word") – that you suffer more than most people could ever bear. But you have got a strength, and it will bring you through it all, if you give it its chance. And then you'll be great. You've already decided that you cant go on as you are. God! if I could help you to shake it off. Tell me if I can help you. Once, I could give you strength, you said. Isn't there any way I can do it now? Any good straight way: talking to you – seing you, or writing. I'll do anything, except lie to you. That I cant do, because I'm not clever enough. And I have a deadly fear of lies – for poisonous things.

You mustn't insist & insist. Its simple enough: – I won't marry you, because I dont love you and dont believe I ever did or ever could. But, if I ever do, I'll marry you. Its just that, that I cling to, things being so, I am right & I wont let you persuade me.

I can see the horror for you, now you think I'm wrong. But I can see a far more desperate horror, which would swamp us both, if we were married, & I hated you. You will never persuade me to allow that to happen. Thank goodness I have power to prevent it.

Till I change. The only thing is for you to be able to face whats left. And dont tire yourself trying to change me, you cant do it, it can only happen in time.

O, I wish I could show you the heaps of good things that are left. You must see them. There are still things in you and there are thousands of good things outside you. You *must* live.

I have felt the strong life in you, when we met on hills & in woods & walked about together. It cant have left you. You Rupert must still be there – all warm & awake, ready to stand out again, soon.

Do write & say how I can be agreable.

I'm humble

I'm penitent
I'm fond. & I want to be made use of, or kicked away for a cure, if
I'm not wanted.
Tell me what I can do.

Noel.

Margery & Jacques & Gwen send love.

Annandale Arms Hotel,
Moffat.

24, Bilton Road is my safest address

Monday [2 September 1912]

I am here a day or two, with Norton & his aunt: then we're going on to
other places – New Galloway. I don't know.
I'm sick & angry & tortured – I wrote rudely to you. I was
unbearable. I'm not necessarily so. You make me, partly. I want to know
if, when, & how, I'm going to see you. At present, I'm merely loitering
about in a stupor, waiting.
If we camp, once more, I can get my tent, for two & I can borrow
others from Justin, & procure the things . . . Yorkshire, they say, is
magnificent: the finest country in the world – I invite you. The immense
gains from my poems belong, in part, in the eyes of eternal justice, to
you – so we decided. So I shall, shall spend them like that. I will pay
your fare & your food & your tent & your bloody fare back, if you
come. Whom do you want? Are you going to bring a sister? I fancy you
won't camp alone . . . Have you anybody lying about? Shall I get poor
Lucy?[1] . . .
You must think of someone. I'm too dead & far off.
I *do* love you, always.

Rupert

---

1 Gordon Hannington Luce, who graduated from Emmanuel with a First in Classics in 1911. He was
one of the Apostles who had been at Goring and Everleigh.

Sanquhar
[Dumfries]
(pronounced Sanker – you know about
the young lady of Sanquhar who went
to sleep in a yacht when at anchor?)
Thursday [5 September 1912]

Dearest Noel,

I don't know what to write.
Your letter seemed, even to me, fine, in a way; and your voice, as
I've heard it, came through, more – Thanks for it.
These days drag by – an intolerable hell. I must see you sometime.
I feel it might clear things – you have, yes, "given strength" in the past.
That might happen. Or I might suddenly find I wasn't in love with you
at all, – a blessed release! or you might see sense. Or, of course, I might
just be driven more desperate than ever. And then there's always the
background of an irrational feeling that things *can't* be madly &
impossibly wrong, in the end, between two people like you & me, &
knowing each other as we do, with all the past behind us.
I keep myself up with that hope, that I shall know what to do after
I've seen you – , even if it's only for a day, perhaps.
At present I rock endlessly about in my mind between the various
alternatives I can see – supposing you won't come round. Sometimes I
feel I can be fairly callous, & go off for a year, & then come back
bearded & burly & make you marry me. Sometimes I feel I'd like to
chuck the whole thing up, & – without loving her – marry Ka, & try to
work. But mostly I feel, quite blankly & seriously, that I can't stand it.
It's all very unlucky. In December I was able to get away from you
– it hurt like Hell & nearly drove me mad – & yet see things left – have
only the idea of going on somewhere in front of my mind. But now it's
different. I suppose I am ill & exhausted, rather. Also, I've a different
view of things.
You lie, Noel. You may have persuaded yourself you don't love
me, or engineered yourself into not loving me, now. But you lie when
you say you never did & never could. You did – Penshurst &
Grantchester & a thousand times. *I* know you did; & you know it. And
you could.
You see, another thing I don't quite swallow, in general, your talk

of your "toughness" & "hardness". It's some of it true in a *sense* –
though not in the wide way you make out. But, you know, I know you
very well. In April, when I told you my dreary tale (& when you were
so astonishingly good to me), & again at Limpsfield in June – I've
known you cry . . . Oh child, I do know you really!

"Fatherly Rupert!" you once called me; how much in contempt, I
don't know. It's true enough, that there's that, with all the rest. It
seemed to me worth while reminding you, lest, in all this bitterness of
my blaming & cursing you, you should excusably forget it; & lest I
should, – telling you, that is, that I'm not merely selfishly wanting you,
wanting to monopolise you & tie you up, wanting to get what I want,
but that I do always, at back, "care" most achingly & passionately &
unendingly about your happiness & your good. Child, I do.

There's a lot to say; but I'm too tired to do it now.

I'm very sorry you're camping with James: – because he "counts
on it" (didn't I?). I hope it'll be short. I'm glad you're not seeing him or
Adrian next term. I even confess to hoping that you won't see Virginia
more than your once in three months – though I suppose she'll try to
make it more.

I see & share your objection to camping with me. My hope for
being able to carry it off lay, as I said, in the peculiar out-of-the-
worldness of camp life. And considering who we are & what we've
been, it seems, in some ways, as if a longer period than a day might let
us feel the position more sanely. It might dispel whatever pitiful &
abhorrent image of me you have stuck up in your mind. Mightn't we
start friendlier? I mistrust the hysteria of a single meeting.

And, by God, if I do kill myself, I'd like to do it with one fairly
decent memory just behind.

I go South in a few days. I want to avoid Rugby. I'm thinking of
going to Justin, who's in a cottage near Leylands, till about the 16th. But
of course this is all in subjection to any arrangements with you.

Try to think of something. I suppose if I had any energy I should
insist on camp . . . Anyhow, consider "one day's" discussion really
only means three hours – one can't keep it up. Two tea-parties'd be
better.

Goodnight. Your last letter was very nice (besides being rather
magnificent.) I'm thanking you for it: (as stiffly as I can –)

By the way, you're not to funk meeting me. It's not as if I'm a
stranger, Adrian or such.

I'm in a most bloody Hell still.

Monday morning will find me at *The Post Office. New Galloway*

September. 12th. [1912]

I was glad to get your two gentler letters. One we just snatched from the
postman as we drove away in a dog cart from Prunoy. The other was
here, it is distressing, but hints that there may be ways through this
slough.
     I've been trying to contrive a plan. Its very difficult, otherwise I
should have written sooner. Finally I think, that the sooner we can
talk the better. Camp seems impossible this weather – and I still
believe it would be a dangerously complicated undertaking. Wouldn't
the best thing be for you to come to Limpsfield for two days, or three
(as long as we needed to clear things up)? Inconveniently, there is no
room in the Champions now; Hugh has to have a room kept free for
him. And everyone is very busy & absorbed. But perhaps you
wouldn't have liked to be surrounded by the family. I've been thinking
that you mightn't mind living in "The Grasshopper" at Moorhouse
Bank, about a mile & a half from here – thro' the woods on the way
to Westerham? Maitland used to stay there, & seemed very satisfied;
they gave him a chop for lunch every day. I could come out & go for
walks in those woods. If you thought that too remote, there is the
"Carpenters Arms" across the common, but it has no recom-
mendation; or again you might just get a room & come here for
meals: but I havn't suggested that to Mother, I thought I'd suggest "the
Grasshopper" first.
     If you agree, come either for this very week-end: Saturday &
Sundy; or better: Tuesday, Wednesday, till Thursday next week (I go to
London on Monday with Mother, & could meet you there & bring you
down). The week-end after we are all going to devote to James near
Haselmere – after that I'm again free. But I dont think we'd better let it
slide too late. If there is any chance that I can help to reduce the
hellishness of your Hell, we'd better try soon. Besides I want you to
escape from England as soon as possible.
     I wont be argumentative now. And when we talk, I'll try not to be
harsh & dogmatic – that oughtnt to be the necessary result of attempts
at honesty – But you *must* try not to be too upsetting. You can reduce
me to dumb helplessness through despair, when you explain all your
misery. I *must* help you, if I can.

Let me know, whether my plan is at all agreable or possible. I hope you like being with Justin.

love from
Noel

[National Liberal Club]
Monday [16 September 1912]

My dear Noel,

I think I was very tired, yesterday. And it becomes harder, then. There seems so infinitely little reason to do, or not do, or choose, or reject, anything, if all ways lead to the same unending dreariness – no – not that.

And my pride battles with me – to be put into the class of your rejected suitors – with, good heavens, James & Adrian! – oh, to be put there, mightn't matter, but to come down to that. I've been so proud all these four years. – No, it's not that I'm wanting to write about.

I'm really a good deal "better" in some ways. I'll come by that 10.25 tomorrow. It starts, as usual, at 10.40: & gets in at 11.30. I shall start up towards you from the station. You may meet me anywhere. If I get as far as the common, I shall sit there.

I shall bring a thing or two in my rucksack, I expect. In case I want to stay the night in the country. But don't let the possibility tie you. You can think of somewhere to go to, if you like.

Staying in rooms & being allowed to come to dinner, two or three days . . . No. I daresay I could behave. But I don't care to go in to be laughed at by all those women –

But there's always the general grounds for talking – for us, anyhow, – or our ghosts. How stupid & ineffectual pride is.

And I do, occasionally, want to see your after all human mind, – what you've been at – And you've got, finally, to face your responsibilities – which you can't do unless you *see* what everything is & costs –

I am, I think unreasonable about all this. In most things in my life I've been reasonable, but I seem I'm not quite, now. There's no *evil* in all this case of ours; as there sometimes is. We ought to be able to get things as straight as they'll go. *We We We* it is an unsustaining diet to come down to, pride.

You're only 19 and a half –

with love

Rupert

Upon meeting Rupert, Noel's resolve remained firm, and seeing that she would not waver, he decided to leave for Germany.

Before going, he spent a week lodging with Eddie Marsh in his Gray's Inn flat. The two men began planning a new enterprise, an anthology of contemporary verse, entitled Georgian Poetry, *which Marsh would edit. At this time the editor of the* Poetry Review, *Harold Monro, was planning to open* The Poetry Bookshop, *which would promote new writing through poetry readings and also act as a publishing house. Rupert and Eddie put their ideas to him, and he agreed to assist them and print the new anthology.*

Eddie was also busy working as private secretary to the First Lord of the Admiralty, Winston Churchill. During the months that followed, Rupert was to spend an increasing amount of time socializing with Eddie and the set of friends that centred on Asquith at 10 Downing Street.

Bei Dudley Ward
Charlottenburg
Berlinerstrasse 100
Berlin

November 12 1912

Well, I've left you in peace a good time, haven't I? (and you me –) – I hope you're grateful.

It *is* comic. It's extraordinarily comic that you've been in some address over a month – And I haven't the remotest idea what it is.

I went to London, and then home for a bit (as far as I can remember); after my last interview with you. I was rather exhausted. It was somewhat melancholy unpacking the clothes I'd carefully packed for camp, all unused, and the books I'd thought might be nice to read there. I wept at the pathetic figure I'd made, trailing them round Scotland & London & God knows where . . . One is like a child, in the important little way one trots round with one's dreams – so unrelated to reality. When I was eight or nine, I used to have a long private imagination about a steam-roller – I went about eating & living in the ordinary way, rather mechanically, but this was my real life – I kept planning how I'd one day get hold of a steam-roller, & start it, & career about the roads killing all my enemies (or the enemies of England, were they? I wasn't quite sure. They were dim figures. Enmity was their common – and only – characteristic. Pale, beastly, people). I fought thousands of such battles, charging them down, rolling them under, triumphant, my hand on the lever, the wonder of the world. Sometimes they'd get hold of another smaller steam roller. Then *I'd* get up a hill & let her rip – & we smashed them into smithereens. There was always admiring crowds: and everybody was very proud of me. It filled my life for so long, the imagining and planning that. I lived more or less on sufferance, on my own sufferance occupied with my triumph. Waiting, with an unperturbedness I could afford, for the great day when I should get control of a steam roller – It seemed very inevitable. – It never has, as a matter of fact, happened. And it's getting rather late. I'm very old. (aren't I?). And the worst is, I don't even *want* to achieve that triumph now, much; and don't even feel confident I *could* . . .

I've gone astray. I don't know what I was originally talking about. I shan't turn over the page to see.

Dudley sits yonder clacking his typewriter; making history. Every half-hour he asks me for an equivalent of some phrase he's used already & doesn't want exactly to repeat. My superb lordship of English rarely fails him.

His wife leads a quiet existence. She is very large with child. I hope it won't kill her – she's very tiny. I work indoors most of the time. Sometimes I go out of an evening to a theatre. And every other day I go out to lunch in a *café*, rather dignifiedly, to show I'm independent.

I now remember that I started this letter with autobiography. Rugby I endured for a fortnight. Then London, Cambridge, London, and here. Rugby London and Cambridge were exactly like Rugby London and Cambridge. I avoided the more pestilential parts of London fairly well: though when Virginia got out of them to Clifford's Inn, I went & saw her. She seemed calmer for her marriage. I felt infinitely removed from her.[1] Adrian seemed brighter than in the summer, a little. I also went a walk with Jacques in the Chilterns.

---

1 Virginia Stephen married Leonard Woolf on 10 August 1912 at St Pancras Register Office. In October they moved to rooms at 13 Clifford's Inn, though they still spent time at Asheham House in Sussex whenever they could.

I quite realise that this is very dull. I will stop. Berlin is full of the best things in old & new art. The only painter I can bear, however, nowadays, is Kate Greenaway. Prof. Reinhardt's productions are execrable. But tomorrow I'm going to see him do *The Dance of Death*.[2] (You may remember hearing me delightfully read that, once.). Dull. Dull.

Good bye . . .

What I really want is, on a card, your address. I won't misuse it. But I want to *know* it. – You see, there are so many fires reported in the papers . . . . . . I suppose you *are* alive (roughly?)

Goodnight.
Rupert.

P.S. I had some very dreary poems in this month's *Poetry Review*[3] I told them to send you a copy – I hope you didn't mind. And I hope they did send it. I expect not –

2 *The Dance of Death* by August Strindberg (1849–1912) had opened on 27 September at the Deutsches Theater, Berlin. When Rupert was invited the following February to speak to the Heretics Society in Cambridge on Contemporary Theatre, he opened his talk by attacking 'that energetic fraud, Max Reinhardt', going on to talk at length about the brilliance of Strindberg's work. His ideas on Strindberg later appeared in print on 11 October 1913 in the *Cambridge Magazine*. It seems likely that Rupert's praise for him was inspired in part by the feeling that here was a kindred spirit, 'a passionate lover . . . born into an age and a community tragically unfit for passionate lovers'.
3 The poems published were: 'Song' (All suddenly the wind comes soft) , 'Mary and Gabriel', 'Beauty and Beauty', 'The Old Vicarage' and 'Unfortunate'.

UNFORTUNATE

Heart, you are restless as a paper scrap
That's tossed down dusty pavements by the wind;
Saying, 'She is the most wise, patient and kind.
Between the small hands folded in her lap
Surely a shamed head may bow down at length,
And find forgiveness where the shadows stir
About her lips, and wisdom in her strength,
Peace in her peace. Come to her, come to her!' . . .

She will not care. She'll smile to see me come,
So that I think all Heaven in flower to fold me.
She'll give me all I ask, kiss me and hold me,
And open wide upon that holy air
The gates of peace, and take my tiredness home,
Kinder than God. But, heart, she will not care.

The London (Royal Free Hospital) School
of Medicine for Women,
Hunter Street. W.C.

Tuesday: Nov 26th? [1912]

Dear Rupert.

This is one of my addresses, the one I'm most proud of. The
other is
20 Portsea Place
Connaught Sqr
W.
I live there with Ethel, as I said I shd, under the care of Mr & Mrs
Murray. He waits at table and is determined against the insurance act and
very Scotch. She calls me every morning and talks until I'm well awake; If

that doesnt suffice she give me a sweat to suck, whilst I'm getting my eyes open. There are three children, one of them in arms. And then there are the other lodgers, various married pairs, who are out all day & most of the night; and some bachelors. One of the pairs is foreign – German we think, – and the man much older than the lady; these two quarrel, and Mrs Murray has had to go & restore peace in the small hrs of the morning on occasion: "hey Lord, yo're keeping all the folks awake!" Its a more successful place to live in – as far as work goes – than that Loudoun Rd Studio. Even my most careful expectations of gaiety: – concerts with James, tea with Virginia about twice, havent come off. I see only Ethel & Bryn in the week and Margery at Limpsfield every Saturday & Sunday. Sometimes I've found people at Limpsfield. Jaques was there once. Harold has come up from Rugby, complaining of the gahstly grind there, about twice; Eva & Bill were there for two week-ends, and Bekassy came flying down & spent a very active Sunday. We planted irises & talked & he discussed with Bill, & held forth and read us Lucy's poem & then ran a man hunt in the evening, with Margery & Bunny & me; finally he fell on his head in a pit, & became more quiescent.

I rush over all these things; I daren't embark on discription; you were so stern last time I tried.

You once suggested a method for me to write you letters; perhaps you remember, I was to write on scraps of paper, whenever I had a minute or an inclination, & then collect them.

It seems the only way to get it done, now. The awful thing is, that you are probably back in England again, & I may meet you round a corner on the way to post this. I must risk it. The worlds very full of rejoicing, because Eva has produced her daughter Diana, about a fortnight before anyone expected it, it was such a noble thing to do. Daughters are so common, & daughters which dont arrive in time are an old story; but this is a little exciting. I suppose the next lady will have to die, in order not to be dull in producing offspring.

The night before it happened I had a very lovely dream, in which I found I'd had a baby, suddenly, in bed, and no one there to help; I lept to the wash stand with it, & washed its face, and when it had opened its eyes & grinned, I knew by its expression that it was girl. Then mother came, & she seemed please, but surprised; and I was at the height of glee, when I could answer her question about its parentage, quite honestly, by saying I knew nothing about it, that as far as I knew, the child had not father, nor ever had, & I supposed it was, just simply, one of these virgin births, a second Christ perhaps.

That seemed to satisfy her & everyone else. So I carried it out into the wood & showed it to Bryn & Teddy Pye & his fiancee;[1] and they were all very amazed & moved, and I felt very like a saint.

I woke feeling more really kind than I had for years – oh *ever*.

I get harder & harder; and if I could be consistent, I'd be careful to an extent of hating any young man. I almost comitted suicide, when it turned out that Bekassy had got it too (Love, love –) I'm in despair about James.[2]

Bunny & Harold are the only comfort. Both very different: Bunny so sympathetic that he can be moved to affection without being hurt by it. And Harold strong & safe as to his heart & yet boisterous with all his charms – so well known. (You wont be liking all this I'm afraid – Aah! I dont want to be liked to a passon again.)

I get nearer to the convent. Last Saturday I went to Vespers at Westminster. They sang an anthem & another thing, and several salms & chants: All the priests were dressed in brown & gold capes with white dresses coming out below, they sat in two rows at the sides of a platform below the high alter – a long way up the church – and every now & then one from each side got up & trotted to the middle of the stage, bowed there together, & trotted back again. It wasn't really like a play, because they were all so absorbed in what they were doing & it wd obviously have gone on just as properly & concisely if there had been no audience. Obviously it was well established & had been going on for years; and the faithful who waited in a que outside the confession box, were well *in* with it all. I felt sorry to be so outside. But I recovered when I got out, & only was pleased by the music.

I must let this go, I suppose. Its pretty bad. Thank you for writing. Give my love to Dudley & Annamarie (I still cant spell her name).

Are you well?

Noel.

Nov. 28th.
P.S. I forgot. Your poems were sent. I was glad to see them, I thought I rather like the newer ones; but I cant be sure.

---

1 Edwin Walter Pye had read Classics at Trinity. He was the younger brother of Sybil and Ethel, and had just got engaged to a girl named Mildred.
2 Ferenc had seen Noel on 27 October and told her how he felt: 'I wonder if you thought the way I talked Sunday evening was too ridiculous? I have a sort of uneasy feeling it must have been very absurd.' By chance, he saw James the same day: 'He was fairly miserable . . . and as far as I could see, though I may just conceivably be wrong, it was all about you. I don't think I can be wrong. Don't hate me for writing this. He thought I didn't see who it was all about, and wanted me to sympathise which I did, rather hypocritically I suppose.' (Olivier family papers)

London (oh, only for a moment!)
Tuesday [28 January 1913]
Later on in the night –

Dear child,

     I didn't know whether to think you more admirably tactful or dignified.

     I *had* to stand in that accursed *foyer*, because one of my party had dashed off & stationed me there till he returned – [1]

     Were you (as far as you were anything) annoyed to find me in England? But I suppose you did know, if only from the fact that some books appeared for you. Perhaps they haven't appeared. Perhaps you sent them back. If you don't want to have them please burn them. There were two Donnes in the only edition. You know about Donne. They're merely to look well on the shelf.[2] But you might dip into the Butler notebooks, some day.[3]

     It was good of you to write to me in Germany. Did you mind – or did you notice? – that I didn't write to you? I occasionally thought of it. But I nearly always was in a condition of hating you a great deal; so I didn't trust myself to write. I'm hastily taking advantage, now, of a friendly lapse –

     Yes: I knew about Bekassy. He went off to stay a weekend with you in the Autumn term (when he should have been at the Society), and my intuition suddenly told me, quite definitely. It was rather awkward, for I'd just then got rather fond of him, & – for instance – he'd sent me his poems to read; &, of course, I immediately hated him, & sent his poems back without comment.

     I'm sorry you should be so bothered by so many people falling in

---

1 Noel and Rupert had both attended the Fabian Society Shaw/Belloc debate held that night at Queen's Hall. In a letter to Mrs Patrick Campbell on 27 November 1912, Shaw describes the forthcoming debate: 'Not an advertisement has appeared and the hall is nearly sold out already. (And actresses talk to me of their popularity!). Belloc shall perish . . . . ; a tempest of blighting, blasting, withering arguments bursts out of me . . . ' *Collected Letters of Bernard Shaw*, vol. iii, *1911–1925*, ed. Dan H. Laurence (London: Max Reinhardt, 1985), p. 128. Rupert, in a letter to Ka, writes of how he 'unluckily ran into that swine Noel. However we put up our noses and cut each other, which was good fun.' (*KCA*, ?30 January 1913)
2 Rupert had sent her the newly published Clarendon Press two-volume edition of Donne's poems, edited by H.J.C. Grierson. After returning from Germany he had stayed with the Cornfords and had written two reviews of the book, one for the *Nation* and one for *Poetry and Drama*.
3 *The Note-Books of Samuel Butler* had been edited by Henry Festing Jones and published in 1912 by A.C. Fifield.

love with you. I'm sure your feelings do you credit. I quite agree; Love's an entirely filthy business.

I think Bekassy's all right. He seems quieter, & disconcerted, and no doubt – supposing you're obdurate, and you torment him an average amount, not too much – he'll be pained for some months, or a year or two. But I think its only calf-love – I know about it, it's what I had for you, *gnädiges Fräulein*[4] – Calf-love that goes wrong only hurts so-so – a remedial & finite business, merely a hand or foot off; not both legs.

Calf-love's what young men have; young women's complaint is called green-sickness, a different affair. Both make a person very unpleasant. I have come more & more to see you've had a deal to bear from me in the past. I've always been horribly unpleasant. Good God! You were really very tolerant – Calf-love goes over, draggingly. It's a pity you've always elicited the worst side of me –

next day)
I beg pardon: I preach. Preaching & irritability are the two great things middle-age brings: as you'll one day find. I'm by way of staying with Jacques. But irritability is so great, with him, that I don't think I can do it much longer – One sermon I'd like to deliver, though, on the text of your last letter, as I remember it. Your form of green sickness helps to drive you into, really, rather wrong ideas. I mean (I'm not trying to sway you!) you've flown a bit too far into worship of "hardness" my dear. It *does* end in thinking Harold much better than – say – Jacques or Gwen or me or Keats or Bekassy or any fine person. You know, – as a man of the world to a woman of the world – it won't do. Will it? there must be a flaw in it. You're in a state where you shrink a little too far from people being in love with you, & that drives you to fantastic valuations.

I've, (you may have noticed!) not much of an ear for music. In consequence, I can hear discords unmoved, which fairly comb the nerves of musical people. What superb hardness! You'd almost fall in love with me, if you could see me at such moments, unmoved where everyone else is shrieking, Noel! – It doesn't really mean that I'm far better – in the musical world – than musical people, my dear. I'm not talking about myself. I'm contemptible enough in other ways. But, on the general question, I discern a tendency in you to be silly on the question of "hardness". Don't. Be clever – (though I sympathise with half of it – your hatred of "softness".)

---

4 My dear young lady.

Well: I may write a letter sometime, with gossip and so on. Unless you dislike it. I tell myself, and everyone else, most of the time, that you're the bloodiest & pettiest person in England. But I suppose I don't believe it. One has to say something, – in order to – well, you know as well as anyone the furtive way one builds up armour plating in personal relationships.

Poor old Noel, you did look *so* very solemn at Mr Belloc's jokes last night –

It was really rather nice seeing you. Well, not *"nice"* – But it lifts the really very low level my unaided life attains – all I mean is that I don't care *what* happens, as long as you stay fine, are fine. If you betray that, I swear I'll kill you. One must invest one's money *somewhere* –

Child, I wish you well. Good be with you. Be happy, incidentally –

I'm trusting you that you'll tell me if ever you want any help about anything or need anything or are in any difficulty. I'm almost infinitely powerful –

I say, there's one thing. Please read this part, & don't pass it over in unconcern – & don't misjudge it. It'll relieve me so to impress it on you. It's this. So many people get kidnapped nowadays: & you're always drifting about alone. Please, I'm perfectly serious – be careful. When I lie awake at nights – Don't ever, on any pretext, go off with people you don't know, however well authenticated, or get into cabs – it's impossible to be too careful. I demand this.

Also, bewahr Dich Gott![5] What I hope is that, at some crossing, when you're just going to be run over by a motor-bus, one of these days, I may pull you out of the way, & get run over myself. It'd be a good way out of a bloody world for me: & I should go with the satisfaction of knowing that you'd feel horribly awkward for a great many weeks, or months.

And how my book'd sell!

With love
Rupert

---

5 So, may God preserve you!

20, Portsea Place
W.
Wednesday evening [29 Jan 1913]

Dear Rupert

    You are still kind. And I am very glad to have Donne – I hope
you don't hate my writing about it. But such a big parcel, & from the
Poetry book shop, with your scrawl inside, was the most sudden &
agreable thing that had turned up for terms.
    I'm affraid, of course, that that other book – Samuel Butler's notes
– is a mistake and you'll be wanting it back. I'll send it; but as it's come,
I'll read it first – oh & perhaps I'll not send it unless you intimate that
you want it.
    The other is rich is good and it's a great comfort (like the Arabian
Nights in Bryn's flat) from time to time – when there's just a moment to
be refreshed in. Thank you. I'll try & conform to your cutting terms.
    But it's going to be pretty silly, if you go on going about in
London. We've had good luck (I'm affraid) up till now. And I must
leave you to take all the trouble. I'll try & be restrained & not bother
you. Last night it was a pretty close thing; I don't know how many more
such, I'll be able to bring it off.
    Margery was very thrilled } at seeing you about.
                        pleased
    Well . . .

                                                        toujours
                                                        Noel.

PRIVATE

c/o E. Marsh
5 Raymond Buildings
Gray's Inn W.C.

Wednesday [12 February 1913]
(ending, Friday)

The chronology and coincidences of this world, – that we should not write for three months, and then our letters cross! Anyhow, I'm glad you liked the books. Though if they were really the "most agreable thing which had turned up for terms" you must have a very dull life of it. – But you like a dull life, (very rightly) – So all's well. Unless, as I suspect, the phrase was merely the false & sugar-tongued politeness of a society woman. I find such in London.

But you, poor brown mouse, can't, in the dizziest heights of murian imagination, picture the life of whirl glitter & gaiety I lead. A young man about town, Noel, (I've had my hair cut *remarkably* short –). Dinners, boxes at the opera, literary lunch-parties, theatre supper-parties (the Carlton on Saturday next) – I know *several* actresses. Last night, in the stalls at the Ballet,[1] Eddie [Marsh] & I (I'd wired for my white waistcoat) bowed & smiled – oh, quite casually – at

Queen Alexandra
The Marquis de Soveral
The Duchess of Rutland
Countess Rodomontini (or such)
Mrs George Keppel[2]

and a host more. And in the interval Mrs Humphrey Ward shook me very warmly by the hand, under the impression I was some one quite different from what I am. But as I'm an anti-Suffragist, I was, of course, rather flattered.[3]

---

1 Once again Rupert had gone to see the Ballets Russes at Covent Garden, this time performing *Les Sylphides*.
2 Eddie was acquainted with Queen Alexandra, the Duchess of Rutland and Mrs George Keppel. The Marquis de Soveral, who was the former Portuguese Ambassador in London, was another figure of High Society and a favourite target for Max Beerbohm's caricatures.
3 Mrs Humphry Ward (1851–1920), novelist, journalist and philanthropist. She was the grand-daughter of Thomas Arnold (1795–1842) of Rugby and niece of Matthew Arnold (1822–88), and inherited their spirit of conservative reform. Whilst being an active campaigner for higher education for women, she was opposed to women's suffrage, and in 1908 organized the Women's Anti-Suffrage League, dedicated to 'bringing the views of women to bear on the legislature without the aid of the vote'.

And one day I had lunch with three editors,
The Editor of *Poetry and Drama*
The Editor of *The Daily Herald*
The Editor of *C.B. Fry's Magazine*
So, altogether, I live entirely for pleasure, & very much despise you
– (You, no doubt, were at the ballet last night, in the Gallery. I didn't
even trouble to look for you.) Farce enters my life, too. I gave a reading at
The Poetry Bookshop, from the poets. Thousands of devout women were
there, & some clergymen. perhaps I told you. An elderly American
female cried slightly, & shook me by the hand for some minutes . . .

Your letter . . . you don't know how it moves one to find that
"afraid" has two "f"s still. There are some things in the world
unchanged* I had thought, nothing; and my feet were tired of the
absence of firm ground.

Yet the world does rattle on. Alix Florence has heart disease.[4] And
Dudley's son is a week old today. It hit me very hard, this last, when I
got the wire. Funny.[5]

Oh! don't be too dreadfully & conscientiously worried about the
awful trouble you take in evading me, holding yourself
in, . . . etc. You hint that the anxiety makes you thin
. . . you don't catch me *that* way. I'll warrant you
against loss of weight.

You may bow to me, if the worst comes to the worst, my Dear. I'll
even give you leave to say " . . . . . . Hullo! . . . . . . " or " . . . Wie
geht's? . . . "

Oh, You've treated me very badly. There have only been two
occasions when you behaved decently towards me. One, – but this is
doubtful – is when, once, you kissed me. The more certain one is when
you hit me (fairly hard) on the face. There should have been more of
that – At least, I deserved more. Funny that I should have been quite
wrong about everything, always, & you quite right; & yet you're so
stupid & I'm so wise.

Oh. I really beg you're pardon. – What I meant to say, when I got

* "seing" for instance.

---

4 Although Alix Sargant-Florence's condition was diagnosed as 'degeneration of the heart', it seems
fairly likely that she was in fact suffering from anorexia nervosa. The robust, healthy girl Rupert had met
at the Fabian Summer School in 1910 had become frighteningly emaciated and had been sent to
recuperate in Freiburg, Germany.
5 The news that Annemarie had given birth to a son, Peter, on 7 February was related to Rupert by
Jacques. To Ka he admits that: 'It was, quite unexpectedly, an awful blow for me – the news. Queer. A
sort of jealousy, I suppose.' (*KCA*, February 1913)

onto that, was, – what was it? I believe I remember how fond you are of poetry.

> There was an old man of Khartoum
> Who left two black sheep in his room;
>   To remind him, he said,
>   Of two friends who were dead:
> – He could not quite remember of whom.

was told me yesterday. Known to you, no doubt. I won't repeat Mr Belloc's version of the National Anthem – You'd know that –

Who asked me after you yesterday, d'you think? Albert Rothenstein.[6] I fairly shut him up.

May all good be with you – I hope you're very happy, and very good. No, that's not quite true. I hope you're *rather* happy, and very good.

My thoughts surround you with nobility. I wish you all the fineness in the world –

                                                        Rupert

                                              [20 Portsea Place, W.]
Sunday. 16th. [February 1913]

Dear Rupert

The envelope looked so agreeable; & the inside was so disheartening. But even from that there was a little cheerfulness:

---

6 Albert Rothenstein (1881–1953), painter and set designer. Rupert first met him when he designed the 1908 production of *Comus*. They were now both working with Middleton Murry (1889–1957) on the modernist periodical *Rhythm*.

What a life you lead! This *moving* in rich *circles* must be rather charming, and stalls in a white waistcote is the ideal life of a gentleman (I should think) Pourvu that you appreciate it.

I wasn't even in the gallery that night of your meeting with Mrs Humphrey Ward. I saw Electra,[1] in the afternoon; it was the last performance & stupendous. I hope you saw it once.

Your literary life sounds sadder: all those maids – unless they are, perhaps, the true cultured public.

O I hope you are'nt having a beastly time.

And as you feared; I am perfectly & utterly happy. I just go about pleased all over; and nearly cry, often, for the joy of walking along the street alone. There is never a hint (unfortunately) of kidnapping; people don't like my looks. Still I hope it may happen one day. It isn't dull, but anything wd be fun.

They've just come back from Jamaica, with relics. M & I spent last night cheering the black butler; comforting the dogs & persuading the little grey cat (very ugly), but mother's so fond of it) that The Champions was its home. This morning the man has gone to church. But the dogs are restless & the cat looks sad. M & I are jaded too. Managing retainers is as great a responsibility as it's possible to bear.

I meant to write quite a different letter. Does this one express how amiable I feel?

I'm beginning to appreciate the wonder of the perfect sadness of it all (if you see what I mean)

yrs with love. Noel

[5, Raymond Buildings, Gray's Inn]

[Postmark 17 February 1913]

Well, if you found that "so disheartening", what the devil *do* you want? and don't joke about kidnapping.

Rupert

---

1 The opera Elektra by Richard Strauss (1864–1949) had been conducted at Covent Garden by Thomas Beecham (1879–1961).

While Rupert was in London he renewed his acquaintance with the actress Cathleen Nesbitt, to whom Eddie had introduced him just before Christmas. He had been initially attracted to her when he saw her playing Perdita in The Winter's Tale at the Savoy Theatre in September, and had asked Eddie to arrange a meeting.

Despite the new attractions of his life in London, Rupert decided that he needed a complete change of surroundings and decided to spend a year travelling in North America and the South Seas. He felt that not only would he benefit from a complete break, but that Ka would find life easier if he were on the other side of the Atlantic.

On 8 March the news reached Rupert that he had at last been elected a Fellow of King's College. He had pulled together his dissertation on John Webster and Elizabethan Drama into a lively and well-argued piece of scholarship, and its originality had greatly impressed those judging. As the position did not necessitate his actually teaching or even being in Cambridge, he decided not to alter his plans to leave the country.

5 Thurloe Square[1]
South Kensington

6531 Western

Wednesday [14 May 1913]

My dear Noel,

You are not a good correspondent. You will be – I shall not say sorry, and I will not say *glad* – oh, leave it, politely, at interested – to

---

1 Rupert was lodging for the month in Albert Rothenstein's flat.

hear that I'm going to America in a few days.[2] Do you want to see me before I go? I daresay I shall be back in eight or nine months; but perhaps not. I have a half-sentimental & half-aesthetic feeling I'd like to wind things up by having tea with you. But if you don't want to; or haven't time; don't let's. If you do I shall be in London Monday Tuesday & Wednesday next week (19th–21st), fairly busy, but able to squeeze in an hour. You can have tea here, or dinner with me at Simpson's, or lunch, or anything. Or you can just telephone; that would be a good joke.

For myself, I get along very well without you: & lead a fairly happy life. I have a dreadfully consistent and faithful disposition, I'm afraid; a nuisance, I find it, in many ways. However, as time goes on Love grows potential and not actual. A comfort. And I've succeeded in hardening my heart against you. So I don't fear seeing you occasionally, or for a short hour – (But I wouldn't see you for long, again – I'm not going to repeat my summer treat again ever. Oh no!) As my dislike for you grows, grows also many other things (some gratitude, among them) a great sympathy. I must have been pretty horrid very often. Child, I apologise –

Yours respectfully
Rupert

On Board S.S. Cedric

May 25 1913

My dear child,

My dear dear dear child –
It was nice of you to come and have dinner with me.[1]
Was I horrible? I was rather tired and pressed that night.

---

2 Just before leaving, Rupert was officially hired as an overseas correspondent for the *Westminster Gazette*, the only professional post he ever held.

---

1 They had dined on 21 May, at Treviglio's in Church Street, Soho.

And I funked, of course, at the last moment, asking you how your feelings were.

Young woman, you shocked me. – Not so much by your frank and unshocked revelation of family disgrace, as by your sallow and hideous appearance.[2] I do not desire you to be ill. – Perhaps it is a sign of age: but certainly a spasm of affection did shoot into my withered heart. Can't I cure you?

I was overwhelmed, as I started, by messages & tokens of sisterly affection from most of your family. I wept between Euston and Liverpool. Now, however, I am very healthy, and happy. I eat enormously & sleep profoundly. The weather is lovely. I sit at table with a professor of ethics, a young engineer from Vancouver and the proprietor of seven New York theatres. And three separate lovely young ladies have fallen in love with me. And I have come to the conclusion that if I'm always so happy out of England, it is absurd ever to return.

It's awful how constipated one gets at sea: But the colour of the deep water is an extremely rich and beautiful blue. And the air is fresh.

I had, in all, sixty-seven introductions. And I left them all in Kensington. But I dare say I shall get on all right.

What is there to say? I wish . . . Yes: if there's anything . . . oh, dear! what I mean is that I should always enjoy doing anything for you.. That sounds thin too.

And, also . . . don't pick up too many of our mannerisms. You're very nice without.

with love
Rupert

---

2 The family were gradually coming to realize that Margery's mental stability was seriously diminishing and that she could no longer simply be regarded as a harmless eccentric.

23, Marlborough Road,
N.W.

June 23rd [1913]

Dear Rupert

Thank you. It was rather nice getting your letter. I hope all the gayness wasn't put on. I like to think that you're enjoying yourself.

But somebody (Bekassy perhaps, or James) said you complained to *them* of boredom; so I rather suspect you. Never mind: one's mood changes. I know. And consistentcy, they say, is stagnation.

There's nothing I can describe, which will interest you at all; but I thought I'd better write one letter, to try & perfect your joy in *righteousness*.

You'ld like to know – or have it confirmed, even if you did know – that I did cave in, pretty thoroughly in the long run. When you said: "What *do* you want?" It seemed pretty clear that I'd no business to have ever interfered with you, or ever felt at ease doing it.

I didn't know *what* I wanted, & didn't get much satisfaction; so it was all pretty bad. And it's now pretty obvious that there's no point in such a person being about.

Toujours gauche, I grovel to the best of my ability (my joints are still stiff), & own up that I haven't an *idea* of how one ought to live, & so far – & at your expense – I have muddled it. I agree that you are much better – there is a straight line about you, & you are fit to walk the earth with others. You keep your level, because of your confidence.

And I've dropped through. Still very torpid & muffled, I feel whats called: *ashamed*.

I'm even sorry, about a few things, Sorry you got so injured. Sorry I wasn't nicer. But chiefly sorry, that the world's too difficult to fit in to. (And too much of a habit to get out of)

And as a result of all this. There isn't much prospect of the future being very grand.

I see us both:

You, an English gentleman, having become le grand indifferent, will have the success of the man who pockets his heart & can devote his energies to prattle & flash. Then – being really rather an agreeable old dear – & not skillful enough to keep up the illusion for more than a year or two, & rather hating it, on the whole; you will drop all that &

very determinedly set up a family in England; bully them rather, &
write pamphlets; & all the old friends will say you found your level &
visit you from time to time.

My case is even worse. There won't even be that progression of
attitudes. It'll be damned monotonous.

I shall go on, enjoying life thoughtlessly most of the time; I shall
get on v well w acquaintances, (except some, who will dislike me,
because they can't see any sincerity or aim in me.) I shall be affectionate
& often irritable with my family, taking them rather as a matter of
course.

And also – as I go along the streets – from time to time, I shall
remember, that it's all rather a fraud; and note that I don't like anything,
or any of them very much, & it's wonderful how indifferent I am to
what the rest are all getting at & how unsympathetic with their "love"
& their "souls" & all. And I shall see all their faults.

And so on, until I have rather a worse stomach ache than usual &
do die. Not very grand that.

But I hope you accept my humiliation and my confession: that the
world being what it is, you are right & I am wrong. And the Gods will
treat us accordingly

Noel.

THERE'S WISDOM IN WOMEN

'Oh love is fair, and love is rare;' my dear one she
  said,
'But love goes lightly over.' I bowed her foolish head,
And kissed her hair and laughed at her. Such a child
  was she;
So new to love, so true to love, and she spoke so
  bitterly.
But there's wisdom in women, of more than they
  have known,
And thoughts go blowing through them, are wiser
  than their own,
Or how should my dear one, being ignorant and
  young,
Have cried on love so bitterly, with so true a tongue?

                                                    Château Frontenac
                                                    Quebec
July 8 1913

You're a Devil. By God, you're a DEVIL. What a bloody letter to write to
me!
    Not but what it was very nice of you to write at all. It has just come
on to me – here – Look here, young woman. I don't like your mood –
But first about myself, as you're so sollicitous –
    Bekassy & James, who, you say, tell you I'm bored, lie, on the
whole. Certainly they can't know. For I've had no communication with
James. And I only write to Bekassy for an address (which he never sent)
As a matter of fact, you'll dance to hear that I'm enjoying myself, & in
extraordinary good health. I was very happy in America, where I made a
lot of friends; and occasionally miserable in Canada, where I scarcely

know anybody. That's because I'm getting old, & more dependent on human companionship. So once or twice I've been homesick. I'm alone you see. I've nothing immediate to worry me. I've had to cut away from Ka, & the thought of her hurts. But I try to pretend it's well with her. I'm not in love with you. I've no intention of playing *le grand indifferent*. I'm going to marry very soon and have a lot of children. I'm practically engaged to a girl you don't know to whom I'm devoted & who is in love with me. And if I don't marry her, I shall very swiftly marry one of two or three others, & be very happy.[1]

A later day.)
I've read your letter over again: and you <u>are</u> Bloody –
    Where was I? Oh yes, I am just explaining that all is well with me, so you needn't worry about *that*. As I mayn't be happy with you, I'm going to be happy without you. (Not but what, if you opened the door again, I mightn't very quickly find my way – . . . . . But you've shut it. So that's not the point.)
    As for my attitude towards you – if I've kept a distance lately (and now!) it's not because I was keeping up that silly special pleading against you I indulged in to work off my feelings at one time. It's only that I'm getting rather parsimonious-minded about my health wealth and happiness. You see, my dear, it's this way.
    I think you very beautiful –
    I admire very much (I'm so sorry) a lot of your temperament and character. (I do know you pretty well, in a way.). And, most of all, – I'm the most conservative person in the world – I <u>can't</u> get out of the habit of being very very fond of you. Quite irrationally. Just your voice – or gait (for instances) I happen to like so much more than nearly any other similar things in the world – You know how it is, affection – So many years of regarding you as queerly mine, & me as queerly yours, leave a mark – I won't go in to that, sentimentally. I'm sorry –
    Well, it'd be nice for me then if (if you liked it) we were "friends" – Last June & July, for instance, – before that Wiltshire place of Keynes'[2] – you were very nice to me, & we seemed to roam about

---

1 Despite his love for Cathleen, Rupert's experiences with Noel and Ka seem to have left him wary of commitment, as he explained in a letter to Eddie Marsh: 'My general position, you know, is queer. I've had enough and too much of love. I've come to the conclusion that marriage is the best cure for love. If I married, perhaps I could settle down, be at peace, and WORK. It's the only chance. Therefore, marry soon. Anybody. Cathleen's character is very good, and I'm very fond of her. Why not her? – On the other hand, she's an actress.' He adds as an afterthought: 'This is the sort of letter that doesn't look well in a Biography.' (*KCA*, 6 September 1913)
2 The Crown Hotel, Everleigh.

contentedly – oh, *do* say that they seemed pleasant to you, Noel, those friendly days –

But – I'm susceptible, &, as I say, reactionary. I'm afraid of getting in to that mess I was in August, September, October – when I was desperately in love with you. It isn't good enough. I will NOT go into that Hell again.

I've tried loving a woman who doesn't love me, you; & I've tried loving a woman who isn't clean, Ka; & it doesn't pay. I'm going to find some woman who is clean, & loves me.

So, my dearest old Noel, you're one of the few things in the world I'm devoted to. I'd do anything I could for you, & I want to. But, I think it's safest to keep the other side of the street, or the world, from you.

But all that doesn't mean that I blame you, as you've so lately learnt to blame yourself. That's the part of your letter that really is bloody silly, & that really riles me. (Your ingenious malice against me got under my guard, & made me wriggle, once or twice, I'll confess: & I always wince when you say you got "precious little" out of the four years I tried to give you.) But what's wrong? I suppose you're tired & overworked; you looked it on the evening of May 23rd. But you're *hateful* about yourself.

You old silly, it was very unfair of me to say "What are you at?" to you, – implying, for the deception of an innocent little girl, that all other males & females knew well what they were "at" the whole time. Noel, I will tell you a secret. No one ever knows what he or she is at. It's really so. In outline, you behaved precisely & boringly like any other girl in the world; as I did like any other boy – Really, child, – I think parts of you, & things you've done, wrong. But very slight affairs – you're just a little too irresponsible. That's all. The main evil was that we didn't, after all, love each other; and for that no one is to blame. Or, if anyone, I: for having been very often so very unpleasant; as I now see I was. Even that was inevitable to my age & temper, perhaps. But oh! how unbearable I was! You know, Noel, we were at odds about a good many things; & in almost *all* of them I've come to see that you were right. I don't know that you had *thought* much more wisely than my able self. *You* only had a cleaner mind and a better nature.

O dear, I'm so irritated. Chiefly with you, because you're in a dreadful mood, exasperating & depressing to me. All this about the world being no place for you . . . My dear, what's up? I'll accept, & discount your characteristically made apology for things not having gone well. You have no need or right to make it. But – what's up? Have you a pain anywhere? Are you ill? In as far as you think you don't fit the world, just because you rather muddled our business, – it's nonsense.

All that proves is that you knew nothing at all about men, just as I knew nothing at all about girls. And so both suffered, the more because we (especially I) are unusual people. But, I'm not so conceited as I was; & I don't believe that's what is chiefly bothering you. (It *might* be: you're so queer: but I guess not.). Well, what is it?

I continue this with the spray of Niagara falling lightly upon me. A fitting place! But oh, oh, oh! Last night there were blueberries (I forget what you call them) on the *menu*: blueberries & cream. So I ordered & ate them, slowly & sacramentally, & sentimentally, thinking nobly of the woods by the Teign. Materially, they were singularly tasteless. My punishment came: for all night I dreamt of you. Brr . . . I don't like it.

Your picture of your future self is what I finally detest. You see, you don't know *at all* what you're like. You've not the remotest conception of the things that have given me pain & pleasure in you. As for what you *feel* like; I don't suppose that'll go on being so unsatisfactory. You will, – as you put it with that devilish literary power that was always & so fatally one of your charms "go along the streets" – but it's quite a good thing to Do. I approve the thought of you going along the streets, as I used to approve the reality. A sweetly pretty picture: tossing your not very brown, & fairly delightful head. We – the world – will accept it. Many nastier people go up & down the streets, and few nicer. From your *own* point of view – you'll find it's quite a pleasant occupation. – My romantic darling, what *do* you want? To play Cleopatra? No, no, you're for better things, you childishest of children. You'll love somebody sometime: I've little doubt: & find it isn't whatever horror or delirium you suppose, but just great friendliness & trust & comfort – ordinary things. Nor do I doubt you'll marry – when I hear of it I'll have a bad hour or two, & then be too busy with my own lovee to think about it – & have children (it's always been my thought what lovely children you would have, most of all if they were mine). These things come round the corner on one . . .

I quite sympathise about this messy "love" & "soul" business people pour out. I plagued you worst that way; so I feel much ashamed. It's partly that you know people distinctly older than yourself; you'll sympathise *slightly* more with them when you are their age. – And partly, as I repeatedly say, your male friends haven't been at all a good lot lately – *quorum pars maxima ego.*[3] (or have you forgotten all I taught you from Catullus, on the lawn?) I'm quite serious about this. But the world's really a jolly place, full of healthy & merry people . . .

It's so very hard, trying to write humanly. All these damned

---

3 Of whom I am the greater part.

affectations get in the light – they leap from the end of the pen. Diffidences, sham jokes, – Stracheyisms all. Disgusting. (You may sympathise: you're afflicted, too.)

I so wish, sometimes, I could get near you – that I dare trust myself – There's so much good. And we could talk – But I daren't – you must be tired of trying to read all this. I get more incoherent as I get older (and I shall be twenty-six before this reaches you!) I'm in such a tumult between rage and – love with a small l. So, goodbye – What I want to do, in sum, is, I think, this:

to thank you *very much* for your letter;

& not at all for your way of writing it.

Is there anything else? I searched Toronto for your cousin. I met him continually: to two or three people I said "Are you the result of . . . etc. . . . etc. . . . " They all denied it. But sure, there are a lot of people in Toronto who have a passing resemblance to you. I *expect* I saw him.

I go on to Winnipeg, Regina, Saskatoon, Edmonton, the Rockies, Vancouver, 'Frisco, & the South Seas. Rugby is my address.

If, Noel, you can spare a minute from your own woes, *and* if you happen to meet Ka, will you please be nice to her? I think she is so particularly in need of it; and you *can* be so nice, if you'll let yourself be. Don't mention me to her at all. I'm cut off – I had to – Do.

Love to the family.

Noel, I always thought it was a funny name . . . not very English. Splendid Noel – silly little child – my friend, my penultimate word to you is, don't be a fool: my ultimate one, eat Ovaltine.

With love
Rupert

July 28
But I shall write again perhaps: about my Adventures.

I always so desire to repeat that tiresome demand that you should invoke my assistance whenever you need it – may it be taken as written at the end of *each* letter, till I revoke it?

[POST CARD]

from Somewhere in the Sierra Nevada

[Postmark 16 Sept 1913]

1

Of beauteous dames of noble birth,
Many, thank God, shall walk the earth:
And many fair as stars have been;
But none like Princess Angeline.

2

For Deirdre men have suffered Hell;
And some loved Helen all too well,
and Cleopatra, that dark queen;
I loved the Princess Angeline.

3

Keats hymned his Fanny (more fool he!),
And Browning sang of Mrs B.,
And Longfellow, Evangeline.
I sing the Princess Angeline.

4

Shout to the sackbut, shrill the flute!
Whisper it low upon the lute!
Strike loud, strike loud, the tambourine!
I love the Princess Angeline.

5

Some like'em young: & like'em pretty,
Winsome & round & red & witty:
They love a pert & plumpy quean,
And tend to find *my* angel lean.

6

Some love a love divine, & bow
To white hands, & an ivory brow
And pale unmoved immortal mien;
And mock the earthy Angeline.

7

But laughter's better than loveliness,
And wrinkled cheeks than youth, I guess,
A gay heart than soul serene,
– *So I stick to Princess Angeline.*

One could go on for ever – Rupert

[The Champions,
Limpsfield,
Surrey.]

September: 25th. Thursday [1913]

Dear Rupert

When your letter came to me, I was having a camp with the
Bloomsbury group in Suffolk, We had four tents & a fire place in a
ragged field with woods on two sides of it and the Ouze in marshes
near by. There was Daphne & Margery & Maynard, Adrian & Vanessa
& Duncan, Bryn & Hugh for a weekend, Roger Fry,[1] Clive Bell,[2] Mrs
McCarthy,[3] & Ka for short times at various intervals. Only D[aphne] &
I & Adrian & Maynard were there the whole time – some twelve days.
We all got very used to one another and I thought that Adrian turned
out to be a great bore; that was probably unfair of me, & only because
he tried to please. I was pretty placid & cheerful & liked to see Duncan
& Vanessa at their pictures out in the field, Daphne absorbed in
Dotztoyevsky[4] & Maynard always busy with his writing. Then there
was also the cooking & the airing & the endless washing up. It was
nice, as camps always are; but not one of the nicest.

I was very glad to hear from you; the letter was so good & – on the
whole – such a comfort, though at first you seemed too angry with me

---

1 Roger Fry (1866–1934), painter and art critic, who organized the two famous Post-Impressionist
exhibitions, held at the Grafton Galleries. The first opened on 8 November 1910 and introduced the
work of Cézanne, Gauguin, Matisse and Van Gogh to an outraged and disgusted British public.
Reviewers at the time hailed it as 'a pornographic show', which was the work of 'lunatics', and Robert
Ross announced that it proved 'the existence of a widespread plot to destroy the whole fabric of
European painting'. It was also Fry who set up the Omega Workshops, which opened on 8 July 1913.
Here he succeeded in introducing the Post-Impressionists' use of rich colour and strong design to the
applied arts, employing artists such as Vanessa Bell, Frederick Etchells, Duncan Grant and Wyndham
Lewis.
2 (Arthur) Clive Bell (1881–1964), art critic. A Cambridge friend of Lytton Strachey, Leonard Woolf,
and Thoby Stephen (1880–1906), whose sister Vanessa he had married in 1907. He had worked
closely with Fry on both Post-Impressionist exhibitions, despite being aware of the affair that his wife
and Fry began in 1911.
3 Mary MacCarthy ('Molly', 1882–1953), writer. She began in 1918 what became known as the
Memoir Club, where members of the Bloomsbury group would read papers of their personal
recollections; it went on meeting until the 1960s. She was married to the literary journalist Desmond
MacCarthy (1877–1952) and had accompanied him and Fry to Paris, to choose paintings for the first
Post-Impressionist exhibition.
4 By this point, Bunny's mother, Constance Garnett (1861–1946), had completed three of the twelve
volumes of her celebrated English translation of Dostoevsky's work.

for writing so horridly to you before. But finally I noticed the friendly part & was very pleased.

You shouldn't be anxious about my cynical atitude. Surely its very natural that I should think life a difficult thing to get along with? I'm so slack that I shall never *insist* on making it a success, as you do so splendidly. And I must be disheartened, that some of the best things that happened (with you) should lead to such a disgusting mess, inevitably. Even now, there seems no prospect of getting on any better.

The irresponsibility you mentioned is still here, as well as a pathetic affection for everyone, which does no good at all.

Now my last hope is a new plan: to give up having anything to do with people of more than 21. It's these buffers of from 24 – 35 that are the ruin; in future I shall speak only to girls at the school of medicine, to relations & the very youngest friends (Nicholas Pease,[5] Horsely minor[6] etc). If that fails or proves intolerable, I shall have to give it all up and go in to a convent or something. (You would say: "get married"; but one must marry some *one*, & I can't see who) I am very well, pretty fat, teeth newly repaired, hair washed and all that. I keep up the athletics and swam a lot with my friend Mary [Newbery] at Walberswick, I am excessively proud of a dive I did off a wier eighteen feet above the river at camp. I am still fond of the family.

———————————   ———————————

Now I've read your letter again. It *is* nice. And it's mean for me to go on answering so bitterly. I want so much to be friendly too. And I want more letters. Especially I wish you would tell me (finally) exactly what it was *you* think I did wrong with you. You disapprove so vaguely, mentioning "mere trifles" that I feel uneasy, & try to think which things they were. Please say; I won't go on punishing myself about them, but it would be very enlightening to know. And I "won't be a fool"; as you suggested. (though to eat Ovaltine would be indecorous for one of my weight)

I talked to Ka at camp. I always liked her, but I don't see how to be especially kind. How can one do more for people than love them. I love Ka, though she *does* pretend rather to be so old and experienced. Perhaps I shall see her some times in London, now she's settling down

5 Nicholas Pease was the son of Edward Pease (1857–1955), one of the founders of the Fabian Society. His elder brother, Michael, had been a member of the Cambridge Fabian Society Committee, with Rupert. The Pease family lived in Limpsfield, in a converted oasthouse, close to The Champions.
6 Oswald Horsely, a Bedalian friend of Noel's and younger brother of Siward. Oswald was killed in a plane crash in 1918, and when his brother died two years later, Bedales named their new laboratory Horsely, in their memory.

to her publishing business – whilst I go on with my medical career. But she told me then, that she was happy, and would hardly ever be unhappy. I think she was telling the truth. At any rate she was very fat and rosy, and apparently pleased with the adventures she'd had in Poland.

Today Bryn showed me a letter she's just got from you – re Mrs Flower. You still make jokes.[7] It was your peculiarly unpleasant sense of humour which finally killed me off, of course. But no more of that. I hope you are at any rate as jaunty as you sound. You profess – I expect – to despise top gayety, but it seems to me about the one thing that keeps us all going – bar the religious people. Perhaps you're religious?

This summer I canoed up the Severn[8] with Daphne & Bunny & Harold & Pauly Montague[9] – did I tell you? – It's very distant now & a very tender memory. I've been to the O.B. meeting at Petersfield, I've camped with the "Jews".[10] I stayed with Mary's family by the sea for a fortnight; I've packed & unpacked & travelled & I've just been staying in Scotland with James for three weeks. And Bryn & Hugh & Lytton.

Each place has been perfect, every lot of people has become very familiar & agreeable to my mind, & each parting was anguish. It seems almost a preposteous way of spending the holidays: – living with people & tearing one's self away five times; as well as little blinks at Limpsfield & the Family in between. But it's very rich, it's equivalent to five summers & would be good if only I remember it all.

Everybody seems very nice in their way, and very harmless since I've begun to develop the faculty of *not* imitating every remarkable person about.

The Strachey – the long dreaded [Lytton] Strachey – turned out to be a good-natured, slightly dotty buffoon; & in so far as the ridiculous makes the world brighter – an excellent fellow. I haven't yet detected the poison in young Strachey, though his attachment to me and my deadly slight affection for him is the most distressing thing (I hear you managed better by being snappy). No one can help.

_____   _____

I musn't write too much; it would be such confusion for you to read. Already, I seem to have created a beastly jumble of hints & vague

_____

7 Rupert had apparently filled the letter with appalling botanical puns, after he had met this old acquaintance of Bryn's in Canada.
8 They had canoed in July from Bridgenorth to Shrewsbury.
9 Paul Montague, the O.B. who had read Natural Sciences at Caius College and had a passion for Elizabethan music.
10 i.e. the Bloomsbury camp described earlier. In fact, since Leonard Woolf was not present, no one Jewish had taken part. Noel is merely borrowing Rupert's own loose terminology.

impressions. Forgive that literary style which may have been fatally one of my charms (I don't know anything about that), but which wads over the meaning and fuddles the mind (even of the writer).

Letters aren't much good – and conversation isn't much better.

I was very moved at your farewell supper with me, I almost cried again; you seemed to be in such a wretched state, with your editor coming in half an hour and your forty superficial friends with Beer at twelve.[11]

It didn't seem real that your appearance should be so familiar & your soul (or whatever it's called) so strange. Perhaps your acting made you even more foreign than ever. (Your soul's turning out to be like Milton's, was always another difficulty) I can't think how it came to such a scene.

That musn't ever happen again. If you think you can't stand it, you had better not see me again. I don't want to see you, it makes me uneasy now. But I agree that it would be nice to stroll along peacefully, as we did here, again; if it could be done. When I'm twenty five & you thirty perhaps we shall be calmer, more restrained people, & will be able to.

I love you much the same as usual. I'm a constant & tepid creature. I wish you well, and thank you for kind help & offers and your letter.

Goodbye
Noel

---

11 After Rupert's supper with Noel on 21 May 1913, he had met up with the editor of the *Westminster Gazette*, J.A. Spender, and then gone on to his farewell party with Geoffrey Keynes and Middleton Murry.

LINE TO HONOLULU
S.S. "SIERRA"

S.S. Sierra, At Sea,
October the eighth (I think) [1913]

My dear Noel,

I've just had, a little to my own surprise, so good and substantial a dinner. It's not that the O[verseas] S[hipping] C[ompany] don't provide the most admirable food, – not thence my astonishment. But I've been feeling so really queer all day, so much – not victimized by, but compromising with – the fairly Pacific but very regular rolling & pitching of S.S. Sierra, so much, in fact what you must always feel like, by your own account, quiet, dull, stodgy, & stupid. But my success at dinner has emboldened me to fly a little higher than sleep & turning over the pages of Miss Austen, which has occupied me all afternoon. So I turn to a letter to you, which is easier than writing one of those damn things for the Westminster, but harder than going on with these tinkly decasyllables on *Friendship*.

I wonder how you're getting on. I often think of my absent my friends in England: about once every three weeks. Lately, I've pictured you all trudging through slush & grime & cold & rain to your various tasks. With me, it has just been one golden blaze of sunshine, ever since I blew in to California, four weeks ago, nearly. Vast brown hills that turn purple in the evening, & an air that seems queerly to have gold sifting & filtering down through it, and women with golden skins and great piles of hair – there's something in the climate that makes all girls grow to six foot high, deep bosomed, and rather *beautiful* – and then the Golden Gate – which stares out at Asia and Africa, through which romantic portal, I sailed out yesterday.

Do you know that feeling of slight surprise when one finds oneself doing something one has planned to do. I have it now. Last week I said that at this time I should be out in the Pacific. And, oh dear me, I *am*. It happened in this way. On Tuesday they said to me, "Where are you going on to next!" "Oh", I said, irresponsibly, "The South Seas".. "When?" "Next week". "Where?" "Ah!" I said, mysteriously: & went home & looked at a map. So next day I could answer "Honolulu: & thence, no doubt, by brigantine or schooner to Fiji or Samoa or

Tahiti" – . I wandered in to a shipping office later & found there *was* a boat for Honolulu this week. So on Thursday I could tell them my passage was booked. Friday to Sunday was taken up with farewell lunches & dinners. On Monday they met me and said, "I suppose you've packed?" So I said "Yes", & hurried home & packed, rather frightenedly. And, finally, yesterday morning, Tuesday, they all came round & said "We're going to see you off!": and they did. So here I am, due in four days to reach Honolulu & wondering what I shall do there. Surf-bathe, I fancy, with a plank. And flirt with the natives. Thence, the South, I suppose –

This boat is filled with Americans & with a baseball team & a rifle team of Hawaians, returning to Honolulu. They are youths of a brown complexion with a touch both of Japanese & of nigger in them. Their own tongue sounds like Italian. But in dress and language they're very Americanized. Raucous.

It's queer, travelling on and on. One's mind becomes blunted to new impressions. I pass through all sorts of new scenery & queer novelties and neglect to notice them at all merely through satiety.

yours
Rupert –

My dear old Noel,

It ended rather abruptly, that letter, didn't it? The truth is, I got to Honolulu, & was too lazy to continue it, and then, the last half hour there, before going on towards Samoa, my mail came, & in it, a letter from you. On the ship (I'm in my bunk now) I read it; & I realise I can't go on with the old letter. Not that I'll try to answer yours now. I will, sometime. All those questions about what you "really did wrong" . . . Lord! Lord! I'll try, one fine day. But it's seven thousand miles away: –

The same old handwriting. A little squarer, perhaps. But then you're a little squarer, I gather. – oh, Noel; you wouldn't deceive an ancient lover, would you, & say you were fat, if you weren't? I'm depending upon you. And – it's horrid of me to open up old sores – but – the old spelling. Or more extraordinary. *Really*, my dear, . . . your rendering that of that exotic epileptic Dostoieffsky, only adds romance to him. But when it comes to "wier" for "wire" . . . I wonder shall I *ever* understand you. You seem better. I hope you are. You *did* look rather bad in May, you know. A nice long dislocated letter. With lots of things in it I want to comment on. Only, three months old comment is thin stuff. But may I peck about in it?

Please don't let your incessant diffidence prevent you being kind to Ka. And don't ask in that hopeless tone of a Cambridge logician "How can one do more for people than love them?" My dear, *you* mayn't have reached a time – you never will perhaps – when you need such things. But, I pray you to believe me, the vastly greater proportion of the world *does*. Not only as comfort, but for the building up of health. There *are* ways of expressing love – if it's only in sitting & grinning. Surely, don't you *know* when the current is flowing? I can't help Ka. But I'm very anxious about her, And I so desire that people who don't want to sponge on her, as nearly all her friends do, people with strength in them, like you, shall show her love. It's the food she needs. You are richer than you make out Gnädiges Fräulein. Don't worry about it, but when you *do* meet her in the streets of London, I pray you, grin, & ask her how she is.

Noel, you hit hard, – & so unexpectedly. The Last Supper – I'd thought it was so nice. (Except that I wanted to shake hands with you, & you completely evaded it, coming & going.). And now it turns out that it was ghastly failure. Oh, Lord! Was I *very* unpleasant? – It was unpardonable of me to be so late, I know. And I was nervous & silly. But I *did* think I was, on the whole, being so nice. I so much wanted to try to make out that, after all, we had our point. My mind was full of "parting friends" & such like ideas – And now it turns out that you hated it all, & that I was "acting", & that my "soul was strange" (I *was* acting, I suppose, but a pathetically well-meaning part.) . . . Well, well, one more little white cross in the cemetery.

> "One more task for the undertaker,
> 'Nother little job for the tombstone maker",[1]

I'm very sorry. Please think it wasn't so very bad; & wipe it out of your mind. I do despair of literature & history when I read your letter. I can see how utterly impossible it would be for a person to get within a million miles of what you're like who read that letter alone & hadn't seen you. I suppose all our judgements are like that.

I dislike your summer. You seem to see a bloody rotten lot of people. I applaud your intention only to see people under 22. Horsley minor sounds utterly charming. How beastly of James to invite you for

---

1 Unidentified.

three weeks with Lytton about! & how very beastly (to James) of you to go! I am very fond of James, though I disapprove of him so strongly that I have to keep away – & I wish he could get clear of you. No doubt, though, he'd only get himself in a mess elsewhere –

(Really the unrelieved *sordidness* of that man's career – loving me for nine years & you for the rest of his life! I sometimes think God has been a little *too* hard on him, dreadful as he is.)

You think Lytton a "harmless buffoon", & I know he is Judas Iscariot. So let it rest. Or you'll feel that I'm as irritating as Ka, in my assumption of age, experience, & knowledge.

I alternate in reading your letter. Often you seem very hard & cynical & bitter, & then I rather hate you; & again you keep turning out to be your very nice, lovely, & rather silly self, and I melt in to a heap of – in a good sense – laughter.

I watch you, from afar & in these intermittent glances, with the kindly anxiety of the elderly, intensified by the fact that I loved a younger sister of yours, once, a long while since, and by another sea (quotation from my new sonnet).[2] I realise that your own accounts give a one sided view, & that, if I went by them I should be leaving out of consideration the important things – which I should see well enough if I was dangerously at hand. I mean, that queer mixture of your (oh hell!) beauty and (if you promise to try sympathetically to understand this) your incomparable solidity. *That's* what the world's richer for, though it mayn't alleviate your disgust with life. But, at this distance, I am rather more concerned with the world's happiness than with yours; the more than I am a part of the world & not at all a part of you.

Yet – it *would* be a pity if you get spoilt. I suppose it's very hard to be 21 gracefully. How little I succeeded! I have been very unpleasant these past few years. Don't you be, please. I detect signs of it. Be malicious, sulky, a Suffragette, a murderess, or what you will, but for God's sake do not be like me. That would be the last straw.

This is not a letter: but a note-book. Yours was coherence to it. I'll write, sometime, of my travels. And even to "explain" things – but I find it so hard to remember. You see, my Noel, I've been through a bad storm since most of *our* little affair; & that puts things so far back. The truth of it all is, we weren't fitted for each other. You had the sense to see so, & the luck not to love me. So I thank you. We made a "mess" of things. But there have been worse messes. I'm very glad you exist, &

---

2 He had just finished 'Waikiki'.

that I know it. I hope you're happy, & seeing decent people. Please, please, believe that you are "successful". – Oh, dear me, I feel so painfully fond of you. Thank you for writing, for being friendly, & for being nice to Ka. Love to your family. I kiss your fingers.

with love.
Rupert.

WAIKIKI

Warm perfumes like a breath from vine and tree
    Drift down the darkness. Plangent, hidden from
        eyes,
    Somewhere an *eukaleli* thrills and cries
And stabs with pain the night's brown savagery;
And dark scents whisper; and dim waves creep to me,
    Gleam like a woman's hair, stretch out, and rise;
    And new stars burn into the ancient skies,
Over the murmurous Hawaian sea.

And I recall, lose, grasp, forget again,
    And still remember, a tale I have heard, or known,
An empty tale, of idleness and pain,
    Of two that loved – or did not love – and one
Whose perplexed heart did evil, foolishly,
A long while since, and by some other sea.

Wastdale Head
Cumberland.

Dec: 31st 1913

We're all up here climbing. A list (as usual) will probably give the vividest idea of us: Margery, Daphne, me, Bill, Ethel, David,[1] and Mr Bishop, who is a scraggy climbing man of Sheffield. We spend a week & then go home. And you wouldn't appreciate any account of how we spend it, (I once told you, with some care how much I enjoyed two days, snowed up in an Alpine hut; & you cursed me for a curate, for telling you. I was very hurt (pride hurt) that my letter hadn't carried you more *with* me; & I shd be hurt again, if a similar thing happened.

But we were in awful bad tempers summer 1912)

I was delighted to get your letter. I mean – it was very nice. Only it was rather sickening to find that answer to my most disagreeable remarks. They should have been ignored I expect. Allusions to the old life turn out depressing & gangreenous, now 'a' days. Please don't struggle to remember & explain anything more about it; its too long ago to be even valuable as an object lesson anymore.

I wish *I* could write without either making speeches or drivelling, & without all these phrases. *What* it is to make it one's chief business, finding out how to write what one means! (given one means something).

Oh – I'm twenty-one.

It came without a pang, & it's already gliding past without a qualm or a spark of improvement – like all the other ages. Probably I shall find out sometime that one *does* get older; but I can't see, yet, the difference between this & fifteen. Everything since fifteen has been sordid & very similar. I'm talking about the personality (Badley would say "Character"; and Jacques: "Soul" – until he remembered that, of course, the little beast hasn't got one yet). Also my memory is as bad as ever – and only tonight I said a lot of silly things, whilst arguing on the meaning of "priggishness" or rather "a prig", because I *forgot* what I and they had said at first, & even which side I was on.

Perhaps it's fortunate; but it really is a fact, that I can't believe you,

---

1 David Randall Pye (1886–1960), a Fellow of Trinity and later knighted for his work on the internal combustion engine. He was the eldest of Sybil and Ethel's brothers.

when you say I've got intellect – nor Mrs McCarthy, when she says I'm "more Napoleonic than Bonaparte" nor any of those who pretend I'm in the least remarkable on the right side. "Wellmeaning, careless, muddleheaded, selfish, dense, bad-tempered, cursed with an acute love of Property, mean, cowardly, vain." oh all such words, also "incompetant & lazy" (which you'd agree to –) are true of me. And they describe best the various parts which, combining this way & that, produce: the way I behave and the effect. I swear there is nothing bigger – not yet. Let us only hope that you are all prophets. You praisers.

And after this, you may as well add: "dishonest hypocrite" because I go about feeling smug and well satisfied with myself most of the time; rather charming too, I trust.

Were you like this at twenty one? You warn me not to be like you. Probably there is very little chance of it; because, you know, it's hardly possible. Just think of you – with all your feelings & rages – *think* of them, – no *don't* think about them. But anyhow I've none of that, & that's what was so striking in you – you said. *That* and the "charm" of person.

"You'll be seing the New Year in, if you aren't careful" says Bill.

So I will go away & make some resolutions, & come back to you again. Trying to be less lugubrious in 1914.

Goodnight.

Limpsfield

Jan 3rd 1914

We came home yesterday. It was a long travel, starting at half past five & stumbling up to the Sty Head pass in the dark. It was hard & uncomfortable, what with the stones & the thawing snow; and we went on along a road & then in a railway train. It's eight hours from the north to London. Daphne & Margery were both pale & tired, D[aphne] peevish, I thought (we left the rest up there) & I became more & more critical. I dozed & thought how ugly they were; and talked, thinking how stupid, & when I watched their ways, I thought how clumsy &

disagreeable their manners. I also read Peter Simple,[1] which made me
think that the ideal person was a "gentleman". (Margery was no equivalent to a gentleman). And so on. Till I became intolerable to myself &
cursed me for sneering & being so beastly; finally there was nothing left,
but to feel gloomy. So it's a good thing I didn't write to you in the train.
Now I am better.

You must hear about the autumn. I couldn't work properly this
term; I was lazier than ever & also took on lots of activities & joined
heaps of the school clubs, amongst them, the Debating Society of which
I was made secretary; I gave it too much thought & worried about it, so
having more excuse for laziness. Really it was an effort to throw off the
older generation & move with the adolescents; but it was a poor effort,
not replacing but adding to the distraction of the grown ups, (I hope all
this won't bore to irritation)

I started well. After Scotland, James & I became very sane & very
courageous & said goodbye. He wrote no more notes & I never called.
When we met by chance it was taken fairly calmly & quite silently, &
one of us went away at once. I found it very dreary, never being able to
talk to him. And he found it worse. (In a few days he's going abroad for
six months) It was extraordinary, what a poor comfort, the satisfaction of
having taken the only possible way, was. Prudence does not seem to be its
own reward. I – in my zeal – tried to induce Békássy to become a
stranger too. But he pointed out that it was nonsense & would be unfair,
and I agreed. We saw him in Cambridge when D[aphne] & I went up one
week-end (we saw forty friends altogether). And he was wonderfully
nice. He entertained in his continental room, so empty & tall; & rode &
talked; I thought he was probably superior to anyone I knew. But I like
everyone so much that it would be hard to stick to that idea.

Békássy is safely of my time. But the *Stephens; there* was a fall!

Vanessa so graciously asked me to Asheham, that I went. I met Mr
Desmond McCarthy there, and, this time, was *enchanted*. He was in a
good temper, and talked gaily, in the best manner of the nicest people
of 40–50; and there was a great rest in his absence of modernity.[2] Old
'Nessa, sitting on the floor in a blue skirt and emerald green sweater
peicing together an "Omega" table top, inspite of her fine breeding,

---

1 A novel by Captain Frederick Marryat (1792–1848), published in 1834. The book details the
nautical adventures of its upright and honest, but decidedly foolish, eponymous hero.
2 Desmond MacCarthy (1877–1952), literary journalist and husband of Molly MacCarthy. Upon
leaving Cambridge he began his distinguished literary career by writing for the *Spectator*. He went on to
become literary editor on the *New Statesman* and in 1928 senior literary critic on the *Sunday Times*,
receiving a knighthood in 1951.

seemed false. Adrian, who turned out to be there too (I was so angry about it) appeared a fool. And I shewed, ignorant, without taste, & immature; wch being a revelation of the truth, I appreciated. Leonard Woolf bicycled over from some house, where Virginia was being looked after by two nurses, & by visits from Ka.[3] I still respect him very much. We played hockey. All the time I worked up an odious indignation against the good Adrian; not even to be calmed by his radiant beauty, as it appeared, when he dined in pyjamas (though it touched me considerably) my hate only subsided after I had left him, in Bloomsbury, on Monday morning. Later on, I felt much more amiable. I attended two or three parties at Brunswick Square, & played Poker with him & the Pophams & such as Maynard & [Gerald] Schove & Mr Sidney Turner.[4] We played late: till twelve and a half past three and four. One evening your Brother Alfred came in – it was extraordinary – with Maynard & two other gentlemen, they played at another table & bet high, your brother winning, though he had come prepared to lose. I dont like Alfreds face, you know. Yours is much better; you did have *some* of the luck, although he appears so far more prosperous a man.

Finally there were the dances; you wouldn't understand: I got very keen & went to lots with Maitland,[5] and learnt the Tango. (which the Queen has now banned & lots of other Society ladies, so I don't know if it'll be much use)

And an exhibition of pictures by Blake at the Tate. *Still* I don't like them. This time I explained my dislike to Maitland by saying I didn't *believe* in them: they all depend on Blake's strong feeling of the existence of Evil (it showed very clearly in a beastly thing with angels of Good & Evil repelling one another). And Evil is a thing I havnt deffinitely realised yet. They all tell me I shall later – so I wait; & then I'll go and look at Blake again.

I wish you would write more of your travels, & what you *really* find on

---

3 Early in the evening of 9 September 1913, Virginia Woolf had attempted suicide, by swallowing a lethal dose of veronal. She was found unconscious by Ka, who had been helping Leonard look after her. Swift medical attention from, amongst others, Geoffrey Keynes, saved her life. On 20 September she was moved to Dalingridge Place in Sussex, where she very gradually began to recover.
4 Saxon Arnold Sydney-Turner (1880–1962), civil servant. He read Classics at Trinity and gained a double First. While at Cambridge he became an Apostle and began lifelong friendships with Clive Bell, Thoby Stephen and other members of the Bloomsbury Group.
5 Maitland Radford, the son of the Garnetts' friends Ernest and Dollie Radford, who had briefly fallen in love with Bryn while camping at Clifford Bridge in 1911.

them. Weren't those islands very wonderful, inspite of all the obvious strangeness, to which – you say – you are becoming senseless? I can't believe that you just go along looking right & left & jotting down quaint conversations, & writing it up for the Westminster, every week, & that all. We all read the Westminster of course; but I want to hear if you've *liked* anything.

It absurd, to let this get so long, I shall have to spend pounds. And I havn't said any of the important things yet.

I *must* say: that I think you *ridiculous* in your attitude towards Lytton & James. Your comparison to Judas (or some such) didn't mean much to me, of course; but I realise that you agree with Jacques about them. I can *just* understand your thinking them evil; & I could understand your *disliking* them and avoiding them because of *that*. But why be afraid of James, if you *do* like him? You can so easily understand him. And if you understand & love the fellow, it's only silly & unkind to run away. This fear of "contamination" is surely only a phrase.

A person barricaded with principles, as you are, & with their eyes open, *couldn't* be injured by a simple – even if weak & somewhat mistaken – James.

I shall always be sorry too, that you miss the great fun of seing Lytton & his jokes, & enjoying the most extraordinary of creatures and his strange amiability, even though he is an old devil.

You said, "how beastly"; but I must save James from your disapproval on this point. He didn't want L[ytton] to come to Scotland; & only let him come when we, & I especially, said we were longing to meet him. Also my beastliness in going, I don't admit.

These old bones are getting rather dry though, aren't they? It will be your turn next. I saw Jacques for five minutes in Cambridge, well & hearty. And Dudly adorable in London for three.

Bon Voyage, mon vieux. Write again

With love & from the family

Noel.

I read & heard what you said about *loving* & *expressing* love (to Ka). (I heard & I will obey)

P.S. Justine is well again & working in tea. We saw him at Cambridge & a Bedalian dance.

Great Hall
Kings' College

February 4th [1914]

Dear Rupert.

If you are passing New Calledonia at any time, you might look in & see Pauly Montague, who is collecting welks & butterflies in the interior (Besides him, there are some French convicts and the cannibals) His address is

> Post Office
> Noumea
> New Calledonia

I recommend him as a relief from every other person you have met on your travels – he is fresh & genuine, being mad.[1]

Here is a man lecturing to the public at Kings College (London) on the philosopher Bergson. This evening he is very difficult to listen to. The chairman is sleeping, so are a gentleman & a lady on my left. Daphne isn't really attending, she only rouses herself for the phrase: "the point at which body & spirit meet is *Action*" And shakes her head, because she can't bear action & is affraid that he will soon say: – "The object of Life is Action" To which sentiment she is strongly opposed. Contemplation is preferable (& not to be classed as action) – Ursula [Cox] is here too, & not attending either, not even for a moment.

"Let us try to remove our thoughts" – from this lecture hall; which is sordid & probably incomprehensible to *you* in the South Seas.

I meant to write a better letter than the last, which went all wrong – I remember. And I didn't mean to give any advice; – but there is *one* thing that I can't help saying, I keep on thinking it:

Two days later at 11.Briardale Gardens Hampstead: –
What I can't help saying is this: I do wish you wouldnt travel at such a rate. From what I gather, you seem to go quickly from one well known town to another; in each you spend only a very few days, and all you try to get from each is a superficial impression, a vague outline of what

---

1 Paul had left the previous October on this biological expedition to New Caledonia and did not return until April 1915.

appears to a stranger to be the political industrial local, etc characteristics, suitable for description in the Westminster Gazette in England. And in the people you meet, it is only the superficial, queer & obvious things you look for; & if you find them to be what you like to think is typical of the country, you are satisfied & leave them, with a few notes re them in your pocket book.

I don't want to be unfair. I think that your articles in the Westminster were admirable – very much better *from that rapid point of view* than anything *they* could write; & I don't think it a pity that you should write them, they were charming & I hope you were very proud of them. But what grieves me, is that the *whole* of your attitude – as you travel – is that journalistic one; and your letters expressed that. It *is* such a waste. I don't know how much your arrangement with the travelers swap society binds your movements; but surely you would be allowed to stay a little longer in one or two of the places? This eternal going from place to place, must be beastly, & the main impressions in your life are trains & hotels & ships & luggage & other travellers with rugs across their knees. I can't bear to think of the horror & discomfort you must suffer; it is such a very poor improvement on your life the last months in England.

Good Lord!

Rupert I'm sure you must hate it, don't go on. You would perhaps find something so much better if you chose a lodging in a place, unpacked your bag – to the bottom – hung up your clothes & put your books on a shelf & *lived* there for a few months. You would get something solid, in finding out what the people were *really* like & the place & liking some of them, instead of being merely amused by them. And it would be a great rest if they came to treat you not as the poet & journalist from England, but as – at least – Mr Brooke, a queer nice man, quiet & lazy & friendly at heart.

I should rather like to think of you in a farm in the country (not doing any one of the work, you know) but I suppose that is too blatantly sentimental of me.

I see I *am* sentimental – romantic (as usual) but I do think I'm right this time. Because it *is* possible & would obviously be better for you to stop living in a nightmare – this particular & unnecessary nightmare.

And seing another part of the world from Europe might be such a splendid experience, if you did it the right way. Gracious! It is a waste of the chance, to do it as you are.

But I've said quite enough about it. Please don't be angry at my criticising again. I want the suggestion to be useful

_____

Limpsfield Feb: 22nd. Sunday night in bed.
I've been waiting for days to get a little while when I should be in sufficiently good temper as well as having the time, to go on with this. Now there's only half a minute, if I'm going to be able to wake up & catch the train tomorrow.

I want to write very amiably. To impress on you how glad your friendly letters (the ones that came months ago) make me. And how much I hope you will write more, & not mind my scribbling back occasionally. I could promise never to come near you again, & take a great deal of care not to be spiteful, if you would allow letters: – & you seemed inclined to like them & writing.

I agree with you: I think its pretty certain that, if ever you came back to Europe, we'd better not call. Its certain from my point of view as well as from yours. I am amazed at the clear head I ever kept a year ago even. I grow more & more wavering, quavering, dotty, jigety & unsound, – more incapable of behaving when "allowed out" – I suspect. I pull through, it is true, but I'm damned clumsy & I tread on anybody's toes which happen to be in my way. I don't want to tread on yours any more. I should like to be a friend, without being unpleasant, if it is possible. If it isn't; then it's awful. So write & *say* it is possible.

<u>Please.</u>
Goodnight.

Hampstead Feb 25th
I'd better send this stuff off, it's getting worse & worse.

This is the news: –

Brynhild had a tea party this afternoon and Justine was chief guest; he seems quite well & chats gaily about his tea business & old days & one person & another. Maitland was there & was pretty whitty & very nervous, (there's a slight malentendu between him & me just at present) Also Adrian was there & all four. It ended in Poker; I settled down to lose; Daphne went off to see Die Meistersinger,[1] Justine went back to Reading & Maitland to his fever Hospital.

_____

1 The Wagner opera had a run of five performances in February and March at Covent Garden.

The Pophams are very charming, I've just come home from supper there. Bryn seems more & more beautiful & I get fonder of Hugh every time I meet him. The lady doctor has injected Margery with Tuberculin, it is supposed to insure her against consumption; but at present she feels very ill with the dose & is a sorry sight. (She lives with B[ryn] and H[ugh]).

I don't see much of anybody. Ka for about five minutes since Christmas; Gwen & Jacques for one weekend on their estate, Adrian from time to time & that's all. No more Vanessa; no more Stracheys, since James has gone to Moscow.[2] Only father & mother & Daphne & Ursula, who lives with me.

I must devise a new letter about these people (unless you wire to stop me) later. Goodbye.

with love from Noel.

El Tovar Grand Canyon Arizona
Don't believe it.

April 25 [1914]

My Dear Noel,

In San Francisco recently I found my November – February mail. My October mail is still in Samoa: my March mail in New York. But that batch contained immense New Year's letter from you. Sweetheart (that's the ordinary form of address in Tahiti where I've been living), sweetheart, it was extraordinarily nice of you. I can't tell you, moreover, how happy I was to find that your style has dropped those few Stracheyisms and Brookologies that I'd grievously seen creeping in in the past eighteen months, & was now modelled

---

2 James arrived in Moscow on 14 February 1914, having taken in Berlin *en route*. Before leaving, he wrote to Lytton saying that if he should die he wanted Noel to have his books 'if she should care for them'. (Cf. *Bloomsbury/Freud*, ed. Meisel and Kendrick, p. 21)

exclusively on Mr. Bradshaw[1] and the late Rev. G.S. Shuckburgh, who wrote a *History of Rome* (& indeed, lived in the Old Vicarage Grantchester, in the 'forties) – [2]

It gave me an immense bird's eye view of the past nine months. In the South Seas I'd suspected that nothing was happening anywhere, – just because nothing, blessedly, happened *there*. But oh! everything went on. And your catalogue method just showed it going on. One or two details puzzled me rather. You as secretary of a Debating Society. Did you *really* make debating speeches Noel? I somehow don't see you at it.

Rt. Hon. Miss N. Olivier, (brilliantly) "The hon. gentleman (or lady) has said that this is a very disastrous affair. (*laughter*). I agree with the hon. (gentleman/lady) – it *is* a very disastrous affair. (*more laughter*) It is very disastrous – for the hon. (gentleman/lady)! (*Loud laughter, and cheers.*)."

That's what's called a debating point. No, no, Noel. I can't fit it in with the world I know. Tell me, please, that your activities were mostly scribal.[3]

I was so much touched by your plea for James; & your dropping out that he was going abroad for six months, that I wrote to him. I was alarmed for his health & happiness. After all, the poor creature *is* lonely: & he's not the sort that can stand loneliness. And he does, in his fashion, attempt spasmodically to protest against the more obvious nastinesses of Lyttonism. He has been brought up not to know what good is. But he *means* well. And that's something. And in the last seventeen years I've grown to like him. Well, I shall see him, just as I shall see you and everybody else – some day. Meanwhile, I hope he's fairly well.

You know, I can't satisfy your demand for a 'real account' of my wanderings; not just funny conversations for the Westminster. You know, the Westminster articles weren't meant for you intellectuals – they were just for ordinary people who like that sort of thing, – people

---

1 George Bradshaw (1801–53), who devised and published Railway Time Tables. By 1841 these became known as *Bradshaw's Monthly Railway Guide*.
2 Rupert is probably referring to the classical historian Dr E.S. Shuckburgh, who had been a Fellow of Emmanuel College. He did live in Grantchester until his death in 1906, though in Grove Cottage, not the Old Vicarage.
3 Although at the London School of Medicine for Women Noel's activities were restricted to keeping the minutes, she had been heard on the debating floor at Bedales. At the Senior Debate in March 911, Békássy in 'his inimitably explicit style, opposed the motion "That the predominance of sentiment in modern fiction is deplored by this house".' He was seconded by Noel, who 'almost timidly spoke forth. Sentiment in *good* books is not overdone; it is a necessary tool to give the desired effect.' Bedales Chronicle: vol. iv, no. 8, p. 90.

who read the Westminster – , people, in short, like myself. For, I can't
disguise the fact, what I related in the W[estminster]. G[azette]. is all that
happened to me, pretty well. Had I been an intellectual . . . But I'm quite
commonplace & I cannot write prose, & Canada's a bloody dull place.
There was more romance in the South Seas. More colour, certainly. I'm
tempted to return there: But those things – dull enough in the relating –
must wait for the relation till you & I & the rest meet at that delightful
dinner party at Bryn's, that'll celebrate my return this year or next, – a
dinner party to which – I can't disguise it – I, occasionally, in my
solitary wanderings, look forward to with a notable quickening of my
heart . . .

What I'm doing now, is really equally difficult to tell. Yesterday I
threw an orange a mile. That, I think, ought to make you respect my
body, if you don't my mind. But oh Dear, it was a mile downwards.

But that's something, isn't it? Oh, there's really no news about
myself that I don't put in the Westminster. Except one thing, & that I
couldn't put in, because Miss Royde Smith,[4] Daphne's friend, is so
particular. Its not, anyhow, of interest to anyone except me: but – it fills
my mind & life to an extraordinary extent. It's about my arms, & the
Tropics. The effect the Tropics has on them, – only from the elbow
downwards – is that they've grown an immense mat of hair very thick
& long & mouse-coloured. It creeps out a little on to the back of my
hand, so I'm very shy in company, & sit with my hands up my sleeves,
like Tagore,[5] or a Chinaman. I suppose it's the result of going about half
naked for several months. But it didn't have the same effect on my
shoulders – which would have been delicious. There it only took all the
skin off, & left great raw patches, into which the sea-water got, & which
were hardly cured, even though beautiful brown maidens rubbed them
assiduously with coconut oil.

There's about me: egotism to egotism, to balance your self-
reflections. I was moved by your account of you all discussing
"priggishness" in a hut on Skiddaw. My dear, if you knew how
impossible it was to find young people discussing anything in this land.
The American girl is so bright, so vurry vurry bright: & oh God! so
boring. She shrills & shrills & shrills all in a glittering mechanical
flirtation. She has no curiosity, no desire to learn, or to teach, the truth,

4 Naomi Gwladys Royde-Smith (d.1964), the novelist, who at this point was literary editor of the
Westminster Gazette.
5 Rabindranath Tagore (1861–1941), Bengali poet and seer whose work had achieved fame and
popularity in Europe and America after he visited London in 1912. He received the Nobel prize for
literature in 1913 and was knighted in 1915.

no sense of following an idea, seriously or humorously. "Badinage" is all, gallons & gallons of badinage; & none of it *at all* good. I suppose English young ladies will very soon be like that. 'Tis the end of Feminism & Plutocracy. But at present – oh, I wouldn't say that you're all either as charming or as intelligent as the damsels of the South Sea Islands – but you *do* shine in comparison with the American female. Noel, I do not think you clever. I have given up every kind of admiration for you – everything, indeed, except a sort of affection. I will agree that you are averagely stupid. I'm even glad you are. But sweetheart, there are times, after conversation with a 'clever' American young woman, when I *long* to sit at your feet day after day, just drinking in wisdom. So, when we meet, if you notice my round eyes & dropped jaw of admiration, as I hear you say "Shakespeare was a great man" or "Marriage is a difficult problem", do not be misled, lady. It will pass, it will pass. 'Tis but relief.

There was high comedy in your poker game: to which enter "Maynard, Alfred, & two other gentlemen". I'm so glad you didn't like Alfred. I suppose he's got worse since I saw him. He was very swiftly on the downhill slope then. Praise me, my dear, that I didn't go like that. I so easily might have. – It *is* funny about his prosperity, isn't it. I can't understand it. I've a theory some rich woman is keeping him. But I think I shall ask him for his tailor's address. I fancy I could be made to look a little like that: & I certainly want to. I could get a better price for my sonnets, if I didn't look down at heel . . . But, oh!, I *wish* I'd been there –

I shall cease to write to you: & go out & look at the Grand Canyon. It is alternately alarming & restful. It is the biggest in the world . . . Noel, I am sick of immensity, I've seen the biggest buildings in the world, & the biggest lake in the world, & the biggest volcano in the world & the biggest river in the world & the biggest canyon in the world & the biggest – I forget the rest. They are not interesting, or not for long. I desire small hedges & medium sized people & average intellects & tiny hills & villages & a little peace. I shall come back to England – I intend to live the rest of my life with my mother who is the only person I really like. But I shall take occasional holidays in London or Cambridge: so I may run across you again. Be good. Thank you for writing.

with love
Rupert

The London (Royal Free Hospital) School
of Medicine for Women,
Hunter Street. W.C.

May 1914.

My dear Rupert

I think I have been strangely blessed in knowing so many extraordinarily nice people; & among them – you. My affection for you, on getting your April letter & now – is boundless & (through it) my serenity is complete.

I am trying to write you another in the style of Mr Baedecker. Though I am a little sorry that I failed to keep up the Strachey touch.

I've been less depressed for the last month or so; or – in fact – since Bryn's son was born. That was March the 11th; & being frankly an aunt, steadies one & keeps one smiling. He (Hugh Anthony – called Timothy) makes me dotty with pleasure & amusement. Bryn you can imagine: beautiful & more charming than ever, hurrying about the house (at Limpsfield) doing heaps of things: & even idioticer than she's ever been – talking aloud to herself – or him (it is reported) when no one is listening.

I won't sicken you with any details of the Governors & her Ladyship's doting. Though personally I find it all very touching.

However, I was saying: everything's been going very nicely; James writes from Russia, Vienna & Italy to Margery; always pretty gaily – so I don't know really how he's getting on.

Békássy met him abroad in his new beard & thought he looked very distinguished: & he evidently was actively getting a lot out of his galleries & concerts & gypsies etc. Perhaps he'll meet Mary [Newbery] in Florence or Venice. But I'm afraid that would hardly make a match.

Adrian has finally done away with any illusions he had about our family; he no longer asks us to operas & poker parties. He's rather happy I shd think – though as tall & slow as ever. You never knew him as he ultimately turned out: – more & more distinguished.

I can't give everyone in full: –

Virginia and Woolfe havn't been seen at all.

Vanessa is in obeyance.

So's Maynard.

But Justine lives at Brunswick Square & with a new lease of life – jumps about & skweaks & trots out to dances or his tea business & is prepared to sing. His poor little mustach isn't much good I'm afraid –

he's still 23 inspite of it; and I find I've been spelling his name with an e at the end all the time! He's very vexed.

Bryn and Hugh – (they've got a baby) & were very pleased when they heard you were coming to dinner there soon.

Margery's decided to go in for medicine! She's to start this October & is as keen & earnest & determined as anything. Nothing could shake her. Her great capacities are now running the furnishing of our new house – where we're all going to live for the next 26 years.[1]

Daphne goes her ways.

I'm going to tea with *Ka* in a few days. I haven't seen her as often as I've wanted to; its very difficult to; she goes on so many visits to aunts & friends & her cottages in Wiltshire & when I meet her in a concert, she is always in a hurry to get home. But her acount is that she's very happy – doing nothing & reading the newspapers. She is extra-ordinarily ardent about the political situation. And I cant see through, so I suppose her account is true. But I shall persevere. One day, I hope, she will uncoil & be – oh angry or anything, but a little less kindly & elder. She's built up such ramparts in her long & eventful life, that its difficult to know how to attack them – even with the best of intentions & sympathies. As you say – one knows when the currents running – . It's been off so far I'm afraid.

Each time I write, it's in the hope of obliterating the impression of the letter before. I'm always surprised at how well you bear them. I was glad you didn't like the Americane so well as us. But your rumours about the South Sea ladies – are very serious. I know them to be the handsomest & best in the world. *One* is married to the Professor of Anatomy here; & she is evidently a perfect human being & superlative wife. You'll probably have gone back to one of them by now. God bless you.

Oh – There's one piece of news: Peter Watson is at your Vicarage till June. You'll have to disinfect it with sulphur fumes – I should think – when you come back.[2] And I hear there have been all sorts of other horrors: Poor Carey;[3] a Quaker gentleman & I don't know who all,

---

1 Sydney Olivier had finished his term of office as Governor of Jamaica in January 1913 and had returned to England to work as Secretary to the Board of Agriculture. The family had just taken the lease on 19 Marlborough Road, St John's Wood, which they retained until 1917.

2 Elliot Lovegood Grant Watson ('Peter', 1885–1970) was an O.B. and close friend of Ferenc Békássy. He was several years older than Noel, but after finishing at Cambridge in 1909 had returned to Bedales as a science master. He had recently written *Where Bonds are Loosed* and other stories, and his second book, *The Mainland*, was published in 1917.

3 Clive Carey (1883–1968), Rupert's old singing teacher, who had appeared as Chorus in the Marlowe Society's first production of *Dr Faustus* and as Papageno in *The Magic Flute*. He later became Director of Sadler's Wells, and in 1946 was appointed Professor of Singing and Director of Opera at the Royal College of Music.

besides Anthony Neeves in & out & haunting all the time. Lord what ghosts the place is accumulating!

But Peter has written lots of stories & a book, & is rather remarkable – though still ludicrous. You might like his stories – I was very struck. And another book, not read, maybe going to be a masterpiece. You can afford to be encouraging to him.

Your Sonnets in New Numbers were very much respected – I heard extraordinarily high praise of them; & liked them in my quiet way too; as much as any of yours, & better than the other peoples'.[4]

It's amusing how established you made yourself – in those hellish months of charm-mongering. It was completely successful. I congratulate you, I bow to you, & send my love to you

Noel.

Write again

I want to add, that St Johns wood is Paradise. We three aunts live there in atics, & work. I am absorbed in anatomy & Pharmacology & shall fail in my exam in July; but I shall love doing the work again.

Re Debating Speeches. I must confess: – my voice has not once been heard in argument. I write the minutes and misspell. So your world is still the right way up. Vale!

---

4 Edition no. 1 of *New Numbers* in February 1914 included the sonnets: 'Not with vain tears . . . ', 'A Memory', 'One day', 'Today I have been happy' and 'Mutability'. The other contributors were: Lascelles Abercrombie, John Drinkwater and Wilfrid Gibson.

Rupert arrived back in England on 5 June and was met at Euston by Eddie,
Cathleen Nesbitt and an old schoolfriend, Denis Browne. After staying the
night at Gray's Inn, he set off to spend a few days with his mother at Bilton
Road. During his visit to Rugby and after his return to London, he made no
attempt to contact Noel. Then, on 18 June, he attended the first performance
of Stravinsky's Le Rossignol, and bumped into her in the interval. Writing
to Jacques, he makes this report:

> Noel is *not* a bloody little bitch. At least . . . not *quite.* I feel
> very kindly towards her just now. I met her the other day &
> didn't recognize her for some minutes. That *was* a triumph.
> Haven't felt so pleased with myself since Father died. I went
> home & laughed about it for an hour . . . Oh dear me, think
> what the poor girl – Noel – has had to go through. Proposed
> to by me, Adrian Stephen, & James Strachey! Wouldn't it
> turn anybody sour? I think she's a miracle to have outlived
> that at all.[1]

19, Marlborough Road, N.W.
Monday. [6 July 1914] 8.P.M.

Dear Rupert

They say there was a vague & general message of love from
you, this evening; & I've fastened on it, Margery being out.
In spite of our very stern meeting in a theatre corridor, I should
like to send my amitiees & best wishes.
I've got just a week before my exam; its going to be a very difficult

---

1 *KCA*, 20 June 1914 [wrongly dated July 1914]).

one; & I'll fail but it will absorbe me for the nex three weeks, & for that time (nearly) I shaln't walk about in the foyers. I'm begining to really look forward to being a doctor, this exam is the last bar between me & hospital, & then it will all be very alarming & wonderful. I shall live surrounded by ill & broken people, & by the nurses who are all in a great hurry & appear to know exactly what they're doing (that's so disconcerting) & the doctors will be very precise & severe; & I shaln't be able to help offending them & doing the wrong thing. It will be even worse than trying to keep the little boys at Bedales in order, & even more engrossing.

There'll be a good deal of horror too; watching the people being hurt (physically – that's what I cant bear) & standing through those awful silent operations.

I shall be settled so, till I'm twenty five, after that, I shall go from Hospital to Hospital earning little salaries – I shall have a banking account, it will be most remarkable. And the wonder is, that it cant fail to happen, its all consecutive & innevitable & even my insuperable laziness cant stop it.

It makes me very pleased, that fate is clear in the main. I can *quite* sympathise with Englishmen, who like to know exactly whats going to happen next.

Now you're about, I cant give you the news, you probably even know all about me; but I don't mind repeating that. Wherever I go, the ladies say; & so *I'm* going in for medicine, that must be very interesting, how long will it take me, & how long will I be in the hospital, & will I practice afterwards? And I start off in a monotenous voice & tell them all the facts – like I do you – & finish up by saying "I like it very much" in flat tones. Thats the only thing which distresses me, that in spite of being so keen, I should have so inexpressive a voice & conversation.

Today, whilst you were at Bryn's, I was having tea at Brunswick Sqr, with 2 or 3 of *them*. I still love everybody – I'm incurable. And they are all very pleasant & friendly.

But I missed Dudley.

Goodnight. I'm going to learn the arteries.

Love X
Noel.

After war was declared on 4 August, Eddie used his influence to obtain Rupert a commission in the Royal Naval Division, and by the beginning of October he took part in a brief, abortive expedition to try to save Antwerp from the advancing Germans. Here the full horror of war struck him for the first time:

> It's queer to think one has been a witness of one of the greatest crimes of history . . . how can such a stain be wiped out? . . . The eye grows clearer and the heart. But it's a bloody thing, half the youth of Europe, blown through pain to nothingness, in the incessant mechanical slaughter of these modern battles. I can only marvel at human endurance.[1]

Rupert and Noel's last recorded meeting was on 16 October, when they arrived together at the Pophams for a play reading. His subdued manner was noted by his friends, as was his newly cropped hair. The pacifism of the majority of Noel's Bloomsbury friends had served to make Rupert dislike them even more. In December the five famous sonnets in his '1914' sequence appeared in the last issue of New Numbers *and he was drafted to the Hood Battalion, stationed at Blandford, Dorset.*

---

1 To Eddie Marsh, quoted in *CH*, p. 466.

Hood Battalion,
2nd Naval Brigade,
Blandford,
Dorset.

Christmas Day [1914]

My dear Noel,

How old you must be! The Christmases fairly crowd past. And in what queer places I sing *Adeste Fideles* in your honour! Last year Waikiki: this year the R[oyal].N[aval].D[ivision].: next year beyond Acheron[1] – I hope you're getting on well with – whatever you're getting on with: & that Margery's better & Daphne's still well. Here it rains all day & every day. God be with you. Send me all the woollen things you weave –

with love
Rupert

Love to everyone –

19, Marlborough Road, N.W.

January 7th 1915

O, dear Rupert

Yes, I'm twenty two, & it *was* nice of you to suspect something of the kind & write.

Perhaps we shall meet, in a week or two, in what you call, "beyond Acheron". I've been trying to enlist too & may die as soon as you do. But that's not *certain*, as my services haven't yet been accepted. There is a hospital going out to service.

---

1 i.e. in the Underworld.

Yes I rather doubt whether they'll want me.

So I shall go on, walking down the grey's Inn road at 10.10 A.M., & walking through the wards till four, until 1917 – when I shall be twenty five, which I've heard is the prime of life. And then anything may happen, thank God.

The family is slipping, slipping: . . . Daphne & I spent Christmas with Lytton (with Bunny for padding & Francis[1] & Duncan & James) & even Daphne liked it awfully.

We never see Jacques and Gwen, & probably there is no health in us. But it cant much matter, if we're all to be killed.

Between the lines, is all rather monotonous, & cynically put. I beg your pardon. Believe me, that I'm really most genial.

I do hope I shall go to service. Did I tell you that I received through Switzerland, a letter from Békássy, written in September, saying he was going to be sent to fight in five weeks. Perhaps its all over now.[2]

Gerald [Shove] doesn't like Toynbee hall, so he cam hurrying back to Bloomsbury last night to a party of Vanessa's, to refresh himself with the company of all his evil old friends.[3]

I don't know why I shd inflict the information on you though.

Goodbye. God bless you.
Noel.

---

1 Francis Birrell ('Frankie', 1889–1935), journalist, drama critic and bookseller, who had become a friend of Lytton's while at King's. He was also a friend of Bunny's, and later this year they went together to work in France for Quaker Relief. It was after Bunny had introduced Frankie and his other friends to D.H. Lawrence that Lawrence made his caustic outburst, in which he declared that they were all despicable and made him dream of black beetles.
2 Ferenc's last letter to Noel was written in May 1915: 'I'm going gladly, I know it's very worth taking the risk, and I am to get something good out of the war unless I die in it . . . Everything is beautiful now, there are some evenings in which all the lovely things are heaped together, flower-smells, clouds, water, chestnut-trees, and young corn. There are very beautiful sunsets, and all this makes it somehow easier to go . . . By the time I go, there'll be roses, and I shall go with a crest of three red ones on my horse's head because (but people won't know the reason) there are three over the shield in our coat of arms. This isn't at all the letter I meant to write, but I can't help it. I long to see you, and all of you again. I often think of you. And we shall meet, Noel, shal'n't we, some day?' He was killed in a cavalry engagement in Bukovina on 25 June 1915, aged twenty-two.
3 Gerald Shove was another conscientious objector, and after he had worked at the East End settlement he went to work on the land, at Philip Morrell's farm.

The Hood Battalion,
Royal Naval Division.
Jan 10 [1915]

My dear Noel,

You were good to write. The manner of your letter was far
nicer than the matter. But perhaps it's natural, in the absence of men,
for you to seek the company of the other sex.

I'm afraid you'll die long before me. My brigade is ready for
service, but will have to wait three or four months for the rest of the
division. You'll be quite an *habitue* over there. You'll show me about –
(and the sonnet'll be dreadfully falsified). Or will you marry a wounded
lovely Serbian, and become the {Baness/Banette} of some Slavonic
place?

This is really to say: if your family takes in an illustrated paper (the
Sketch, Tatler, or what not) if it sends it me when finished with, week by
week, it'll be lovely for my platoon.

It's very bloody about Békássy. Thank God, he'll be fighting in a
different part of Europe from me. After all, there's a ten to one chance of
him coming through. Dreadful if you lost all your lovers at once, – Ah,
but you won't lose *all* –

But please send me a card if you *do* go abroad. I rather hope you
do.

It's bloody dull, here: not fighting.

With love
Rupert

Epilogue

On 28 February 1915, Rupert set sail for Gallipoli.

A few weeks later, on Easter Sunday, Dean Inge read out his sonnet, 'The Soldier', in St Paul's Cathedral, helping to ensure his subsequent fame. Meanwhile, Rupert was suffering from a mild case of sunstroke, on board the *Grantully Castle*. The doctor treating him noticed a small swelling from a mosquito bite on his upper lip, but he left it untreated and it appeared to clear up. However, by 20 April the inflammation returned and he was diagnosed as having septicaemia and transferred to a French hospital ship.

His fellow officer, Denis Browne, stayed by his bedside as Rupert lapsed in and out of consciousness. On the afternoon of 23 April, 'with the sun shining all round his cabin and the cool sea breeze blowing through the door and the shaded windows',[1] he died. He was buried the same evening, in an olive grove on the nearby island of Skyros, 'one of the loveliest places on this earth, with grey-green olives round him, one weeping above his head: the ground covered with flowering sage, bluish grey & smelling more delicious than any other flower I know'.[2]

Noel's grief at Rupert's death was exacerbated by that of Ferenc and the continuation of the war, and by September 1916 she was severely depressed. Writing to James, she said there was now no chance that she would marry for love and tells him of a recurrent dream she has of Rupert, just before waking. Like many of Rupert's friends, she was appalled by the way his death had become a timely piece of war propaganda. The fame of Rupert's '1914' sonnets was compounded in the public imagination with Winston Churchill's tribute to him in *The Times* on 26 April, which described him as: 'Joyous, fearless, versatile, deeply instructed, with classic symmetry of mind and body, he was all

---

1 Denis Browne to Mrs Brooke, quoted in *CH*, p. 510.
2 Denis Browne to Eddie Marsh, 25 April 1915, *LRB*, p. 685.

that one would wish England's noblest sons to be in days when no sacrifice but the most precious is acceptable, and the most precious is that which is most freely proffered.' The mixture served to create a mythical, idealized figure; a patriotic golden-haired youth, who could be held up as a worthy emblem for his country. She refused to be associated with his posthumous glory both at the time of his death and throughout the rest of her life. She made no contribution to Eddie Marsh's *Memoir*, which appeared in 1918 and caused anger amongst Rupert's closest friends. Bunny found the book unreadable, so distorted was the picture it gave:

> James – who knew him better than anyone else . . . is silent – he is mentioned once as having been on a walking tour with him – Noel is of course not mentioned. You might as well write a life of Keats and leave out Leigh Hunt, Fanny Brawne and the influence of nature on a townsman.

He goes on to add:

> I am amazed at the underlying assumption of the authors.
>   That is: We like our boys to wear their hair rather long – to dabble in Socialism, to dabble in 'decadence' . . . to fancy they really care about ethics – but all the time we know they are SOUND: SOUND TO THE CORE.
>   When the time comes they'll go off heroically and forget their wild oats and die in a Greek island and then we can wallow in sentiment . . . but the wild oats of Mr Marsh are really the important things in life. Rupert even though he did go to the bad some time before his death at one time cared about the important things and was able to understand them . . . [1]

Later, Noel did assist Christopher Hassall when he was writing Rupert's biography, though typically she refused to let him or Geoffrey Keynes acknowledge this in the introduction.

She became a fully qualified doctor in 1917, and two years later fell in love with a Welsh colleague, Arthur Richards. They shared a love of music and nature, and Noel was won over by his fiery but humorous temperament. They enjoyed a passionate physical relationship and had

---

1 Undated letter to Constance Garnett. Garnett family papers.

a son, Benedict, in 1924, followed by four daughters: Angela, Virginia, Tazza and Julia. They both followed busy and successful medical careers, with Noel becoming a Member of the Royal College of Physicians in 1922. She specialized in paediatrics and was appointed Consultant Physician at Westminster Children's Hospital.

In 1932, over twenty years after James Strachey had first fallen for Noel, the two started having a love affair. Over the next decade they exchanged hundreds of letters and would meet in London to go to concerts and plays together.

Despite this liaison and Arthur's own unfaithfulness, the Richards' marriage remained a strong and happy partnership. For many years Arthur had suffered from Paget's disease, and as his condition worsened Noel left work to devote herself to caring for him. Although she knew full well the severity of the illness, his death, in 1962, came as a great blow to her.

Even in old age she remained physically active, and it was while pruning the vine at her Sussex home that she suffered a stroke, dying on 11 April 1969.

Biographical Appendix

Békássy, Ferenc Istvean Denes Gyula (1893–1915), poet. Son of a rich, liberal Hungarian aristocrat, Ferenc, like all his brothers and sisters, was sent to be educated at Bedales. In 1911 he went up to King's College to read History, and soon became friends with Maynard Keynes, who ensured his election to The Apostles in 1912. At the outbreak of war, Ferenc determined to return home, to fight for the Austro-Hungarian Empire, despite the pleas of his friends, especially Maynard. Seeing he could not be dissuaded, Maynard eventually lent him the money for his fare, and by July 1914 Ferenc was back in Hungary. Having fallen in love with Noel at school, he remained devoted to her throughout his life. Of all her admirers, Noel felt she had the most in common with Ferenc, and after his death she remained in touch with his family, and would often speak warmly of him to her children.

Brooke, Justin (1885–1963), businessman and farmer. He was educated at Bedales and Emmanuel College, where he read law. After leaving Cambridge he spent a brief period articled to a solicitor, before entering the family firm of Brooke Bond in 1913. He lost touch with most of his Cambridge friends, and when Noel met him in 1916 they found they had little in common. He married in 1917 and settled with his wife and four children in Bath. However, an affair with his children's governess led to divorce, and his brothers asked him to leave the company. He married the governess and they moved to Suffolk, where he became a successful fruit farmer.

Cox, Katherine Laird ('Ka', 1887–1938). The second daughter of Henry Fisher Cox, a Fabian and a stockbroker, by the time she entered Newnham College, both her parents had died; she developed a maternal, caring attitude to both her sisters and her friends. At Cambridge and after, she was courted by Jacques Raverat, but refused his repeated marriage proposals. According to Cathleen Nesbitt, Ka became pregnant by Rupert but miscarried the child, which added greatly to her distress in 1912 when their affair ended. During the war, Ka worked with Serbian refugees in Corsica and then as a civil servant on Allied shipping. In 1918 she married a naval officer and painter, Will Arnold-Forster, and they had a son, Mark. They moved to Cornwall and in 1928 Ka became a JP and later a member of Cornwall's education committee. She gradually grew apart from her Bloomsbury friends, who were not impressed by Will, but she and Noel corresponded and visited each other until her death in 1938 of a heart attack.

Garnett, David ('Bunny', 1892–1981), novelist and critic. Bunny grew up at the Cearne in Limpsfield, the only child of the publisher's reader Edward Garnett and his wife Constance, translator of the Russian classics. He studied at the Royal College of Science, Kensington, then, as a conscientious objector, went to France in June 1915 to work with the Friends War Victims Relief Mission. On his return to England, he began working on the land, living at Charleston, Sussex, with Duncan Grant and Vanessa Bell. In 1919 he started a bookshop in Bloomsbury with Francis Birrell, but after the great success of his novel *Lady into Fox* in 1922 he lived entirely by his pen. He became literary editor of the *New Statesman* and wrote many more novels, one of which, *Aspects of Love*, has subsequently been made into a musical. After brief affairs with Daphne Olivier and Alix Sargant-Florence, he married Ray Marshall in 1921, and they had two sons. Ray died of cancer in 1940 and Bunny married Angelica Bell, the daughter of Duncan Grant and Vanessa Bell. Bunny was Noel's oldest friend and their two families spent many holidays together, and later, after he moved to a farmhouse near Cahors, France, her children and grandchildren would go out to visit him.

Keynes, Geoffrey Langdon (1887–1982), surgeon, scholar and bibliographer. After gaining a First in Natural Sciences in 1909, Geoffrey began a distinguished medical career at St Bartholomew's Hospital, London, where he would later become Consultant Surgeon. In 1917 he married Margaret Darwin, Gwen Raverat's younger sister, and they had four sons. He spent three years as Hunterian Professor at the Royal College of Surgeons (1923, 1929 and 1945) and in 1939 began six years as Senior Consultant Surgeon in the RAF. As one of Rupert's Trustees, Geoffrey spent much of his time loyally preserving his friend's memory, and edited both his poems and letters. He also published bibliographies of several English authors, including William Blake (1757–1827), on whom he became a respected authority. He was knighted in 1955 and in 1958 became Chairman of the Trustees of the National Portrait Gallery.

His memoirs, *The Gates of Memory*, were published in 1981, when he was ninety-four.

Keynes, John Maynard (1882–1946), economist, Fellow and Bursar of King's College, Cambridge. The elder brother of Geoffrey Keynes, he was a close friend of Lytton Strachey, Leonard Woolf and Ferenc Békássy. During the war he worked for the Treasury and was their principal representative at the Paris Peace Conference. He resigned in June 1919 and his famous work, *The Economic Consequences of the Peace*, was published later that year. After his relationship with Duncan Grant ended, in 1914, Maynard grew more interested in women, and in 1925 married the Russian ballerina Lydia Lopokova (1892–1981). In 1936 he published *A General Theory of Employment, Interest, and Money*, which greatly influenced the policy-making of Western governments for many years. In 1940 he was asked to rejoin the Treasury and in 1942 was made a peer. A great supporter of the arts, he founded the Arts Theatre at Cambridge in 1936, largely with his own money, and became the first chairman of the Arts Council in 1945.

Olivier, Brynhild (1887–1935). The second daughter of Sydney and Margaret Olivier, she was the sister to whom Noel felt closest. After the birth of Anthony, Bryn and Hugh Popham had two more children; a daughter, Anne (who later married Vanessa Bell's son Quentin), and another son, Tristram. However, in 1917 she met Raymond Sherrard, the handsome and charming son of Dr Caesar Sherrard, who at that time was treating Margery; they soon began an affair. Bryn and Hugh were divorced, and she married Sherrard, with whom she had three more children. Financially, Bryn's new life was not at an easy one. After their marriage the Sherrards moved to Rushden, near Letchworth, where they tried, unsuccessfully, to farm. Then, in 1933, with a loan from George Bernard Shaw, Bryn bought Nunnington Farm at West Wittering, Sussex, hoping that a more prosperous farm would bring them financial security. Coupled with their money problems, Bryn was now suffering from Hodgkin's Disease, which her parents and Noel unsuccessfully sought to cure by sending her for treatment in Zürich, in 1934. They felt that Sherrard had let her down, when she most needed him, by leaving her and their small daughter Clarissa to be taken care of by Bryn's teenage daughter, Anne. Noel had her admitted to St Bartholomew's Hospital and it was there that she died on 13 January 1935.

Olivier, Daphne (1889–1950), educationalist and third daughter of Sydney and Margaret Olivier. Daphne read English at Newnham, but her great interest was always singing, which she was taught by Vaughan

Williams. After leaving Cambridge, she had an affair with Bunny Garnett in 1915, but remained unmarried until her mid-thirties, when she fell in love with Cecil Harwood, with whom she had five children. Harwood had studied at Christ Church College, Oxford, where he became a friend of C. S. Lewis (1898–1963) and one of 'The Inklings'. Daphne had heard Rudolph Steiner lecturing in Torquay, and persuaded Cecil to accompany her to Germany to work with him. On their return they founded the first Steiner school in England, in 1925. Together they ran the New School, first in Streatham and then later, as Michael Hall, in Sussex.

Olivier, Margery (1886–1974). The eldest of the four Olivier sisters, and the most intellectual of them. After graduating from Newnham, Margery could not decide on any one career and fruitlessly pursued a number of options. Her growing eccentricity began to seriously alarm her family, and in 1916 she was taken to see the neurologist Sir Henry Head, who had treated Daphne after a nervous breakdown the previous year. In 1921, her parents tried for a time to look after her at their new home, Ramsden Hall in Oxfordshire, but Margery grew worse, becoming convinced that her father was evil and viciously attacking him. Margery's mother and sisters took turns in helping to take care of her, but her psychosis did not decrease. Finally, in 1922, it was agreed that she would be safer in a mental hospital, and Noel, who was now qualified, had her committed to Camberwell House. She remained institutionalized for the rest of her life, visited and taken on excursions by her sisters, all of whom she outlived.

Raverat, Gwendolen Mary, née Darwin (1885–1957), painter and wood-engraver. She was the elder daughter of Sir George Darwin, Professor of Astronomy at Cambridge, and granddaughter of Charles Darwin. She studied painting at the Slade School, under Wilson Steer, but it is for her woodcuts that she is best remembered. She was a founder member of the Society of Wood-Engravers, and exhibited with them from 1912 onwards. She married Jacques Raverat on 27 May 1911 and they had two daughters. After his death she had an unhappy love affair with the French painter Jean Marchand and returned to live in England in 1925. Her recollections of childhood, *Period Piece*, were published in 1952.

Raverat, Jacques Pierre (1885–1925), painter. Son of a wealthy French businessman, Jacques was educated at Bedales and the Sorbonne, before arriving in 1906 to study mathematics at Emmanuel College. In 1908 Jacques had a severe breakdown, and his father took him home to recover. At the time he was diagnosed as having had a nervous breakdown, but it was later realized that his condition was caused by the early stages of multiple sclerosis. Whilst abroad he carried out his courtship by letter of Ka Cox, but on his return he soon realized that she would never marry him. In 1911 he married Gwen Darwin and began to paint full time, exhibiting in 1918 as a member of the New English Art Club. Jacques' health deteriorated, and in 1920 the Raverats returned to the milder climate of France, settling near Vence in the Alpes-Maritimes. In 1922 Jacques renewed his friendship with Virginia Woolf, and they continued corresponding until his death in 1925.

Stephen, Adrian Leslie (1883–1948), psychiatrist, the younger brother of Virginia Woolf and Vanessa Bell, who, though fond of him, were much closer to his elder brother, Thoby. He studied law at Trinity College, Cambridge, and then went to Lincoln's Inn in 1907. He and Virginia shared a house, 29 Fitzroy Square, where they held Thursday evening 'At Homes'. They later moved to 38 Brunswick Square and were joined by Leonard Woolf, Duncan Grant and Maynard Keynes. Adrian had a tendency to be extremely lethargic, and after Noel's rejection of him this was exacerbated, much to his sisters' annoyance. In 1914 he married Karin Costello (1889–1953), sister of Ray Strachey, and they had two daughters. The couple trained at University College Hospital and both became successful psychiatrists.

Strachey, James Beaumont (1887–1967), psychologist, the youngest of General Sir Richard and Lady Strachey's thirteen children. After leaving Trinity College in 1909, he took a job as assistant to his cousin St Loe Strachey (1860–1927), who was Editor of the *Spectator*. He was a conscientious objector, and his opposition to the war led to his resignation from the paper in 1916, after which he began relief work with the Quakers. Having courted Noel for many years, he married Alix Sargant-Florence (1892–1973) in 1920, with whom he shared an interest in psychology. They travelled to Vienna and became the first couple to be analysed by Freud. On his return, James maintained an active analytic practice, whilst he translated Freud's psychoanalytical writings, assisted by Alix. He was a passionate music lover and in 1934 became a founder member of the Glyndebourne Opera, where many of his programme notes and commentaries are still used. He remained close to Noel throughout his life, and in 1932 they began a love affair, which continued for almost a decade. He became godfather to Noel's fourth child, Tazza, and worked with her eldest daughter, Angela, on the final volumes of Freud's *Standard Edition*. The final volume was published in 1966, winning James the Schlegel-Tieck prize, awarded by the Society of Authors and the

Translators Association. He died in 1967, and Angela Richards finished his great work by compiling a volume of indexes and bibliography, published in 1974.

Strachey, (Giles) Lytton (1880–1932), biographer and essayist. Beloved elder brother of James Strachey, he graduated from Trinity College with a Second in History. Whilst there he became friends with Walter Lamb (1882–1961) and developed a fascination for his brother Henry. It was after Lytton had invited Henry to join the Lulworth party at the beginning of 1912 that Rupert developed his irrational loathing of him. He felt that Lytton embodied all that was perverse and dangerous about the Bloomsbury group, blaming him for Ka's association with Lamb and fearing lest Noel too should be corrupted. The publication of *Eminent Victorians* in 1918 brought him fame and inaugurated a new mode of biography.

Ward, Dudley (1885–1957), economist and scholar. He was educated at Derby Shool and St John's College, where he became a fellow in 1909. On leaving Cambridge, he began working for *The Economist* and soon became assistant editor. The paper sent him to work in Germany with his wife Annemarie and son Peter, and he was there when war broke out. He managed to smuggle them out and to escape with them back to England. He began working for the Treasury, representing it alongside Maynard Keynes at the Paris Peace Conference and at Brussels in 1921. He became Director of the British Overseas Bank and received a CBE in 1922. He was the General Counsel for the European Office of UNRRA between 1944 and 1948, and then the London representative of the United Nation's International Children's Emergency Fund. Peter's birth was followed by two daughters and the family lived in the Old Vicarage, Grantchester, which had been left to Dudley in Mrs Brooke's will. Rupert had sent a last letter to Dudley asked him to destroy certain groups of letters, and Dudley became a loyal Trustee of his friend's memory. Noel retained enormous affection for Dudley and Annemarie, and in her seventies made a final visit to the Old Vicarage to see Peter.

Woolf, (Adeline) Virginia, née Stephen (1882–1941), novelist, essayist, biographer and critic. She was the daughter of the eminent biographer Leslie Stephen and his second wife, Julia Jackson. Both Virginia's brothers went to Cambridge, and it was while visiting the elder, Thoby, that she met his friend Leonard Woolf, whom she married in 1912. Together they founded the Hogarth Press, which published almost all of her major writing, including *Mrs Dalloway* in 1925, *To the Lighthouse* in 1927 and

The Waves in 1931. After Rupert's death, she remained friends with Noel, who in 1919 helped save the life of her newborn niece, Angelica Bell, by sending down her colleague Dr Marie Moralt to replace an incompetent local practitioner. Noel named her second daughter after Virginia and made her the baby's godmother. Throughout her life, Virginia suffered from bouts of nervous exhaustion and severe depression, and on 28 March 1941, fearful that she would become incurably mad, she drowned herself.

Bibliography

Anscombe, Isabelle *Omega and After* (London: Thames & Hudson, 1981)

Archer, Mary *Rupert Brooke and The Old Vicarage, Grantchester* (Cambridge: Silent Books, 1989)

Badley, J.H. *A Schoolmaster's Testament* (Oxford: Basil Blackwell, 1937)

Bedales Chronicle (Petersfield: Bedales School, 1907–10)

Bedales School Record (Petersfield: Bedales School, 1894–1907)

Bell, Clive *Old Friends: Personal Recollections* (London: Chatto & Windus, 1956)

Bell, Quentin *Bloomsbury* (London: Weidenfeld & Nicolson, 1968)

—— *Virginia Woolf: A Biography*, 2 vols (London: The Hogarth Press, 1972)

Bell, Vanessa *Vanessa Bell's Family Album*, compiled by Quentin Bell and Angelica Garnett (London: Jill Norman & Hobhouse, 1981)

Brandreth, Gyles, and Sally Henry, ed. *John Haden Badley, 1865–1967: Bedales School and its founder* (Bournemouth: Bedales Society, 1967)

Brooke, Rupert *Democracy and the Arts* (London: Rupert Hart-Davis, 1946)

—— *Letters from America* (New York: Charles Scribner, 1916)

—— *The Letters of Rupert Brooke*, ed. Geoffrey Keynes (London: Faber & Faber, 1968)

—— *Lithuania* (London: Sidgwick & Jackson, 1935)

—— *The Poetical Works of Rupert Brooke*, ed. Geoffrey Keynes (London: Faber & Faber, 1970)

—— *The Prose of Rupert Brooke*, ed. Christopher Hassall (London: Sidgwick & Jackson, 1956)

Clements, Keith *Henry Lamb* (London: Redcliffe Press, 1984)

Deacon, Richard *The Cambridge Apostles* (London: Robert Royce, 1985)

Delany, Paul *The Neo-Pagans: Friendship and Love in the Rupert Brooke Circle* (London: Hamish Hamilton, 1988)

Dunn, Jane *A Very Close Conspiracy: Vanessa Bell and Virginia Woolf* (London: Jonathan Cape, 1990)

Furbank, P.N. *E.M. Forster: A Life*, 2 vols (London: Secker & Warburg, 1977, 1978)

Fry, Roger *Vision and Design* (London: Chatto & Windus, 1920)

Garnett, Angelica *Deceived with Kindness: A Bloomsbury Childhood* (London: Chatto & Windus, 1984)

Garnett, David *The Familiar Faces* (London: Chatto & Windus, 1962)

—— *The Flowers of the Forest* (London: Chatto & Windus, 1955)

—— *The Golden Echo* (London: Chatto & Windus, 1953)

—— *Great Friends: Portraits of Seventeen Writers* (London: Macmillan, 1979)

Garnett, Richard *Constance Garnett: A Heroic Life* (London: Sinclair Stevenson, 1991)

Harrod, Roy *The Life of John Maynard Keynes* (London: Macmillan, 1951)

Hassall, Christopher *Edward Marsh: A Biography* (London: Longmans, 1959)

—— *Rupert Brooke: A Biography* (London: Faber & Faber, 1964)

Hastings, Michael *The Handsomest Young Man in England: Rupert Brooke* (London: Michael Joseph, 1967)

Henderson, James L. *Irregularly Bold* (London: André Deutsch, 1978)

Henley, W.E. *Poems* (London: David Nutt, 1904)

Holroyd, Michael *Augustus John: A Biography* (London: William Heinemann, 1974)

—— *Bernard Shaw*, vol. i: *1856–1898, The Search for Love* and vol. ii: *1898–1918, The Pursuit of Power* (London: Chatto & Windus, 1988, 1989)

—— *Lytton Strachey: A Biography*, 2 vols (London: Heinemann, 1967, 1978)

Housman, A.E. *The Collected Poems* (London: Jonathan Cape, 1939)

John, Augustus *Autobiography* (London: Jonathan Cape, 1975)

Keynes, Geoffrey *A Bibliography of Rupert Brooke* (London: Rupert Hart-Davis, 1954)

—— *The Gates of Memory* (Oxford: Clarendon Press, 1981)

Keynes, John Maynard *Two Memoirs* (London: Macmillan, 1949)

Lee, Francis *Fabianism and Colonialism: The Life & Political Thought of Lord Sydney Olivier* (London: Defiant Books, 1988)

Lehmann, John *Rupert Brooke: His Life and His Legend* (London: Weidenfeld & Nicolson, 1980)

Levy, Paul *Moore: G.E. Moore and the Cambridge Apostles* (London: Weidenfeld & Nicolson, 1978)

Mackenzie, Norman and Jeanne *The First Fabians* (London: Weidenfeld & Nicolson, 1977)

—— *The Time Traveller: A Biography of H.G. Wells* (London: Weidenfeld & Nicolson, 1973)

Marsh, Edward *A Number of People* (London: William Heinemann, 1939)

—— *Rupert Brooke: A Memoir* (London: Sidgwick & Jackson, 1918)

Masefield, John *Poems* (London: Macmillan, 1930)

Moore, John *Edward Thomas* (London: William Heinemann, 1939)

Murray, Gilbert *A Biography of Francis McDonald Cornford, 1874–1943* (Oxford: Oxford University Press, 1944)

Olivier, Margaret *Sydney Olivier: Letters and Selected Writings* (London: George Allen & Unwin, 1948)

Palmer, Alan and Veronica *Who's Who in Bloomsbury* (Brighton: Harvester Press, 1987)

Partridge, Frances *A Pacifist's War* (London: The Hogarth Press, 1978)

—— *Memories* (London: Victor Gollancz, 1981)

Raverat, Gwen *Period Piece: A Cambridge Childhood* (New York: Norton, 1952)

Richardson, Elizabeth P. *A Bloomsbury Iconography* (Winchester: St Paul's Bibliographies, 1989)

Rogers, Timothy *Rupert Brooke: A Reappraisal and Selection from his Writings, Some Hitherto Unpublished* (London: Routledge & Kegan Paul, 1971)

—— *Georgian Poetry 1911–1922: The Critical Heritage* (London: Routledge & Kegan Paul, 1977)

Sayler, Oliver M. *Max Reinhardt and his Theatre* (New York: Bretano's, 1924)

Shaw, George Bernard *Collected Letters of Bernard Shaw*, vol. iii: *1911–1925*, ed. Dan H. Laurence (London: Max Reinhardt, 1985)

Shone, Richard *Bloomsbury Portraits* (Oxford: Phaidon Press, 1976)

Skidelsky, Robert *English Progressive Schools* (Harmondsworth: Penguin, 1969)

—— *John Maynard Keynes*, vol. i: *Hopes Betrayed 1883–1920* (London: Macmillan, 1983)

Spalding, Frances *British Art since 1900* (London: Thames & Hudson, 1986)

Strachey, James and Alix *Bloomsbury/Freud: The Letters of James and Alix Strachey, 1924–25*, ed. Perry Meisel and Walter Kendrick (London: Chatto & Windus, 1986)

Stringer, Arthur *Red Wine of Youth* (New York: Bobbs-Merrill, 1948)

Swinburne, Algernon *Poetical Works* (New York: John D. Williams, 1884)

Webb, Beatrice *The Diary of Beatrice Webb*, vol. iii (London: Virago, 1984)

—— *Our Partnership* (New York: Longmans Green, 1948)

Webb, Sidney and Beatrice *The Letters of Sidney and Beatrice Webb*, vol. ii: *Partnership, 1892–1912*, ed. Norman Mackenzie (Cambridge: Cambridge University Press, 1978)

Wells, H.G. *H. G. Wells in Love: Postscript to an Experiment in Autobiography*, ed. G.P. Wells (London: Faber & Faber, 1984)

Woolf, Leonard *Beginning Again: An Autobiography of the Years 1911–1918* (London: The Hogarth Press, 1964)
—— *Letters of Leonard Woolf*, ed. Frederic Spotts (London: Weidenfeld & Nicolson, 1990)
Woolf, Virginia *The Diary of Virginia Woolf*, ed. Anne Olivier Bell, 5 vols (London: The Hogarth Press, 1977, 1978, 1980, 1982, 1984)
—— *The Letters of Virginia Woolf*, ed. Nigel Nicolson and Joanne Trautmann, 6 vols (London: Chatto & Windus, 1975, 1976, 1977, 1978, 1979, 1980)

Index

A NOTE ON THE EDITOR

Pippa Harris is Noel Olivier's granddaughter. She read English at Cambridge and became President of the Marlowe Dramatic Society. The Society, which had Rupert Brooke for its first President, is the subject of her next book. Since leaving Cambridge, she has worked in film and video production and is currently producing a classical music documentary. She lives in London.